1988

The Special Child

The Special Child

A Source Book
for Parents of Children
with Developmental Disabilities

by

Siegfried M. Pueschel, M.D., Ph.D., M.P.H.
James C. Bernier, M.S.W.

and

Leslie E. Weidenman, Ph.D.

with invited contributors

·P·A·U·L·H·
BROOKES
PUBLISHING CO

Baltimore · London · Toronto · Sydney

Paul H. Brookes Publishing Co.
Post Office Box 10624
Baltimore, Maryland 21285-0624

Copyright © 1988 by Paul H. Brookes Publishing Co., Inc.
All rights reserved.

Typeset by The Composing Room, Grand Rapids, Michigan.
Manufactured in the United States of America by
The Maple Press Company, York, Pennsylvania.

Library of Congress Cataloging-in-Publication Data

Pueschel, Siegfried M.
    The special child: a source book for parents of children with
developmental disabilities / Siegfried M. Pueschel, James C. Bernier, Leslie E. Weidenman; with invited contributors.
      p.   cm.
    Bibliography: p.
    Includes index.
    ISBN 0-933716-97-4
    1. Developmentally disabled children. 2. Developmentally
disabled children—Care. 3. Developmental disabilities.   I. Bernier, James C. II. Weidenman, Leslie Ellen, 1952–   III. Title.
RJ135.P84 1988
617—dc19   88-1353
                                                     CIP

Contents

Nutritional Interventions
Educational Interventions
Therapeutic Interventions

Prenatal Diagnosis
Newborn Screening
Sweat Test
Chromosome Analysis
Tests for Neurological Disorders
Procedures to Diagnose Neuromuscular
    Disorders
Procedures to Diagnose Sensory
    Disorders
Evaluation of Respiratory Disorders
Assessment of Cardiac Diseases
Diagnostic Procedures Used in
    Intestinal Diseases
Urological Disorders
Physician's Responsibility

Equipment for Children with
    Developmental Delays
Adaptive Equipment for Body Control:
    Posture, Movement, and Balance
When to Consider Adaptive
    Equipment for Your Child
Adaptive Equipment Can Improve
    Your Child's Attitude and Interest
What Kind of Equipment Do You
    Need?
How to Obtain and Finance Adaptive
    Equipment
Methods to Help Compensate for
    Various Disabilities
Good Positioning Does Not Always
    Require Commercially Made
    Adaptive Equipment
Measuring Your Child for Adaptive
    Equipment
Orthopaedic Appliances
Prostheses or Artificial Body Parts
Mobility Aids
Ambulation Aids
Adaptive Equipment for Fine Motor
    Control

About the Authors

Siegfried M. Pueschel, M.D., Ph.D., M.P.H., as Director of the Child Development Center at Rhode Island Hospital since 1975, has worked with thousands of children with special needs. He has published 10 books on various developmental disabilities and has written over 130 articles relating to many types of handicapping conditions. Prior to his appointment at Rhode Island, he initiated a lead poisoning program, became Director of the first Down Syndrome Program, and provided leadership to the PKU and Inborn Errors of Metabolism Program at The Children's Hospital in Boston.

Certified by the American Board of Pediatrics and a Diplomate of the American Board of Medical Genetics, his academic appointments include Lecturer in Pediatrics, Harvard Medical School, and Professor of Pediatrics, Brown University. Over the past 20 years, Dr. Pueschel has been involved in clinical activities, research and teaching, and continues to pursue his interest in developmental disabilities, biochemical genetics, and chromosome abnormalities, particularly Down syndrome.

James C. Bernier, M.S.W., is Director of Social Service at the Child Development Center of Rhode Island Hospital, a position he has held for the last 9 years. A social worker with 16 years experience in counseling physically and emotionally disabled children and their families, he also maintains a private practice. He holds memberships in the National Association of Social Workers—Academy of Certified Social Workers, American Association of Mental Retardation, and American Public Welfare Association. He has also had his writing published in a professional reference on autism.

Leslie E. Weidenman, Ph.D., joined the staff of the Child Development Center's Early Intervention Program in 1979, and from 1982 to 1984, directed the Early Intervention Program at J. Arthur Trudeau Memorial Center in Warwick, Rhode Island. She is currently Clinical Associate Director of the Groden Center, Inc., an agency that provides evaluative, therapeutic, and educational services for children and young adults with moderate to severe behavioral/emotional disorders and autism. She also serves as a consultant to local school systems in Rhode Island, where she is licensed to practice as both a Psychologist and School Psychologist.

Dr. Pueschel, Mr. Bernier, and Dr. Weidenman were assisted in their writing by the following colleagues. When this book was conceived and during the initial phase of writing, all contributors were staff members of the Child Development Center, a University Affiliated Program, located at the Rhode Island Hospital in Providence, Rhode Island. Particular credits appear at the close of each chapter:

Barbara Bush, R.P.T.

Katherine C. Castree, M.D.

Sarah J. Gossler, M.S.W.

Debra J. Lobato, Ph.D.

Leesa H. Mann, M.A.

Daniel T. Marwil, M.D.

James P. McEneaney, M.Ed.

James A. Mulick, Ph.D.

Carol A. Musso, B.S., R.N.

Barbara D. Remor, B.S., R.N.

Ellen I. Rollins, Ed.D.

Edward A. Sassaman, M.D.

Patricia S. Scola, M.D., M.P.H.

Karen E. Senft, M.D.

Janet L. Tobin, M.S.

Ann S. Zartler, Ph.D.

Acknowledgments

We are indebted foremost to the many children with special needs we were privileged to serve in the Child Development Center. The lessons they taught us are invaluable. We also thank their parents, for it was their unassuming partnership, devotion, and encouragement that led to the writing of this book.

We also express our gratitude to our colleagues from the Child Development Center, too many to name, who contributed in numerous ways to this book. We thank the many secretaries of the Child Development Center who have been involved in the preparation of the manuscript. In particular, we would like to acknowledge the outstanding secretarial skills of Linda Crepeau. We also express our appreciation to Pamela and Jeanette Pueschel for proofreading the manuscript. Moreover, we are indebted to Maurice Bernier for the excellent illustrations he contributed. We thank the Meeting Street School, East Providence; the Groden Center and the Child Development Center, Providence, Rhode Island; and many parents for providing us with photographs of their children that were used to illustrate this book. Last, but not least, we are most grateful to Melissa A. Behm of Paul H. Brookes Publishing Company for her ever-ready guidance and support.

Introduction

The Special Child is a book for parents. It was written mainly to help parents of children with developmental disabilities.

Children with developmental disabilities, like all children, are unique individuals. No two are exactly alike, even though they may have the same problem or diagnosis. Because of their disabilities, however, they may have many things in common, such as a need for special education, for additional medical care, or for specialized equipment. Families of disabled children also have similarities; they often require emotional support and counseling. This book focuses on all of these common needs.

The Special Child tells you how to recognize developmental problems and how to obtain an evaluation that may lead to a specific diagnosis. We describe the roles of the various professionals you might meet as your child is evaluated, as well as the types of tests and procedures that can be performed. Other sections of the book focus on families and the adjustments they make when they discover their child has a developmental disability. We also highlight a number of specific disabilities, tests and procedures, medications, treatments, and operations commonly performed. Many other topics of interest, such as going to school, community resources, and legal issues are discussed as well.

Many questions that you will ask about your special child are answered in this book. In fact, this is the reason we decided to write *The Special Child*. Parents so often ask the same questions about various issues concerning developmental disabilities that we realized how valuable a book could be that provided a wide range of information readily.

Obviously, one book will not answer all of your questions. *The Special Child* is not intended to be an encyclopedia. For those wishing additional information, a list of resource materials and a reference section are included at the end of this book. As a further aid to reading, many of the medical terms used in the book are defined in the text.

Remember, *The Special Child* is not intended to replace the individual counseling, support, and guidance you will receive from the professionals who help you care for your child. Moreover, it is not a "do-it-yourself" book that can substitute for your personal physician's advice in specific situations. *The Special Child* is a home reference book intended to complement the professional services you receive.

The authors of *The Special Child* are specialists who work with developmentally disabled children. These experts, with years of experience, include physicians, psychologists, social workers, therapists, and nurses. All work or have worked at the Child Development Center of Rhode Island Hospital, a University Affiliated Program, which is the major diagnostic and treatment center for children with developmental disabilities in southeastern New England.

◀ **PART I** ▶

*Children with
Special Needs,
Their Parents,
and the Professionals
Who Care for Them*

◀   Chapter 1   ▶

Who Are the Special Children?

WHAT'S IN A NAME?

When you hear the words *developmentally disabled* or *handicapped,* you may think of a specific person or kind of problem. Many people have limited ideas about the effects of disabilities. Some automatically think of physically impaired children as in wheelchairs, while others may picture children with mental retardation. The truth is, there are hundreds of different types of disabilities that can affect many areas of a child's life.

Basically, a developmental disability is any physical or mental condition that can impair or limit a child's skills or causes a child to develop language, thinking, personal, social, and movement skills more slowly than other children. *Developmental disability* is such a broad term that it is easy to see how two children with very different problems could both be described correctly as having a developmental disability.

This book uses the terms *developmentally disabled* and *handicapped* interchangeably. These and other similar terms also have technical definitions. The federal government, for example, has defined both *developmental disability* and *mental retardation* in two respective laws (PL 88-164 and PL 94-103). These definitions are found in Chapter 5 on "Mental Retardation."

Most people are unfamiliar with the technical definitions of *developmental disabilities* and *mental retardation* and develop their own ideas of what they mean. Unfortunately, many definitions are inaccurate, based on vague impressions, hearsay, or "horror stories" about individuals with handicapping conditions. As a result, the terms and labels used to describe disabilities often have negative connotations that can cause problems for families and disabled children alike. Problems show up in a variety of ways, such as fears, prejudices, and discrimination, to name a few. When specific terms are heard, uninformed people may imagine the worst and then, out of fear, avoid meeting, associating with, and learning about handicapped persons and their families. In *The Special Child*, we hope to dispel many of these misconceptions by sharing what we know about various developmental disabilities. The best way to begin is simply to keep in mind that disabled children are children first.

They may have disabilities and special needs, but, like all children, they require lots of love, care, and affection.

The problems with labels and terminology lead many parents to ask why the use of labels has not been abandoned altogether. After all, disabled children are more like nondisabled children than they are different. This problem, however, does not apply only to handicapped people; racial, ethnic, economic, and religious labels all may bring out prejudices. Parents also often worry that once a child has been given a diagnosis, the label will remain forever, even if the disability has been "corrected" or if the diagnosis turns out to be incorrect.

Despite these problems, there are several good reasons for using specific terms. For example, if a syndrome has been identified and a child has been diagnosed correctly, then parents can be informed about the condition and told what the future might hold for the child. Moreover, parents can be provided with specific genetic counseling, and they can be advised what their risks are for having another baby with a similar problem.

Diagnostic labels also provide parents and other family members with a name for the child's condition. Friends, neighbors, and strangers might inquire about the child's handicap or ask why the child has not developed like other children. If a diagnosis has been made, the term can help explain the child's problem.

One tangible benefit to being identified as a handicapped person is that once a disability is documented, services often become available. Many government programs base their eligibility criteria for disability benefits on this kind of information. Moreover, early intervention programs, schools, and community agencies often require a specific diagnosis for enrollment of your child in a special program.

RECENT CHANGES IN ATTITUDES

Fortunately, the care and treatment provided persons with developmental disabilities has improved greatly in recent years. In the past, severely handicapped children were hidden away in institutions and all but forgotten. Today, attitudes are generally more positive and more realistic. Even the words used to describe handicaps have improved. No longer are expressions such as *imbecile, feeble-minded,* and *moron* used when referring to the child with mental retardation. Instead, more positive expressions have taken their place, including the *child with special needs* or the *person with a developmental disability.* Condescending and insulting terms, such as *mongoloid,* are less frequently heard these days.

Today, we know that children with many different developmental disorders are able to accomplish much more than was ever anticipated

previously. Not only can they participate in family life, but they can go to school, have friends, enjoy recreational activities, live and work in the community, and much more. This knowledge, and the increased focus on the abilities of persons with handicapping conditions, not just their disabilities, has resulted in many novel programs and services that are now available from an early age on.

Along with the recent changes in attitudes have come insights into how children learn and grow, medical advances, modern technology, and new ideas about the rights of individuals, all of which have revolutionized our thinking and approaches to the care of individuals with developmental disabilities. Multiple new services, treatments, and equipment have been devised to help handicapped children. We are fortunate to live in a time of positive thinking where parents and professionals are striving together to help developmentally disabled children lead happy, healthy, and productive lives.

ACKNOWLEDGMENTS

Contributions have been made to this chapter by Leslie E. Weidenman, Ph.D., Ellen I. Rollins, Ed.D., and James C. Bernier, M.S.W.

Chapter 2

Discovering Your Child Has a Problem

SUSPECTING YOUR CHILD HAS A DISABILITY

Certain disabilities and birth defects are discovered at birth or sometimes even during pregnancy. If either of these is the case, then parents usually learn about the problem from their obstetrician, pediatrician, or family physician. In other instances, parents are the first to suspect that something is wrong with their child. It may be a vague feeling or the realization that their baby is not developing at the same rate as a neighbor's child. At times, questions from close friends or relatives, such as why 3-year-old Johnny isn't talking, 2-year-old Betsy isn't walking, or 10-month-old Kevin isn't sitting up yet, may alert parents to a possible problem. Often, the baby's doctor is the first to notice a developmental disability. Clearly, developmental problems can be discovered in many ways.

Recognizing a developmental disability is sometimes easier if you know something about how children develop normally. If you have other children or have watched someone else's child grow, you may have a general idea of how children develop. Thus, over the years, you may have acquired an understanding of the sequence and ages at which essential skills and abilities generally appear. For instance, you may have noticed that babies usually sit by themselves at approximately 6 to 8 months and start walking sometime around their first birthday.

There are numerous indicators or signs of developmental problems in a child. Some are very subtle and not easily noted; others are more obvious. Careful and repeated observations often are needed before a developmental disability is uncovered. As parents and doctors watch a baby's development, they must keep in mind that the signs of trouble may change as a child matures. Certain behavior that is typical at one age may mean a problem at another. The task of identifying developmental problems is made even harder when you consider that every child is unique and no two children will develop in exactly the same way. We also must remember that all youngsters, handicapped or not, are individuals and develop at their own pace. The job of parents and professionals is to find out if a particular child's progress and behavior are normal or if there are signs of a developmental problem.

DIFFERENT TYPES OF DEVELOPMENTAL PROBLEMS

To monitor developmental progress, doctors and child care professionals look at how well a baby is doing in a number of areas of functioning. These areas include basic senses like vision and hearing as well as important developmental areas of speech, thinking, social interactions, and movement skills.

Signs of developmental problems also are grouped by area of functioning. Certain signs may suggest a visual problem, whereas others may indicate a hearing impediment. Problems with muscle use are identified in still other ways. There are many signs and symptoms that may indicate problems. Only a few of the common ones are mentioned in the list following:

If your baby is not startled by loud sounds, does not turn toward your voice when you speak, or at a later age does not respond to his or her name when called, there may be problems with hearing.

If your baby does not focus on your face, does not follow objects or people as they move, or shows random searching eye movements, there may be a visual handicap.

If your baby is unable to bring his or her hands or objects to the mouth, always keeps the hands tightly fisted, is unable to hold the head up by 3 months, cannot sit independently when placed by 7 to 8 months, or is not walking by 14 to 18 months, there may be a problem with muscles or nerves.

If your baby does not babble or make a variety of sounds, does not use any words by 12 to 15 months, or does not speak in short phrases by 24 months, then you probably should be concerned with his or her language development.

If your child does not smile when talked to by family or friends, stiffens when held, or later avoids making eye contact with you and others, there may be a social/emotional problem.

If your baby shows one or more of these signs, there may be a developmental disability. The best way to be sure is to talk to your child's doctor about your concerns and observations. The doctor then may suggest that you take your child for a thorough developmental evaluation. On the other hand, the doctor might reassure you that your child's progress is within the range of normal development.

WHEN CAN A DEVELOPMENTAL DISABILITY BE DETECTED?

Not all developmental problems are detected at birth or during the baby's first few weeks of life. More often, problems are not noticed until much later, perhaps during the first few years or when the child enters nursery school, kindergarten, or elementary school. Part of the difficulty in detecting developmental problems in young children is that many disabilities are not immediately obvious. For example, almost everyone has heard stories of children in excellent health who had no problems during infancy, but later turned out to be mentally retarded. The opposite situation also occurs, where children who have had difficult births and a rocky first few days of life bounce back and develop quite normally.

Detecting Problems during Pregnancy

Sometimes a developmental problem can be uncovered before a baby is born. A number of procedures are now used regularly to detect problems during pregnancy. A few of the more common tests are described here. (Detailed descriptions of these and other procedures are found in Chapter 22 on "Tests and Procedures.")

One procedure used in prenatal diagnosis is called amniocentesis. Amniocentesis involves removal (by use of a needle inserted through the woman's abdominal wall) of some of the fluid that surrounds the baby in the mother's womb. The cells obtained from the amniotic fluid are grown or cultured in the laboratory for 2 to 4 weeks. Then, the chromosomes (tiny, microscopic, rodlike structures containing thousands of genes) are studied or specific biochemical tests are performed. These tests can tell whether or not the unborn baby has any of several disorders known to be caused by chromosomal or biochemical defects.

The mother's blood and her amniotic fluid also can be tested for a specific protein called alpha-fetoprotein (AFP), which is ordinarily produced by the unborn baby. If too much alpha-fetoprotein is found, the unborn baby may have spina bifida (an opening at the back of the spine) or a related brain or spinal cord defect. If a very low amount of alpha-fetoprotein is uncovered, this may in some cases suggest that the mother is carrying a child with Down syndrome, which is the most frequently observed chromosome disorder associated with mental retardation.

During the past few years, a new technique for prenatal diagnosis has been developed. It is called chorionic villus biopsy. During this procedure, a small part of the placenta (the chorionic villus) is obtained during the third month of pregnancy. (The placenta is the afterbirth, the organ that nourishes the growing fetus in the uterus.) The advantage of chorionic villus biopsy over amniocentesis is that a chromosome analysis can be performed immediately on a fresh sample of tissue without using lengthy culture procedures. Thus, the time period between obtaining the chorionic villus sample and the results of chromosome analysis can be shortened significantly. With this procedure, it may only take a few hours to obtain an answer, whereas cultures after amniocentesis may take 2 to 4 weeks. Another advantage of chorionic villus biopsy is that it can be performed at an earlier time period during pregnancy. In addition to fast chromosome analysis, the tissue sample can also be used for biochemical studies and DNA analysis. (DNA stands for dioxyribonucleic acid, a basic component of living tissue, containing the genetic code.)

Ultrasound, or sonography, is another technique frequently used to identify structural problems in the unborn baby. Sonography uses sound waves to form an image of the baby. In particular, spina bifida, major skeletal deformities, enlarged kidneys, and certain congenital heart defects can be detected during the second half of pregnancy with ultrasound.

Fetoscopy is also used in prenatal diagnosis, usually during the second trimester of pregnancy. During this procedure, a tubelike instrument is inserted through the mother's abdominal wall into the womb. With this instrument, the doctor can see parts of the baby and look for abnormalities. This same instrument also can be used to obtain blood samples from the developing baby, which then are tested in the laboratory.

Prenatal diagnostic tests are not recommended for everyone, because each test involves some risk to the unborn baby and the expectant mother. Doctors recommend prenatal diagnosis only in certain circumstances. For example, amniocentesis or chorionic villus biopsy are suggested for pregnant women who are 35 years and older, for those who have a known chromosome problem, or for those who already had a child with a genetic problem or chromosome disorder. Fetoscopy is used only in rare situations such as a suspected blood disorder in the unborn baby.

For the most part, the results of such tests during pregnancy will turn out to be normal, which is reassuring to expectant parents. However, when the results are abnormal, meaning that the baby is likely to have a serious problem, you, as parents, are faced with the difficult question of what to do. There is never an easy answer. What is decided will depend on many factors, such as your personal beliefs about complex issues including abortion and right to life. It will also depend on your understanding of the specific disorder detected, implications for the quality of both the child's and family's lives, the types of services needed, assistance and support available to parents of handicapped children, and your personal feelings about raising a child with a handicap. The more informed you are, the better you will be able to make a decision. Whatever decision you make then deserves the considered support of caring professionals.

Birth and Newborn Difficulties

Doctors examine babies as soon as they are born and carefully look for abnormalities during this first examination. Obvious physical anomalies, such as cleft lip or spina bifida, will be noticed right away. Other problems, although present at birth, may not be visible. They may be uncovered later, perhaps in the newborn period or during the first few years of life.

At times, the process of being born can cause developmental problems. If, during birth, the baby does not get enough oxygen, brain damage may ensue, as too little oxygen (a condition called anoxia) can harm nerve cells. The extent of brain damage depends on how long the brain was without oxygen. Babies injured at birth or deprived of oxygen sometimes develop cerebral palsy, seizures, or other developmental disorders.

Soon after the baby is born, your doctor or other delivery room personnel will check the infant's heart rate, respiration, skin color, reflexes, and muscle tone. Based on this quick evaluation of your baby at 1 and 5 minutes after delivery, the doctor develops a score (Apgar Score) indicating how the baby is doing. Each of the just-mentioned physical findings will be scored from 0 to 2, for a total of 10 points. For example, if the baby's heart rate is over 100 per minute, then the baby will get a score of 2, if the heart rate is below 100 per minute, a score of 1 is given, and if the heart is not beating at all, then a 0 score is obtained.

Premature infants born weeks or even months too early are at a higher risk of developing handicaps than full-term infants. These babies often are very sick and require intensive care in a hospital. Most of their problems occur because their vital organs are underdeveloped and are not yet functioning properly. Often, premature infants will need mechanical support systems in order to live. A respirator, for example, may be needed if a baby is born with immature lungs. Other problems common to premature babies are heart defects, feeding difficulties, and metabolic problems. Heart defects may impede circulation and delivery of oxygen to the brain. Feeding difficulties may lead to nutritional deficiencies. Metabolic problems such as extremely low blood levels of calcium or sugar may cause seizure disorders. Any of these problems, if severe or prolonged, may lead to developmental disabilities later on.

Another source of concern for premature babies is their susceptibility to infection. Due to an underdeveloped immune system, infections can be very dangerous for a premature infant. If the infection occurs in the brain (termed meningitis or encephalitis), there may be damage to nerve cells. Some very small, premature infants suffer brain damage from bleeding inside the brain. This also may lead to subsequent development of hydrocephalus (increased water in the brain).

Other concerns in the newborn period require special attention. During the first week of life, all babies are tested for specific metabolic problems such as hypothyroidism (a condition in which there is insufficient thyroid hormone) and phenylketonuria (a disease in which a building block of protein called phenylalanine cannot be broken down by the body). In this country, babies are screened for these and sometimes other metabolic disorders before they leave the hospital. If such a condition is detected, appropriate treatment can begin immediately and developmental disabilities can be prevented. Before screening for and treatment of these disorders were available, affected children often became severely mentally retarded.

Uncovering Developmental Problems during Early Childhood

Also during the first few years of life, parents and doctors may notice signs of developmental problems in a child. Regular checkups by your child's physician can be helpful in monitoring your child's development and finding possibly existing disabilities early. During these "well-baby" visits, your pediatrician may ask how you think your child is developing and when specific developmental milestones were achieved. Most pediatricians value parents' observations and rely on this information to obtain a true picture of the baby's current level of ability.

The pediatrician will also examine the baby and obtain his or her weight, height, and head size (as an indication of brain development). Many physicians often conduct developmental screening tests to assess the child's developmental progress more systematically. With this information, then, the pediatrician can compare your child's progress to the average child's development. If any of the results are out of the average range, the child may need a more detailed evaluation.

In many communities, public health nurses and/or child development specialists routinely conduct developmental screenings. These professionals give brief screening tests that provide an estimate of the child's level of functioning in several areas of development. The results of such a quick assessment can tell you one of several things: they might indicate that your child should have a more thorough examination, they may reassure you that everything is fine, or, if the results are unclear, they may suggest that your child's development be monitored closely and that the screening test be repeated in a few months.

Infants and toddlers, like newborns, also can be affected seriously by infections of the brain (meningitis and encephalitis). Other common sources of developmental problems at this age include childhood accidents, lead poisoning, and chronic illnesses. Surely, your pediatrician will discuss these health care issues with you and the ways many of these problems can be prevented.

Finding Problems in School-Age Children

Mild developmental delays and minor disabilities may go unnoticed during early childhood and only become apparent when a child begins school. It may be a child's inability to keep up with others, immature behavior, or difficulties making and maintaining friends that causes concern. At other times, the teacher may be the one who notices that the youngster is having difficulties in certain academic areas. Learning disabilities and attention deficit disorders including hyperactivity, poor concentration, distractibility, and similar signs are most often uncovered during the first few years of school.

As you can see, developmental problems can be detected at any time beginning with pregnancy and continuing throughout childhood. Keep in mind, though, that all problems cannot be found at the same time. As a rule, the milder the disability, the later it is uncovered.

COMPREHENSIVE EVALUATIONS FOR CHILDREN WITH DISABILITIES

We have previously mentioned that it might be wise to have a child who is suspected of having a disability examined by specialists in a child development center. Such centers, specializing in in-depth developmental evaluations, are located throughout the country. At these centers, youngsters are evaluated by professionals from a variety of disciplines who work together as a team. Generally, these teams include pediatricians, psychologists, language specialists, social workers, educators, physical and occupational therapists, nurses, nutritionists, and others. At times, additional laboratory procedures and special tests are needed to find the cause of the child's problems. Sometimes the exact cause of the disability remains unknown. When the evaluations have been completed, team members carefully consider all of the information gathered during the various assessments. Then, together they develop recommendations for the child's best care and management.

Many evaluation centers provide coordinated follow-up and treatment through special clinics. Individual therapy, counseling, and support services for parents and family members also are available in a number of places. Continued follow-up of the child, together with support to the family, appropriate education, and the availability of other needed services, should help the child with a developmental disability to thrive optimally.

ACKNOWLEDGMENTS

Contributions have been made to this chapter by Siegfried M. Pueschel, M.D., Ph.D., M.P.H., and Leslie E. Weidenman, Ph.D.

◄ **Chapter 3** ►

Developmental Disabilities Are a Family Affair

All of us have expectations and dreams of what our children will do when they grow up, who they will look like, and what they will accomplish in life. Such expectations can help us by providing guidelines for planning our children's future. Most of us modify these plans as our children's unique personalities and abilities unfold.

Discovering that a child has a developmental disability is another matter. No one is ever really prepared to be a parent of a handicapped child.

WHEN YOU ARE TOLD OF YOUR CHILD'S HANDICAP

Being told your child has a disability always is a shock, even if you suspected that something was wrong. It may seem that your hopes have been shattered and your worst fears realized. At the same time, you may not believe what you have been told and think that this only happens to other people.

Parents of handicapped children often describe these and other feelings of sadness and desperation upon learning that their child has a developmental disability. We hope that, when you were told of your child's disability, that it was done with tact and sensitivity. Unfortunately, this is not everyone's experience. All too often parents are hurt unnecessarily by insensitive but well-meaning individuals or by those who are misinformed.

Giving bad news is a difficult job for anyone—professionals included. In your experience, you may have found that certain people are more sympathetic and easier to talk to than others. Some professionals have a knack for relating to people. For others, developing a rapport does not come easily. Also, some professionals are unaware of the impact their style of communication has on parents. In general, professional training has not included communication skills. Fortunately, this is changing. Increasingly, physicians and other professionals are being taught effective ways of talking to and listening to parents and patients.

Inaccurate information about disabled persons is a major source of emotional pain for families. The field of developmental disabilities has advanced rapidly in recent years. What we now know about the potential of children with a variety of disabilities far surpasses our knowledge of only 20 years ago. Unfortunately, not all professionals are aware of these changes, causing them to give parents discouraging information based on outdated views.

Whatever your experience, the initial shock usually is followed by a grieving period during which denial and feelings of guilt and anger often prevail. Subsequently, during the time of adjustment, most parents adapt to the change brought about by the birth of a handicapped child. It is important to remember that everyone adapts in his or her own way. One mother may express her pain and feeling of loss openly, while her husband may suppress his grief by immersing himself in work. Another parent may feel numb or waver between periods of acceptance and depression. Other emotions may surface such as anxiety, shame, hatred, self-pity, and loneliness. You may feel a variety of emotions, each with a different intensity, at different times or all at once. Contradictory feelings occasionally may make you feel out of control or cause you to wonder if you are still able to think straight. Individuals who ordinarily are stable and mature may sometimes feel as if the world is coming to an end. If you are feeling this way, it is likely you are having a normal response to a very stressful situation.

FINDING SOMEONE TO TALK TO

You may find that you are isolating yourself during this difficult time. However, it can be helpful for parents to seek out someone, perhaps a relative or close friend, who will listen and understand. Though you may think that talking only makes things worse, keep in mind that sharing concerns often relieves stress. For example, talking to a parent of a child with a similar problem may convince you that you too can survive this crisis and adjust to the changes in your life. In addition, a parent who has experienced similar disappointment often is more sensitive and can be helpful in ways a professional never can.

Beyond the assistance and support of relatives, friends, professionals, and other parents, the most important factor in the adjustment process is time. Initially, you may feel that you will never be able to cope, but with time you will. One mother describing the first 2 years of life after the birth of a child with spina bifida said: "I can now admit that having Laura is mostly a blessing. . . . much of the experience has been positive, challenging, and rewarding, and I have grown as a person in ways I may not have without her. . . . In fact, the past 2 years have changed me for the better in just about every way. Nevertheless, I still don't want to be the mother of a handicapped child. But I am Laura's mother, I love her deeply, and that makes all the difference."[1]

Although time generally heals, if you are severely depressed or very anxious, you may find that you are provided measurable relief by talking to a professional. For example, psychologists, psychiatrists, or social workers are professionals trained to help people in stress.

HOW DOES THE BIRTH OF A HANDICAPPED CHILD AFFECT YOUR MARITAL RELATIONSHIP?

So far we have been talking primarily about individual adjustment. Yet, the birth of a handicapped child is bound to affect a husband and wife's relationship. The birth of any child brings changes in life-styles and daily schedules. Parents find themselves devoting much of the time and energy once reserved for each other to the baby. And when the baby has special needs, an extra dimension of stress is added to the marriage.

Parents of handicapped children often experience a wide range of intense emotions as they adapt to their youngster's disability. Such emotional distress can affect a couple's relationship. Just how the marriage is affected depends, in part, on its strength before the baby's birth. Even healthy marriages may be stressed for a time as husband and wife struggle to cope with, accept, and understand the changes in their lives. As they adjust, they may discover that they have grown closer and that the marriage is stronger than ever. Some marriages, however, have problems unrelated to the child's disability that may become more evident during this period of stress. Old conflicts tend to reappear. In most instances such problems can be resolved. There are situations, though, where the gap between husband and wife is so great that a resolution is not likely. In addition, during this time of crisis, parents' individual needs often conflict. Each partner looks to the other for support and comfort at a time when it is often difficult to provide.

When a handicapped child is born, parents frequently are faced with many unexpected choices and decisions. Pressures mount and you may feel like everything has to be attended to at once. However, a good rule of thumb is to try to avoid making major life decisions until you have had time to step back and objectively look at your situation. A crisis is not the time to decide your family's future. If possible, take the

---

[1]Sutton, B. (1982). A mother's view. Clinical proceedings. Children's Hospital National Medical Center. *The Child with Spina Bifida: II Psychological, Educational, and Family Concerns, 38* (4), 213.

necessary time to sort out the facts and your feelings. Do not make hasty decisions you may regret later.

WHAT TO TELL THE CHILD'S BROTHERS AND SISTERS

While most of your attention is focused on the disabled child, it is easy to put aside your other children's needs. Remember, people of all ages can feel stress. Even the youngest child can sense when you are sad or something is wrong. Most of us want to know the truth, and children are no exception.

Avoid thinking you must protect your children from emotional pain, though you must remain compassionate. Children, like adults, need accurate, understandable information to help them comprehend what has happened. By discussing the unique needs of the handicapped child and how they may affect family life, parents will help their children adjust. This is particularly important if the disabled child has medical or physical problems requiring much of the parents' time and attention. If no explanation is offered as to why all your time is spent with the disabled child, your other children may draw their own conclusions. For example, they might think erroneously that you are angry with them or perhaps that you love the disabled child more. Without information about the handicapping condition, fears may arise about their sibling's well-being or their parent's sadness. It is important to acknowledge your children's fears and concerns and reassure them of your love and their valued place within the family.

HOW WILL OTHER FAMILY MEMBERS AND FRIENDS REACT?

In addition to the immediate family, other family members and close friends are affected by the arrival of the special child. Just as husbands' and wives' reactions may differ, so will those of relatives and friends. Relatives, upset by the news, may insist that the problem will go away or that the doctors are wrong. Some may argue that "these children" are better off among themselves and therefore should be institutionalized. Other well-meaning friends may point out that Einstein did not talk until he was 4 years old or that "so and so" took forever to walk and now is perfectly normal.

Some family members may look for someone to "blame" for the child's disability. Comments such as "our side of the family is healthy, so the bad genes must come from your side," unfortunately are not uncommon. It is best to avoid such discussions, as they can be divisive and destructive at a time when the family needs extra support from everyone.

At times you may find that close friends and family fail to understand or are reluctant to talk to you about your feelings. They may even avoid you or at the least avoid asking about your child for fear of hurting you further. Some parents find they are unable to tell others of their child's problems because it is too painful. Others cannot talk about anything else. If you want to discuss your concerns and feelings, sometimes it is necessary to let others know that you would like to talk. Remember, grandparents, aunts, uncles, brothers, sisters, and friends are making their own adjustment to the situation and at the same time may be trying to spare your feelings. The best solution is to help each other by providing support and assistance when needed. Like it or not, having a child with a disability is a family affair.

YOU WILL NEED TO SETTLE IN

Once the initial shock has passed and the disappointment, confusion, and grief begin to fade, life will become more normal as you settle into a daily routine. Although it may not be the routine you anticipated, the daily tasks of child care and of maintaining a home and a job do provide a structure that will help stabilize your life.

Every family develops its own system to meet the needs of the individual as well as those of the whole group. This is true whether or not there is a disabled family member. For example, some families sit down together for every meal, while others see each other only at Sunday dinner.

When a child is handicapped, you may find you must fit many additional activities into your family's schedule. Frequent doctor's visits, appointments with therapists, parent meetings, and so on, although important, are very time-consuming. In addition, other duties such as giving medicine or doing physical therapy exercises may be daily chores. Adapting to your child's needs can take lots of energy—intellectual, emotional, as well as physical. Because of such demands, it is important to pace yourself. Having a clear picture of your child's needs will help you settle in and plan for the future.

Have Realistic Expectations for Your Child

Developing a clear understanding of your child's strengths and weaknesses can help prevent unnecessary disappointment and discouragement. Suitable expectations are a protection against the extremes of deep pessimism and overoptimism. Focusing on what your child can do will help you recognize what can be accomplished and how you can help your child progress. Sometimes this is difficult to do. It is not always easy to pinpoint a child's capabilities. At such times, profes-

sionals from early intervention programs or evaluation centers may be of help (see Chapter 4 for additional information).

Establish Priorities

As you identify the various tasks that need to be done, including activities suggested by professionals, it is important for you, your child, and the entire family to establish priorities. No one knows as well as you the demands on your time, as well as your financial and emotional resources. Recognizing the limits of your family's resources is one way to begin. As you plan, consider the time, energy, and cost of each task required and compare this to the benefits. You will want to make sure that the needs of all family members, not just those of your handicapped child, are considered. You also may want to guard against a plan in which one family member makes all the sacrifices. Some compromises should be expected of everyone. A realistic plan will diminish frustration, resentment, and unnecessary anger.

You may find that your priorities shift as your child grows and the family changes. Therefore, as time goes on, the routines and schedules should be reassessed and modified to meet the changing needs.

There Will Be Ups and Downs

As your child grows and enters new worlds, feelings of disappointment, frustration, and grief may resurface. One day you may be on top of the world, only to find that the next day you are short on patience and angry at everyone. At times, feelings of sadness and sorrow may overwhelm you, often without warning. For example, you may experience both joy and a sense of sadness when your child begins to walk or talk. Although you may be thrilled with your child's accomplishments, you also are reminded painfully of how long it has taken. Major milestones in a child's life such as the first day of school, puberty, or turning 21 often are times when parents are reminded of their child's developmental disability.

These feelings usually are not as intense as those you felt when you first learned about your child's disability. And they typically do not last as long as they did initially. As someone explained, "You never get over having a disabled child, but you do get used to it." Some professionals use the term *chronic sorrow* to describe the occasional return of painful feelings. Each family member may experience this at different times and in varying ways.

Your Marriage Is Important

Having a handicapped child should not mean that your marriage is handicapped as well. As we have mentioned, healthy marriages can become stronger, but they also can be affected by the added stress of having a disabled child. Just as your child has special needs, so does your marriage. In a way, it is easy to take care of your child's needs and neglect those of your marriage. Many parents feel there just is not time to attend to everything. Yet, you will be doing yourself and your family a favor if you take the time and give your relationship some extra attention.

How can this be achieved? First, parents need to spend time together. In a busy family, this can be difficult to arrange. There always seems to be something important that needs attention. When time alone is limited, parents may find that they focus only on significant family matters and never get around to just being with each other. Save some time just for yourselves, even if it means postponing other important matters for a while. Allowing yourselves to enjoy something together, when you do not talk about family routines and problems, can do much to relieve stress and preserve intimacy.

Another way of strengthening marital relationships is preserving communication between you and your spouse. Being able to share concerns and feelings and discuss important issues is an important goal, but one that is not always easy to attain.

A good rule of thumb for fostering healthy communication is to avoid making assumptions about your spouse's thoughts and feelings. Likewise, you should not take for granted that your mate knows where you stand on various issues. Even if it is "the same old story," listening to what really is meant and not only what is said can improve understanding of each other. After ample discussion, husbands and wives often realize that their views are quite similar and that the real obstacle was that they assumed too much and listened too little.

It is also important that you and your spouse share responsibilities. There are many tasks to be considered: managing the finances, making decisions about health care, determining the best program for your child, and taking care of household chores. It is not unusual for partnerships to be lopsided. One parent may take on certain jobs and have minimal involvement with others. For example, mothers often take children to the doctor and attend clinics. As a result they may assume the responsibility for managing health care issues. Although it may be necessary for one person to be more familiar with certain problems, this should not mean that the other does not need to show an interest.

Brothers and Sisters Also Have Needs

One question parents often ask is: What is the long-term effect on brothers and sisters when a handicapped child is in the family? Studies of brothers and sisters (siblings) of handicapped children have found that many of them possess a greater tolerance and compassion toward disabled persons than their peers. They also are more accepting of individual differences. Moreover, many of the siblings feel good about their role in the progress made by a brother or sister with special needs. Experience with a handicapped brother or sister has led a number of siblings to careers in the field of human services, including social work, education, medicine, and psychology.

Not long ago, it was assumed that the care of disabled children required an inordinate amount of parents' time. Therefore, many professionals concluded that brothers and sisters might feel neglected. Fortunately, most research has not found this to be so. Many parents do make allowances and consider the needs of all of their children. In addition, studies have found that brothers and sisters do not perceive substantial differences in the amount of attention given to them as compared to their disabled sibling.

How Can You Help Your Other Children? When confronted with novel or unusual situations, children usually model their reactions after those of their parents. Reactions to a handicapped sibling are no exception. As a parent, how you respond to any situation will set the tone for your children. Since your reactions to the needs of your disabled child will be numerous and mixed, you can expect that brothers and sisters will have varied reactions as well.

Before you can help your children cope with their emotions, you should be aware of your own feelings. Typically, children experience many of the same emotions as their parents, although the frequency and intensity might differ. Sometimes, children display love as well as resentment toward their handicapped sibling. It is not at all surprising to find occasional frustration, jealousy, and anger directed toward the handicapped child. These emotions commonly are also seen in children adjusting to the birth of a healthy brother or sister. However, when directed toward a disabled child, these feelings can elicit guilt, fear, or perhaps protectiveness. Everyone needs to know that these feelings are not unusual. Keep in mind that with support from parents, children can learn to manage their emotions as well as resolve problems. As your children grow and mature, their understanding of complex issues will increase. Moreover, their feelings and perceptions will change, and each change may require additional support and guidance.

You may find that explanations must be repeated or expanded upon and that frequent reassurance is necessary. At all times, remember to keep your children well-informed. Without accurate information, fears and misunderstandings can develop, which in turn can affect a child's behavior.

WHEN TO SEEK PROFESSIONAL HELP

There are times when you lose confidence in your abilities as a parent. You may be faced with a difficult problem and find you are unsure of what to do. As we mentioned, talking to a close friend or parent who has had a similar experience may be all that is needed to work out a solution.

Unfortunately, this is not always enough. Concerns can linger or perhaps even worsen. If a problem begins to interfere with your ability to carry out daily activities, getting professional help should be considered. This does not necessarily mean ongoing therapy or counseling. Many issues can be resolved and stress can be reduced in just a few meetings with a professional counselor or therapist. Basically, what counseling does is help you look at a problem from another perspective. It also provides an opportunity to talk to a professional person who has been trained to help people resolve personal difficulties.

To determine if you need professional help, take a good look at your actions and reactions to daily events. If you discover that one or more of the following describes your behavior or the behavior of anyone in your family, then professional assistance could be beneficial: intense unprovoked anger, prolonged grief, marital problems, difficulty holding a job, loss of interest in normal social activities, and abusive behavior toward oneself or others. Chronic depression, excessive drinking, or use of drugs also are signs that help is needed. Sometimes, one family member's emotional problems are a sign that the family as a whole is having difficulty. In such instances, family counseling can be helpful.

It is important to note that not all emotional problems are obvious. Signs of trouble can take various forms. With children and adolescents, the sudden appearance of problem behaviors can be signs of trouble. Symptoms also can be physical. For example, chronic headaches, loss of appetite, stomach aches, and other ailments may be a physical expression of an emotional problem. If a good student's school performance suddenly fails or a sociable youngster no longer gets along with peers, help may be needed. Regression (that is, acting in an immature manner) may suggest a problem. For example, a school-age child may revert to thumbsucking, bedwetting, clutching a security blanket, and so on. It is important to know that children often show their inner concerns through their behavior rather than by talking about them. You can think of these signs as barometers of the family's well-being. When there are significant concerns, help from a professional may be the best remedy. Professional counselors may help you look at problems in new ways and identify resources you may not have considered. However, the actual work involved in making long-term changes will remain the family's responsibility.

LOOKING TOWARD THE FUTURE

Having a disabled child is not something you expected. Although your handicapped child may involve you in many trying experiences, there are also many positive things in your life that happen because of this child. Often you will feel enthusiasm, pride, love, and a great deal of gratification in your role as a parent. You will encounter capacities and strength within yourself that you never believed were there, and you will learn to cope in the face of adversity. You may wish things were different, but you may find that you have grown in ways that you never thought possible.

ADJUSTMENT OF THE DISABLED CHILD

Until now, this chapter has focused on how you and your family might react and adjust to the special needs of a disabled child. You also may be concerned about how disabled children adjust to their own disabilities. Questions like "Will my mentally retarded daughter recognize that her life is different from other girls her age?" or "Will my physically handicapped son become a loner because he cannot participate in sports with his peers?" or "Will my special needs child have friends to play with?" are asked frequently by parents and siblings of handicapped children. Such questions reflect a family's concern not just for themselves but for the feelings of their disabled child.

Personal adjustment basically refers to the way individuals respond to the happy, sad, and challenging moments of their lives. In the disabled population, individuals considered to be well-adjusted generally are those who have a positive outlook on life, who care about others, recognize their strengths, and are proud of their accomplishments. On the other hand, poorly adjusted individuals tend to have a negative outlook, often are bitter and unnecessarily dependent on others, and may be overly critical of those around them.

Helping a child develop into a well-adjusted individual is no easy task whether or not the child has a disability. Countless factors influence one's adjustment to personal challenges. For disabled people, some of the more obvious influences include the type and extent of the disability, the age of onset of the condition, the stability and support available from family and friends, as well as the youngster's inherited traits and biological characteristics. The manner in which family members, friends, and strangers react to the child and the disability is particularly significant for the child's self-attitude. For example, consider the effects on a physically disabled child of constant attention, pampering, and assistance from others. Before long, this child begins to expect such attention and treatment from others. Such treatment, although meant to be helpful, in the long run may be teaching the child to be dependent. If, however, a disabled child is encouraged from the beginning to do as much as possible for himself or herself, an appreciation of the rewards of self-sufficiency and personal accomplishment are much more likely to develop. Remember, the expectations of others do influence our behavior. Thus, parents' expectations for all their children will affect their attitudes and outlook on life. In general, to help disabled youngsters develop positive attitudes, a good rule of thumb is to try to maintain a balance between encouraging independence and providing enough assistance to prevent frustration.

As children grow and mature, the issues of adjustment change. In infancy and early childhood, for example, important influences on adjustment are the characteristics of the child and the interactions between the infant and family members. During this early stage, it is through interactions with the baby that parents learn about what is comforting, pleasing, distressing, or stimulating to the baby. Not all babies will respond the same way, and all parents learn to tailor their interactions to obtain the best results. Certain babies, however, because of their handicapping conditions, have more difficulty than most in tolerating stimulation. Premature infants, for example, are much more easily overstimulated than full-term infants. When overstimulated, these infants respond by withdrawing—perhaps by turning their heads, averting their gaze, crying, or stiffening when held. It is important for family members to adjust their styles of interaction to accommodate these sensitive infants. Otherwise, the youngster will continue to withdraw from human contact, which easily can be misinterpreted by parents as dislike for them. By adjusting the style of interaction to one the baby can tolerate, parents and family adjust to the youngster's needs, and the baby is allowed to begin to learn about the social environment.

During the preschool and school years, interactions with people outside the family begin to play an important role in the adjustment of a disabled child. Teachers, babysitters, neighbors, and peers all become part of the child's everyday life and thus help shape attitudes. Many issues of adjustment appear in terms of learning self-care (e.g., getting dressed or eating without help) and self-control (e.g., sharing voluntarily, learning to take turns in a group). Through experience with groups of adults and children, youngsters learn to control their individual desires. The ways in which people respond to the child's natural attempts to control the situation will influence the child's future expectations and approaches. Affection and consistent, fair discipline are as important with a disabled child as they are with nondisabled children. Feeling sorry for and indulging a child because of the disability is not an uncommon parental reaction. But it is one to avoid if you want your disabled child to be accepted and valued by siblings and peers. Avoiding discipline or stifling a naturally angry reaction to a misbehavior because a child has a disability simply emphasizes to the child how different he or she is from other children. Most disabled children, however, yearn for the daily reminders that they are more like other children than unlike them. They want to be recognized as capable people, who deserve and can tolerate the same privileges and treatments received by others.

Some disabilities make the tasks of self-control more frustrating for everyone involved. But they are important to master, nevertheless. If, for example, parents consistently ignore the early, nonverbal requests of a hearing- and language-impaired child but finally respond once that child throws himself on the ground and cries, then the child will learn that the most successful way of gaining attention is by having a tantrum. This same child might never have tantrums in school because the teacher has learned to respond to the earlier nonverbal signals, or when she missed those, she never "gave in" as a response to a tantrum. If the child has a learning or memory problem, it is especially important that you be extremely consistent in your reactions to misbehaviors. The learning-impaired child has difficulty applying a lesson learned one day or in one context to another circumstance. This child is likely to make the same mistake over again, requiring repeated consequences. If the consequences are the same each time the behavior occurs, the youngster will learn the lesson infinitely more rapidly and will be able to turn attention to new learning.

No matter how carefully the parents introduce new challenges so that a disabled child's frustrations are minimized and his or her accomplishments are optimal, once the child enters school, the lessons the child is expected to learn may not always be so individually planned. In the process of learning the necessary lessons outside the home, disabled children are likely to encounter failure and perhaps rejection. Much research has demonstrated a strong relationship between personality adjustment and achievement. Encountering insurmountable and regular failure often results in an increase in maladaptive behaviors (such as excessive drinking or smoking, yelling, violence). This has been demonstrated repeatedly, even among nondisabled people who beforehand had been considered even-tempered and adjusted.[2] Unfortunately, because of the disability, even routine tasks may be difficult for a disabled child. If the youngster is aware of others' accomplishments, it will be relatively easy for him or her to lose interest and become frustrated laboring over a task that others do without a second thought. It is, therefore, important that the disabled child be praised regularly for persisting with tasks that are difficult but necessary to master. Furthermore, you and your child's teachers should assist the child to find and pursue activities that accentuate strengths so that his or her feelings of self-worth can survive even outside the family.

ACKNOWLEDGMENTS

Contributions have been made to this chapter by James C. Bernier, M.S.W., Sarah J. Gossler, M.S.W., and Debra J. Lobato, Ph.D.

---

[2]Szymanski, L. S., & Tanguay, P. (1980). *Emotional disorders of mentally retarded persons: Assessment, treatment, and consultation.* Baltimore: University Park Press.

◀ Chapter 4 ▶

Parents and Professionals

A Working Partnership

There are many reasons why your child might need a thorough examination involving a number of professionals and specialists. In the past you may not have needed the services of these specialists, so you may be unfamiliar with what each professional does. If this is the case, you may want to know why particular specialists are seeing your child and how they can contribute to his or her evaluation and care.

WORKING TOGETHER

The idea of parents and professionals sharing information and responsibility for a disabled child's care is so important that it merits special attention here. At long last, parents are being recognized as the people who are most important in caring and planning for handicapped children. In a way, parents are the real experts on their children. They often have the best understanding of the ways their children behave and communicate. They know their children's likes and dislikes as well as their motivations. Many parents have become skilled as teachers and advocates and are quite knowledgeable about their children's special needs and problems.

While professionals may be able to suggest many ways to help a disabled child, parents know what activities are practical for their particular household. They can take into consideration schedules, finances, and other family needs when planning for the handicapped youngster. This parental perspective is extremely important and should be shared with professionals when treatment programs are being developed. Recognizing parents' abilities, however, does not mean that their contribution can replace the work of trained professionals. Professionals bring a background of rigorous training as well as specific knowledge and experience to evaluation and planning for handicapped children.

Handicapping conditions often involve complex biological and environmental factors. Advances in the understanding of these factors have come from scientists working in the fields of medicine as well as the social and behavioral sciences. This improved understanding has enabled professionals to develop more effective interventions for the education and treatment of developmentally disabled children as well as programs to prevent future disabilities. The complexity of some of the handicapping conditions and the diversity of the fields of study contributing to the new knowledge, however, make it necessary for professionals to specialize in order to keep up with even part of the useful information. Thus, numerous professionals from various specialties may be required to work with parents and handicapped children at different times.

Children with disabilities benefit the most when parents and specialists work together. Professionals can provide assistance by working directly with children, consulting with parents and teachers, and participating in the development plans for care and management. Professionals also help parents solve specific problems and improve their teaching and caregiving skills. In turn, the professionals may rely on parents for specific observations and current information about their children. This give and take, respecting each other as equally important partners in the child's care, will contribute to a trusting relationship between parents and professionals, which is so important for the child's optimal development.

COORDINATING SERVICES

At times, the seemingly endless rounds of appointments and evaluations for your child may leave you feeling confused and exhausted. It may seem like you are running in circles only to get different, and occasionally conflicting, pieces of advice. Coordinating the services for a handicapped child can help reduce some of the stress this confusion can leave. If an evaluation has been done at a major child development center, then the chances are that one person from the team of professionals has been assigned the role of coordinator. This professional may be a pivotal person you can contact when questions arise about services or upcoming appointments, or perhaps when you want to discuss new problems and concerns. The coordinator may be responsible for making sure that all necessary appointments have been scheduled, recommended tests have been performed, and appropriate follow-up care is being provided.

If you have not been to an evaluation center and do not have a coordinator for your child, there are several options available. One is to assume the responsibility yourself. This would require that you keep accurate, up-to-date records on your child and make sure that all information is shared among the professionals involved in your child's care. This can be time-consuming and, at times, difficult, yet it is an effective way to make sure your child's needs are being met. Another possibility is to contact local associations for individuals with handicapping conditions, such as the Spina Bifida Association, Down Syndrome Congress, or the Association for Retarded Citizens, for assistance. You also may want to ask your child's pediatrician for help. You can request that all doctors and professionals involved in your child's care be informed of test results, treatment decisions, and future plans. Moreover, if your child is of school age and receives special education services, someone at the school may be able to assist you in coordinating services.

FINDING AND CHOOSING SPECIALISTS

Referrals to specialists may be made for a number of reasons, such as:

To evaluate specific skills as part of a complete diagnostic workup
To do further testing once a diagnosis has been established
To assure ongoing treatment once a problem has been identified
To obtain a second opinion regarding a diagnosis, prognosis, or course
    of treatment

Choosing a specialist, like selecting your family doctor, is not always easy. A good place to begin is by asking for recommendations from respected professionals, family members, or trusted friends. If you are new to an area, the public health department, visiting nurse associations, hospitals, the medical bureau, and the directory of medical specialties can provide useful information.

You should feel comfortable with your choice, particularly if you expect a long-term relationship. You should be able to discuss treatment programs, ask questions, and consider the cost of service with the professional without being intimidated or overly embarrassed. Feeling good about the way a professional interacts with your child and the extent of his or her experience in working with children who have special needs are also things to consider. Some professionals might feel uneasy working with a handicapped child or may not recognize how certain disabilities affect a child's behavior. Remember that your neighbor's favorite doctor may not be the right one for you! If you find that you are uncomfortable or that you do not like the way your child is treated, it is up to you to change doctors, therapists, counselors, and so forth. The better you communicate with the professional, the more likely it is that better services will be obtained for your child.

SOME PROFESSIONALS YOU MAY MEET

The professionals described in this section are people you may meet in evaluation centers. Also included are specialists your child may be referred to by your family physician or the child's pediatrician. (Note that many of the procedures mentioned here are described in more detail in later chapters.)

Anesthesiologist An anesthesiologist is a medical doctor who administers anesthesia such as a drug or gas to a patient about to undergo surgery or an obstetrical or other medical procedure, in order to block the feeling of pain. The anesthesiologist examines the patient before an operation; then, in consultation with the other doctors involved, selects the type of anesthesia to be used.

Audiologist An audiologist is a specialist trained to evaluate a person's hearing. A variety of instruments and/or tests may be used to determine a person's hearing ability. In testing a child's hearing, the audiologist may observe the child's reactions to environmental sounds and to specific sound frequencies presented to each ear. The audiologist also may examine the flexibility of the eardrum using a special instrument in a procedure called tympanometry (see Chapter 22 for a fuller description). Nerve responses to sounds can be assessed by examining brainwave patterns measured after an eardrum has been exposed to a sound. This is a special procedure called auditory evoked response (AER), sometimes called brain stem evoked response (BSER). (See Chapter 22 for a more detailed description.) Often, an audiologist will have to test a small child's hearing more than once before an accurate picture of the hearing abilities can be determined. Audiologists frequently work closely with other professionals interested in the child's hearing such as speech therapists, otolaryngologists (ear, nose, and throat doctors), pediatricians, psychologists, educators, and so on. Sometimes, more sophisticated forms of testing may also be used, such as Central Auditory Processing, which assesses a child's listening skills.

If a hearing loss is detected, the audiologist may be the key person involved in planning and coordinating a remediation program. And, if hearing aids are prescribed, the audiologist will teach family members about their proper care, fit, and use.

Cardiologist A cardiologist is a medical doctor who specializes in the evaluation and treatment of diseases of the heart. The cardiologist examines patients for symptoms of heart problems, and, in the process, uses various instruments and procedures. Commonly, the doctor listens to the heart sounds using a stethoscope; and, if necessary, conducts special tests such as an electrocardiogram, echocardiogram, or cardiac catheterization. (For descriptions of these procedures, see Chapter 22.) Children with heart problems are treated according to their specific needs. A treatment plan might include one or more of the following:

careful monitoring of a child's condition, a change in the patient's diet, daily heart medication(s), and surgery to correct a specific defect of the heart. The latter is done by a cardiac surgeon.

Counselor (see also **Psychiatrist, Psychologist,** and **Social Worker**) A counselor is a professional who has been trained to provide individual and/or group counseling services. Counselors may work in a variety of settings such as a clinic, hospital, mental health center, university, or public school, or have their own private practice. In general, counseling aims at helping people improve their feelings about themselves as well as their social relationships with others. A counselor may help an individual pinpoint specific problems and identify potential solutions through personal interviews, individual or group discussions, observation of specific behaviors, or assessment using a variety of tests or inventories. A counselor may work with a parent and a child individually or together, or perhaps with an entire family. It is important to select a counselor based on your needs as well as the counselor's area of expertise. Not all counselors can help solve all problems.

Dentist A dentist is a doctor who has been trained in the prevention, diagnosis, and care of diseases of the mouth, particularly of the teeth and gums. Most people have experienced a dental examination and treatment of common dental problems such as cavities. Most will recall that a dental examination involves inspection of the teeth and gums with various instruments and sometimes requires a series of X rays of the teeth. Treatment of cavities or tooth decay usually consists of drilling out the decayed portion of the tooth and filling the hole with a substance to prevent further decay. Other common procedures used in the treatment of dental problems are: cleaning, pulling of teeth, capping or crowning diseased or broken teeth, root canal treatments, and gum care. Professionals in the field of dentistry may specialize and focus their practice on certain types of dental problems. For example, an **orthodontist** corrects irregular tooth alignment through the use of braces or other dental appliances, and a **periodontist** focuses on treating diseases and problems of the gums surrounding the teeth.

Dietitian (see **Nutritionist**)

Educator An educator is a specialist trained to teach others. Educators or teachers are professionals who have been trained to instruct students in various fields of study. Teachers must qualify to teach in public schools by successfully completing a course of study that meets the state's requirements. Most states grant teaching certificates for specific areas such as elementary education, secondary education, early childhood or preschool education, and special education. The field of special education is the one with which most parents of developmentally disabled children will come in contact. Within special education, teachers can specialize further by focusing their training on profoundly and severely mentally retarded or mildly to moderately mentally retarded people. Students majoring in special education receive specific training in various handicapping conditions such as learning disabilities, hearing and visual impairments, and mental retardation.

Endocrinologist An endocrinologist is a medical doctor who specializes in the study and treatment of disorders of the endocrine, or ductless, glands in the body. The endocrine glands include the pituitary, thyroid, parathyroid, adrenal, pancreas, ovaries, and testes. They are called ductless glands because they secrete their hormones directly into the blood stream. Problems with hormone production may result in either too much hormone being released (hypersecretion), too little being released (hyposecretion), or other glandular disorders.

Gastroenterologist A gastroenterologist is a medical doctor who specializes in the study and treatment of problems of the stomach and intestinal tract. This doctor also might be concerned with other parts of the body related to digestion, including the esophagus, liver, gallbladder, and pancreas. Patients usually are referred to a gastroenterologist for further evaluation, diagnosis, and treatment of stomach and intestinal problems by their regular physician.

General Practitioner or Family Physician A general practitioner is a medical doctor who attends to and treats a wide range of medical conditions in a general practice. The general practitioner conducts physical examinations and may order and/or perform specific tests to diagnose a patient's problem. The general practitioner, often referred to as a G.P., provides preventative care by inoculating or vaccinating patients against certain diseases and by advising people on proper diet, exercise, and hygiene, and methods of avoiding diseases. A general practitioner also may provide prenatal care to a pregnant woman and may deliver babies.

Genetic Counselor A genetic counselor is a specialist trained to advise expectant or potential parents about the risk of their children having hereditary birth defects. People may want to see a genetic counselor for one of the following reasons: they previously may have had a child with either an inherited disorder or a birth defect; someone in the immediate family has a birth defect or genetic disorder; the potential parents are 35 years or older; the mother has had repeated miscarriages or stillbirths; or the couple is worried about exposure to drugs, alcohol, or radiation. The genetic counselor will gather background information about the couple and other family members concerning inherited problems or birth defects. In some situations, chromosome or other genetic studies will need to be done to determine if either parent is a carrier of a chromosomal or genetic disorder that could be passed on to the baby. (Chromosomes are structures of the cell nucleus containing DNA, which transmits genetic information.) Usually, results are given in terms of probability or percent chance that a baby born will or will not have a genetic defect or a birth defect. It must be emphasized that the counselor cannot tell with absolute certainty whether or not a problem will occur. Moreover, the genetic counselor does not tell parents what plan of action should be pursued, but only informs couples about the possible risks.

Geneticist A neonatal geneticist is a physician who is concerned with the relationship between heredity and certain diseases. The role of the clinical geneticist is often similar to that of the genetic counselor and would include performing a complete examination of the patient, discussing all the information obtained in a genetic counseling session, and describing the chances of having a child with a genetic disorder.

Gynecologist A gynecologist is a medical doctor who specializes in the diagnosis and treatment of disorders of the female reproductive system. Gynecologists conduct general physical examinations and special examinations of such organs as the vagina, uterus, and ovaries. They prescribe appropriate health care regimens including medications, exercises, or hygiene procedures. A gynecologist may perform surgery as needed to correct a malfunction or remove a diseased organ. A gynecologist also has training as an obstetrician and may provide care for pregnant women.

Intern An intern is a professional who has just graduated from medical school and is starting to practice medicine under the supervision of licensed doctors in a hospital setting. Internships most often continue for 1 year. The purpose of the internship is to provide young doctors with supervised training and to allow them to gain valuable experience in examining and treating patients.

Internist An internist is a medical doctor specializing in the treatment of diseases of internal organ systems. The internist deals with problems and diseases that usually are not treated surgically.

Neurologist A neurologist is a physician who specializes in the diagnosis and treatment of disorders of the nervous system, including the brain, cranial nerves, spinal cord, and peripheral nerves. The neurologist traditionally deals with problems such as seizures, brain damage, muscular disorders, brain tumors, and so on. The neurological examination conducted by the neurologist attempts to determine how the nervous system is developing, how it is functioning, and if any problems exist. Among other things, neurologists look at muscle strength, motor coordination, reflexes, ability to perceive sensations, and the function of the major cranial nerves, by observing things such as eye movements, vision, and hearing. A neurologist may use a variety of instruments or laboratory tests to assist in the evaluation of a patient's nervous system. The brainwave test (electroencephalogram or EEG) is used primarily in the evaluation of seizure disorders. The neurologist also may order brain scans (see Chapter 22), spinal taps (see Chapter 12), and other tests to diagnose a patient's condition. Parents of handicapped children seeking neurological evaluations should look for a pediatric neurologist who specializes in treating children. A pediatric neurologist is trained to evaluate the developing nervous system and is skilled in assessing problems that may be particular to children.

Neurosurgeon A neurosurgeon is a medical doctor who has had special training in operative procedures of the brain, spinal cord, and nerves. Neurosurgeons usually perform neurological examinations similar to those done by a neurologist. Neurosurgeons are often asked to treat children with hydrocephalus by inserting a plastic tube into the middle of the brain (the ventricle), in order to drain the surplus liquid (cerebral spinal fluid) into the abdominal cavity. Neurosurgeons are also consulted in cases of head injury, brain tumor, bleeding into the brain, and other brain problems.

Nurse A nurse is a professional who is trained to care for those who are sick or injured, or who have disabilities, and to provide advice on appropriate health care and prevention of illnesses. Nurses work in many settings including hospitals, clinics, physicians' offices, and the community. The nurse's specific role depends on his or her training, professional background, and job requirements. A nurse's training can lead to several professional degrees. The most common ones are L.P.N., or licensed practical nurse, and R.N., or registered nurse. An L.P.N. is licensed to care for patients under the direction of a physician or registered nurse. An R.N. is a graduate of a nursing training program who has completed all the requirements for registration and licensure demanded by a state board of nursing. The type of nursing a particular nurse practices often is indicated by the title. For example, the titles district, community, or visiting nurse all refer to registered nurses who work in the community, caring for patients in their homes or in community centers. A school nurse is a registered nurse who provides care to children while they are in school, and a clinic nurse usually works in a hospital setting.

Nutritionist A nutritionist is a specialist in the study of food intake. Nutritionists who work directly with patients most often are found in clinical settings such as hospitals or diagnostic centers. In the field of developmental disabilities, the nutritionist can be an important member of an interdisciplinary team of professionals. The role of the nutritionist generally involves assessing the child's past nutritional history and current status. The assessment might include a study of the child's daily food intake, feeding abilities, food tolerances, and so forth. If a nutritional problem is discovered, the nutritionist, along with the other members of the interdisciplinary team, will develop a treatment plan. Nutritionists are often involved in the care of children with specific metabolic disorders.

Practicing nutritionists usually are registered dietitians, which is indicated by the initials R.D. A registered dietitian has completed a specified course of study in dietetics or nutrition, as well as an internship in a professional setting.

Obstetrician An obstetrician is a medical doctor who specializes in the care of women during pregnancy, birth, and the period immediately following the birth of a child. The obstetrician typically is the doctor who delivers the baby. Obstetric care usually involves frequent visits to the doctor's office during pregnancy. During the visit, the doctor will monitor the growth of the unborn baby (fetus) and examine the mother's condition. The obstetrician also provides valuable advice on proper nutrition and exercise; and the importance of immunization, of getting adequate rest, and of avoiding the use of drugs, cigarettes, and alcohol and the unnecessary use of prescription and nonprescription medications.

Occupational Therapist An occupational therapist is a professional who specializes in helping handicapped individuals improve their skills of daily living in order to function as independently as possible. With children, the focus of occupational therapy, or O.T., concentrates on habilitation or the acquisition of new skills. The occupational therapist may work with children in a number of different settings including hospitals, residential facilities, diagnostic centers, as well as the patient's home. The occupational therapist primarily helps the child improve fine motor skills (that is, the function of the smaller muscles of the body such as those found in the hands and arms). Examples of such skills include reaching and grasping objects, self-feeding, drinking from a cup, and using crayons. The occupational therapist also devises splints or adaptive equipment to improve the child's functional abilities. Occupational therapists may work directly with children on a regular basis or consult with family members, teachers, or other professionals working with the child.

Ophthalmologist An ophthalmologist is a medical doctor who specializes in the diagnosis and treatment of injuries, diseases, and functional problems of the eye. The ophthalmologist examines the patient's eyes and tests visual abilities. The examination may include looking into the eye with a special instrument as well as having the patient look through a variety of lenses. If a vision problem is detected, the doctor may prescribe corrective lenses or glasses.

Optometrist An optometrist is a professional specifically trained to test vision and prescribe corrective lenses when necessary. The optometrist's professional degree is a doctor of optometry, abbreviated O.D. Optometrists are not medical doctors and therefore are not qualified to treat eye diseases or injuries.

Orthopaedist An orthopaedist is a medical doctor who specializes in the diagnosis, prevention, and treatment of disorders of the bones, joints, and muscles. Of particular interest to the orthopaedist are the body structures involved in various movements such as walking or positions such as sitting or standing. An orthopaedic examination will include an evaluation of the patient's muscle strength, range of motion, flexibility, and the presence or absence of any deformities. Often, one or more X rays are needed to determine if an orthopaedic problem exists. Children with certain developmental disabilities such as cerebral palsy or spina bifida may need to see an orthopaedist for evaluation and possible treatment at various points during their lives. These disabilities may affect muscle control, which in turn may cause bony deformities. Orthopaedic treatment may consist of a prescription for exercises, physical or occupational therapy, splints, casts, braces, adaptive equipment, or surgery. Orthopaedists often work closely with physical and occupational therapists who are carrying out the treatment plan.

Otolaryngologist An otolaryngologist is a medical doctor who specializes in the diagnosis and treatment of diseases of the ear, nose, and throat. An otolaryngologist, usually referred to as an E.N.T. specialist, examines the ear, nose, and throat using various tools and instruments such as an audiometer (measures the acuity of hearing), X rays, otoscope (used to inspect the ear), and so forth. Some physicians may choose to specialize further and focus their attention on only the ear, nose, or throat. These doctors are called **otologists** (ear), **rhineologists** (nose), and **laryngologists** (throat).

Pediatrician A pediatrician is a medical doctor who specializes in the care of children from the time they are born through adolescence. The pediatrician provides routine health care services such as regular checkups and immunizations. This often is called well-baby or well-child care. The pediatrician also cares for the child who has become ill or hurt. Parents frequently turn to the pediatrician for advice on many childrearing issues. For example, the pediatrician may be asked questions about behavior management techniques, toilet training, sibling rivalries, discipline strategies, developing independent feeding skills, and so on. Many pediatricians can offer excellent suggestions on these and other topics.

Physiatrist A physiatrist is a medical doctor who primarily uses physical agents to treat patients with physical handicaps or neuromuscular disorders. Physical agents may include heat, light, water, electricity, massage, exercise, and radiation. In the field of developmental disabilities, the physiatrist may be involved with those children who have disorders of the nerves and muscles or other physical handicapping conditions requiring treatment. The physiatrist usually works closely with orthopaedists, and physical and occupational therapists. The physiatrist may be instrumental in prescribing splints, braces, wheelchairs, and other pieces of adaptive equipment for physically impaired children.

Physical Therapist A physical therapist is a professional trained to help handicapped individuals improve and develop skills for balance and movement. The physical therapist, or P.T., is concerned mainly with the function of the larger muscles of the body. These muscles are needed for gross motor activities such as walking, crawling, rolling, and moving from one stationary position to another. Physical therapists can provide therapy to adults and children alike in a variety of settings, such as in hospitals, clinics, rehabilitation centers, schools, and homes. Physical therapists are important members of interdisciplinary teams that provide diagnostic and treatment services to developmentally disabled children. In this context, the physical therapist's role usually involves conducting an evaluation of the child's current level of motor development and determining if there is a need for therapy. As part of the evaluation, the

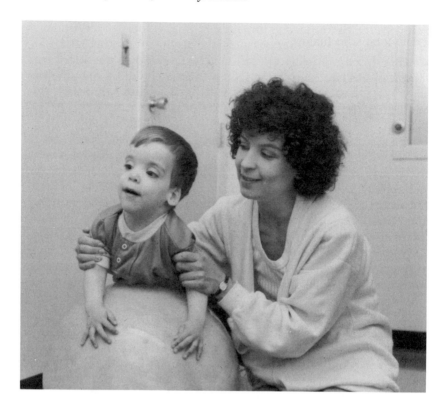

therapist examines the child's muscle tone, muscle strength, range of motion of the joints, reflexes, posture, movement patterns, and motor skills. The physical therapist also will look for any structural deformities.

Psychiatrist A psychiatrist is a medical doctor who specializes in the diagnosis and treatment of mental, emotional, and behavioral disorders. The psychiatrist obtains information about the patient's condition through observation, physical examination, interviews, and testing. Family members and friends of the patient may be interviewed in order to learn more about the patient's medical and personal history. By carefully evaluating all the data that has been gathered, the psychiatrist develops a diagnosis of the patient's problem and formulates a plan of treatment. Psychiatric treatment methods will vary considerably, depending on the patient's problems, and may include the use of prescribed medications and/or participation in one or more types of individual or group therapy.

Psychologist   A psychologist is a professional who specializes in the study of intellectual functioning and behavior. There are many types of psychologists, including clinical, educational, school, child, and counseling psychologists, to name a few. Each area has a different focus and prepares the psychologist for a different type of practice. Despite the different emphasis in training, all psychologists are concerned with the analysis, interpretation, and application of information that has been obtained about an individual, group, specific problem, or area of investigation.

Parents of developmentally disabled children are most likely to encounter clinical, school, or child psychologists. Psychologists working with disabled children are skilled in evaluating the child's developmental, social-emotional, and intellectual abilities. As part of the evaluation process they are likely to administer and interpret intelligence tests. Many psychologists also are skilled in other types of evaluation such as behavioral assessment. Upon completion of the psychological evaluation, the psychologist formulates recommendations or develops specific programs for particular problems. The psychologist may work directly with children or consult with parents, teachers, or other professionals involved in the child's overall treatment.

Respiratory Therapist   A respiratory therapist, or R.T., is a professional trained to help patients who have breathing problems. Assistance can be provided either directly by inhalation and chest physical therapy or indirectly through the use of special equipment designed to help patients breathe more easily. Equipment used in respiratory therapy may include: oxygen masks, respirators, mist tents, and Intermittent Positive Pressure Breathing (IPPB) machines. The latter technique helps breathing by inflating the lungs with pressurized air. Respiratory therapists most often are employed in medical settings such as hospitals and nursing homes, but also work in agencies providing home care services.

Social Worker   A social worker is a professional whose role, in general terms, involves helping others get along in society. Social workers provide assistance in many different types of human service agencies. For example, they are employed routinely by hospitals, schools, welfare agencies, diagnostic centers, residential facilities, and public health agencies. The specific function of the social worker depends on both the job setting and the individual's professional background and training. Many social workers function as counselors and psychotherapists. In addition, they may help families locate and obtain services from appropriate agencies or other available sources of assistance. In the field of developmental disabilities, social workers often help families to obtain emotional and financial support. For example, they may help families contact other families experiencing similar problems; provide individual, group, or family therapy; introduce a parent to relevant national and/or local organizations; or show parents how to apply for appropriate federal or state aid programs.

Speech Pathologist   A speech pathologist is a professional trained to evaluate speech and language disorders in children and adults. In addition, speech pathologists plan and carry out treatment programs for these disorders. The speech pathologist, who also may be referred to as a speech therapist, evaluates speech and language skills primarily by observing the child and conducting specific tests. Speech pathologists, like audiologists, also are concerned about hearing problems and the impact they have on the development of language and communication skills. Many children with developmental disabilities are seen by speech pathologists because of delayed language development. Once the evaluation is completed, the speech pathologist will determine the need for direct speech and language therapy. If a child has not developed vocal communication skills, speech pathologists will examine the type of communication system the child could use—for example, a sign language system or modern communication devices.

Surgeon   A surgeon is a medical doctor who specializes in the use of operative or surgical techniques to treat infections, tumors, and injuries; correct deformities; and improve functioning. A surgeon may practice general surgery or specialize further. For example, hand surgeons restrict their practice to problems of the hand; plastic surgeons use surgical procedures to restore or repair parts of the body that have been damaged, lost, or deformed; and cardiovascular surgeons use operative procedures to correct problems of the vascular system, which includes the heart, lungs, and blood vessels. Prior to an operation, the surgeon will examine the patient, select the most appropriate surgical procedure, and evaluate the risks involved. Part of planning for an operation may include consulting with other doctors who have cared for the patient and are familiar with the specific problem necessitating surgery.

Urologist   A urologist is a medical doctor who specializes in the diagnosis and treatment of problems of the urinary tract and kidneys. The urologist also is the doctor who diagnoses and treats diseases and structural problems of the male and female genital tracts. A urological examination might require use of special equipment such as catheters, cystoscopes, X rays, and other instruments. Treatment of urological problems includes prescribing medicine, use of antiseptics to prevent infection, or surgery. In the field of developmental disabilities, children who have spina bifida or a spinal cord injury may need to see a urologist, since urological problems are common with these disorders.

ACKNOWLEDGMENTS

Contributions have been made to this chapter by Leslie E. Weidenman, Ph.D., and James A. Mulick, Ph.D.

◄ **PART II** ►

Common Problems and Disabilities in Children with Special Needs

◀   Chapter 5   ▶

Mental Retardation

DESCRIPTION AND INCIDENCE

Although most people have some idea of what *mental retardation* means, not everyone is aware that there are technical definitions of the term. The most commonly used definition was developed by the American Association on Mental Retardation (AAMR), a professional organization that specializes in problems of people with mental retardation and developmental disabilities. The AAMR definition reprinted here is written in complex language and has several important parts. Therefore, following the definition, we have explained the meaning and significance of each part. According to the American Association on Mental Retardation, mental retardation is: "significantly sub-average intellectual functioning existing concurrently with deficits in adaptive behavior and manifested during the developmental period" (Grossman, 1973).

"Significantly sub-average intellectual functioning" usually means that the child has an IQ score of less than 68 or 70 on one of the individually administered, standard intelligence tests. The exact score depends upon the specific test that has been used (see Chapter 27 for a discussion of intelligence tests).

"Adaptive behavior" refers to the skills needed for personal independence and social responsibility such as dressing, toileting, feeding, behavior control, independence in the community, and interaction with peers.

"Developmental period" is defined as the time between birth and 22 years of age.

There are four levels of mental retardation: mild, moderate, severe, and profound. Levels are determined by an individual's IQ on a standardized intelligence test. IQ scores are based on an average of 100. How far below average a person's score falls determines whether he or she is mentally retarded as well as the degree of mental retardation. These four levels, as well as normal and borderline intelligence, are described next and are summarized in Table 1.

Normal Intelligence

People are considered to be of average intelligence if they score between 84–85 and 115–116 on an intelligence test. This group makes up ap-

Table 1. Levels of intelligence in relation to IQ score

Level of intelligence	Intelligence test score	% of population in each group[a]
Normal	Between 84–85 and 115–116	68
Borderline	Between 68–70 and 83–84	14
Mild mental retardation	Between 50–55 and 67–69	2
Moderate mental retardation	Between 35–40 and 49–54	<½
Severe mental retardation	Between 20–25 and 34–39	<¼
Profound mental retardation	Less than 20–25	<¼

[a]Approximately 15% of people score above 115–116 IQ.

proximately 68 percent of the population. People who score above 116 would be considered to be of above-average intelligence or gifted.

Borderline Intelligence

An IQ score that falls in the range from 68–70 to 83–84 suggests that an individual is of borderline intelligence. These people are not considered mentally retarded, as they do not have impairments in their independent living skills. This group represents approximately 14 percent of the population.

Mild Mental Retardation

Mild mental retardation applies to IQ scores within the range of 50–55 to 67–69, depending upon the test used. Many mildly mentally retarded people are indistinguishable from the general population, but they usually will learn more slowly in school and may be limited in their choice of vocation. They are frequently quite independent in the community and most often take responsibility for their own basic day-to-day needs. They are often capable of working and living either independently or with a minimum of assistance and supervision.

Moderate Mental Retardation

Moderate mental retardation includes the IQ score range of 35–40 up to 49–54. Moderately retarded children generally will learn the basic academic skills necessary for daily living. As they get older, their school programs often will concentrate on important self-help skills, community living, and vocational preparation. As adults, they may be employed in sheltered workshops or other supervised work settings.

Severe Mental Retardation

Severe mental retardation refers to IQ scores that fall within the range of 20–25 to 34–39. Severely mentally retarded people may have associated handicaps, such as motor problems or significant speech and language deficits. School programs will emphasize basic developmental skills, communication, and adaptive behavior. People who are severely mentally retarded usually can work in supervised workshop settings. Supervision in daily living throughout adulthood is necessary for the severely mentally retarded individual.

Profound Mental Retardation

Profound mental retardation refers to IQ scores that fall below the range of 20–25. Again, there may be significant associated handicaps. Still, with proper training, many profoundly retarded people can learn basic self-care skills. If their functioning is very low, if other handicaps such as hearing problems or visual or motor impairments are extremely incapacitating, or if their health status is precarious, special living arrangements may be necessary.

WHAT IT MEANS TO BE MENTALLY RETARDED

Mental retardation can be a frightening term. Frequently parents are able to recognize and accept other handicaps in their children, but are devastated by the term *mental retardation.* Many people have strong prejudices or misconceptions about mental retardation. For example, they may think that mentally retarded children are very different, that they will not learn or grow or have normal emotions, that their appearance will be unusual, that they always will be children, or that they will be unable to care for themselves.

The various words used to describe a child who is significantly subaverage on psychological tests can be confusing. Parents may have heard terms such as *slow learner, developmentally delayed,* or *learning disabled,* and may not be sure how they differ.

Basically, a mentally retarded child is one who learns slowly. However, the term *slow learner* usually is reserved for children who are slightly below average intellectually, but not so far below to be considered mentally retarded. A young child diagnosed as mentally retarded will continue to learn, change, and grow intellectually, but the speed with which new skills are acquired will be much slower than that of the average person. Mental retardation is not drastically different from many other kinds of learning problems, but it means that a large number of skill areas are affected, especially those skills that are needed for success in school.

It is important to know that mentally retarded children are not helpless. Unless some other disorder or medical problem is present, or the environment is deprived, mentally retarded children continue to progress.

A mentally retarded child also could be considered learning disabled, but only in the broadest sense of the term. Such children are disabled because they have trouble learning or learn very slowly, compared to the average. *Learning disability*, however, is a specific term that refers to a different kind of problem (see also Chapter 7). Learning disabled youngsters have one or more specific deficits in skills necessary for learning, but do not have globally subaverage intelligence. They may be perfectly average or even above average on psychological tests, but fall 2 or more years behind their peer group academically, for reasons that cannot always be identified. In these very important ways, learning disabilities and mental retardation are different types of handicaps.

MENTAL RETARDATION VERSUS
DEVELOPMENTAL DELAY: MAKING AN ACCURATE DIAGNOSIS

Mental retardation is difficult to diagnose with certainty in very young children. Infants and preschoolers who are behind in some or all of their developmental skills initially may be called *developmentally delayed* to describe the lag. This term may imply to some parents that the child will catch up at some point and will develop normally afterwards. Indeed, some developmentally delayed youngsters do catch up; however, others do not. Some children who are delayed at a young age turn out to be mentally retarded. In many developmentally delayed children, it is impossible to predict whether or not they will be mentally retarded until they are older. *Developmental delay* is often the term used to describe a child's below-average functioning until a more specific diagnosis can be established.

It is possible to miss the diagnosis of mental retardation in a young child, because normal development is so variable and unpredictable. Especially if children are normal in appearance and doing well in their muscle development, mental retardation may not be evident until the youngster is 2 or 3 years old or older. For that reason, any suspicion of delays in development, especially in language, deserves a thorough evaluation by a team of professionals.

It is also possible to mistakenly diagnose a child as mentally retarded. Children who are deprived, uncooperative, withdrawn, ill, tired, emotionally disturbed, frightened, on medication, physically handicapped, very young (birth to 3), or who dislike the examiner or the testing environment may be misdiagnosed. Also, for reasons that are not well known, a few individual children can show major variations in test performance over the course of months or years. A child who appears to be mentally retarded at one time might seem to be a slow learner at another time when evaluated by another examiner or when given a different test. The opposite can also occur. Usually, these discrepancies are not serious, but they can be upsetting to parents. Therefore, great care must be taken in testing and labeling children. Routine retesting at regular intervals may be important, and a frank discussion with the psychologist whenever a question arises also may be of benefit.

Does a diagnosis of mental retardation mean that a child is brain-damaged? In most cases it is true that something is wrong with how the brain works in children who are mentally retarded. However, there may not be a specific, identifiable area of damage in the brain to which the retardation can be traced. Not all mental retardation is caused by damage to brain structures. For example, chemical imbalances or "mis-wiring of nerves" can cause various problems in brain function. Certain neurological tests such as the brainwave test, CT scan (see computerized tomography, Chapter 22), and spinal fluid examination may indicate that there are problems, but usually they cannot tell exactly what is wrong inside a child's brain that may result in mental retardation.

CAUSES OF MENTAL RETARDATION

Medical science has discovered numerous causes of mental retardation. Yet, for many persons with mental retardation, the specific cause remains unknown. Mental retardation frequently occurs along with or is a symptom of specific developmental disorders or syndromes. As you will see, many of the disabilities discussed in Part III of this book include mental retardation as one of the characteristics.

Most often, mental retardation is caused before, during, or shortly after birth. Of course, accidents, infections, or injuries to the brain can happen at any time and may result in mental retardation. Known causes of mental retardation during early development include:

Inherited (genetic) disorders or chromosome defects
Abuse of certain drugs or alcohol during pregnancy
Specific infections during pregnancy
Malnutrition during important periods of brain development before and
    after birth
Complications of prematurity
Severe bleeding at the time of birth
Birth injury or lack of oxygen during delivery
Glandular problems, such as hypothyroidism
Serious brain infections
Toxic effects on the brain such as in lead poisoning
Accidents that cause brain damage

PARENTAL EXPECTATIONS

To hear their child diagnosed as mentally retarded can be excruciatingly painful for some parents. However, the concept continues to be applied because it can be useful. When used appropriately, it conveys to parents that the disability is real and that it is lifelong. It can help parents to be realistic about the child's educational program and long-term vocational goals. Yet, it can also be damaging to the extent that it may cause parents to have low expectations for their child, or it may create a self-fulfilling prophecy in which the label guarantees that the condition, that of below-average functioning, will remain.

It can be equally damaging however, to use softer, more vague terms to protect parents from the truth. Avoiding the issue of mental retardation can result in years of struggling with inappropriate classroom placements, poor school curricula, pressure on the child at home, and a long, painful history of failure and frustration on the part of the child. The concept of mental retardation does not need to be discarded. Rather, it needs to be recognized and defined so that parents as well as the public will come to understand what it means to be mentally retarded and how high-quality special education programs can help to remediate the condition.

ACKNOWLEDGMENTS

Contributions have been made to this chapter by Leesa H. Mann, Ph.D., and Leslie E. Weidenman, Ph.D.

◀ Chapter 6 ▶

Attention Deficit Disorders

DESCRIPTION

The term *attention deficit disorder* is one of several terms referring to a group of problems believed to be caused by slight abnormalities in the brain. Children who have attention deficit disorder characteristically have one or more of the following problems: hyperactivity (excessively active), impulsivity, distractibility, disorders of speech or hearing, clumsiness, and perceptual difficulties.

From this list, you can see that attention deficit disorder can affect any one of a number of skill areas. But unlike mental retardation, which causes global delays or problems in all areas of functioning, attention deficit disorder typically affects only a few specific skills.

A variety of terms in addition to *attention deficit disorder* are used to describe children with these problems, including *minimal brain dysfunction, attention deficit hyperactivity disorder,* and *hyperactive* or *hyperkinetic child syndrome.* These terms often are used interchangeably, since clear-cut diagnostic criteria have not been established for each. This can be somewhat confusing to parents and professionals alike.

Signs of attention deficit disorder generally surface between the ages of 2 and 5. Often, parents first notice an extremely high activity level and limited attention span. Descriptions such as "he is always on the go," "he never can sit still for a second," "he jumps from toy to toy," and "he never seems to listen" are common. Children with attention deficit disorder also may be impulsive, very distractible, and have sleep disturbances. Many such youngsters frequently are difficult to discipline, have a low frustration tolerance, and have poor peer relationships. A number of such children also are clumsy and appear more immature than others their age.

CAUSES

Specific causes of attention deficit disorder have not yet been discovered. No one has found a part of the brain that when damaged

results in attention deficit disorder. Scientists are researching various possible causes (or etiologies). Some suspect that attention deficit disorder is caused by too high or too low levels of neurotransmitters, those essential chemicals that carry messages or nerve impulses throughout the brain. Others believe that environmental factors such as severe illnesses, toxic substances, or injuries early in life may cause attention deficit disorder. Still others are exploring the role of genetics in attention deficit disorder. Keep in mind that hyperactivity and poor attention also are found with disorders other than attention deficit disorder. For example, children with seizure disorders may have difficulty concentrating or may be overly active.

INCIDENCE

Attention deficit disorder and hyperactivity are known to occur much more often in boys than girls. It has been estimated that boys are affected nine times more often than girls. Approximately 1 boy in 25 has problems characteristic of attention deficit disorder.

DIAGNOSIS

Making a diagnosis of attention deficit disorder requires detailed information on the child's behavior as well as knowledge of the youngster's educational and intellectual abilities. There is no simple test for attention deficit disorder or hyperactivity. A doctor arrives at the diagnosis by eliminating all other possible explanations for the child's behavior. This process may require giving certain medical, psychological, or educational tests.

Diagnostic criteria have been established for attention deficit disorder by the American Psychiatric Association in the *Diagnostic and Statistical Manual of Mental Disorders (3rd ed.-rev.)*, also known as *DSM-III-R.* According to these criteria, attention deficit disorder with hyperactivity begins before age 7, with children showing several signs of inattention, impulsivity, and hyperactivity. There are some children who have this disorder who do not exhibit hyperactivity.

TREATMENT

Helping children with attention deficit disorder may involve a combination of treatments such as the use of behavior management techniques, medications, a change in diet, and special education. Many youngsters improve in structured environments where consistent management techniques are used. When good behavior is rewarded consistently and undesirable behavior is discouraged, children gradually learn to control their impulsivity and increase their ability to focus on tasks.

Some youngsters, particularly those with hyperactivity, respond to treatment with medications such as Ritalin, Dexedrine, and Cylert (see also Chapter 24). Doctors are not yet sure why these medicines work or why they work only with some hyperactive children. A small group of children with attention deficit disorder seem to improve with a drastic change in diet. Removing sugar, food coloring, and other additives from all foods eaten has helped some children increase their attention span and ability to focus, while decreasing their activity level. Even so, many other children do not improve when given such a special diet.

Appropriate education for these children is essential. Some children will require special education services in the form of resource rooms, tutoring, self-contained classrooms, or perhaps even a private special program.

In addition, families and children with attention deficit disorder often benefit from counseling. Counseling helps family members understand attention deficit disorder better and learn to cope with a child with these difficult behaviors.

PROGNOSIS

Typically, children with attention deficit disorder and hyperactivity who receive adequate treatment are given a positive prognosis (prediction regarding the outcome of the condition) and show improvement as they get older. Many become somewhat less active but may continue to be distractible and impulsive. As adults, most can hold productive jobs and lead normal lives.

ACKNOWLEDGMENTS

Contributions have been made to this chapter by David T. Marwil, M.D., and Leslie E. Weidenman, Ph.D.

◀ **Chapter 7** ▶

Learning Disabilities

DESCRIPTION

Learning disabilities are considered by some professionals to be a subgroup of minimal brain dysfunction. Children with learning disabilities seem to have average potential but have difficulty in specific areas of learning such as reading, writing, mathematics, and language. Some youngsters' problems are the result of difficulties in processing information that is seen or heard. In the Education for All Handicapped Children Act (PL 94-142), a learning disability is defined as "a disorder in one or more of the basic psychological processes involved in understanding or in using language, spoken or written which may manifest itself in an imperfect ability to listen, speak, read, write, spell or do mathematical calculations." Learning disabilities are categorized further according to the area of learning affected. You may hear the term *dyslexia* used to refer to reading disabilities.

CAUSES AND INCIDENCE

Like attention deficit disorder, learning disabilities are thought to be caused by minor abnormalities in the brain, which, unfortunately, are not yet understood. Learning disabilities are more common in boys than girls, occurring approximately four times more often. It is estimated that 10 percent to 15 percent of all school children fall in the category of learning disabled.

DIAGNOSIS

Children who are suspected of having learning disabilities usually are given a battery of tests including intelligence and educational achievement tests. Making the diagnosis is difficult, as symptoms of learning disabilities are also symptoms of other developmental disabilities. Professionals must look for certain patterns of test results in children with learning disabilities before a diagnosis is made. Typically, these youngsters have average or near-average intelligence test scores, but do poorly

in specific areas of educational achievement, such as reading, writing, or mathematics.

Most learning disabilities are not identified until a youngster enters school and begins to have trouble with schoolwork. However, certain problems such as language disabilities now are being recognized at a much earlier age.

TREATMENT

The earlier learning disabilities are identified, the more effectively they can be treated. There are many approaches to helping children with learning disabilities. Some therapies, such as sensory integration therapy, involve exercises to strengthen perceptual abilities. Educational methods of treatment are the most common. Many learning disabled children have responded well to programs designed for the youngsters' specific area of weakness. Usually, such programs are multisensory; that is, they employ all of a child's senses in teaching, as a way to overcome a disability in one area. Emotional problems because of years of frustration and school failure are common for learning disabled youngsters. Many benefit from counseling during their school years.

PROGNOSIS

The outlook for learning disabled children generally is quite good. Most grow up to lead normal lives and to work productively in the community.

ACKNOWLEDGMENT

Contributions have been made to this chapter by Daniel T. Marwil, M.D.

◀   Chapter 8   ▶

Sensory Disorders

VISUAL IMPAIRMENT AND BLINDNESS

Description

Visual impairment simply means less than normal vision. More specific information about the type and severity of the problem is needed in order to determine how impaired the vision is, a diagnosis that is usually provided by an eye doctor or ophthalmologist.

Most people have heard normal vision described as 20/20. This measure of visual acuity or sharpness means that an individual can see at a distance of 20 feet what the normal eye is supposed to see at 20 feet. Visual acuity of 20/40 indicates a mild visual impairment. In this case the individual only can see at 20 feet what ordinarily can be seen at 40 feet. A significant visual impairment would be 20/200. A person with such poor vision would be considered legally blind.

A restricted visual field is another type of visual impairment. When looking straight ahead, most people also see peripherally in a 180-degree field of vision. If for some reason, the visual field is reduced to 20 degrees, a person is designated legally blind, as seen in Figure 1. As you can see, it is possible to be legally blind and still have some sight. If an individual has no vision at all, he or she would be considered totally blind.

Causes and Specific Impairments

There are numerous causes of visual impairment. Any defect in the eye itself, in the optic nerve that carries visual messages to the brain, or in the vision center in the brain may result in a visual impairment. Damage from injuries, accidents, or illnesses to any part of the visual system, and genetic disorders, metabolic diseases, or congenital abnormalities can cause a visual impairment. To understand how a visual impairment can develop, it helps to know something about how we see normally.

As seen in Figure 2, light enters the eye through the cornea (1). It passes through the anterior chamber (2), pupil (3), and lens (4). It continues through the vitreous humor (6) until it reaches the retina (7) at the back of the eyeball. The retina contains light receptors that trans-

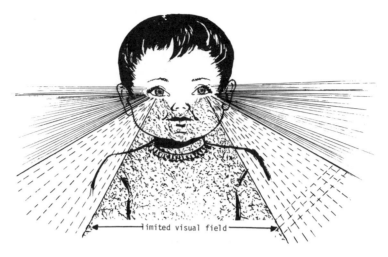

limited visual field

Figure 1. A child with a reduced visual field may be severely visually impaired. Shaded areas indicate various degrees of reduced visual field.

form the image seen to nerve impulses that are carried by the optic nerve (8) to the vision center at the back of the brain. Only then, when the image reaches the brain and the image is interpreted, do we know what we have seen.

Vision is a complex process. A problem at any step in the sequence can result in a visual impairment. Some common problems are described next.

Cataracts affect the lens of the eye by preventing light from passing through in the normal way. Cataracts can increase over time, gradually causing the lens to become opaque. Many people associate cataracts with the elderly. However, children also may have cataracts, including infants who may be born with cataracts.

Premature infants who require extensive oxygen after birth may develop a condition called retrolental fibroplasia (see Chapter 14, ''Problems of the Newborn Period''). The retina may then become damaged and may not be able to respond appropriately to light.

Other conditions affecting the retina and impairing vision are retinitis pigmentosa (an abnormal accumulation of pigment) and retinoblastoma (a tumor of the eye). Also, a damaged optic nerve may be unable to carry the light impulses from the eye to the brain. Moreover, when the eye itself and the optic nerve are intact, it is possible to have visual problems when the parts of the brain that receive and interpret visual images function improperly or are damaged.

An imbalance in the eye muscles can cause a number of visual problems. Coordinated eye movements require that the six eye muscles, which are controlled by three different nerves, work together in perfect balance. It is easy to understand why this complex process may be a problem in very young infants.

Squint (cross-eyedness or strabismus, as it is called in medical terminology) is a common problem in infants. There are two types of strabismus: esotropia (crossed eyes, or eyes that turn in) and exotropia (wall-eyes, or eyes that turn out). In addition, although both eyes may have adequate vision, if a child fails to coordinate eye movements, amblyopia, or "lazy eye," eventually may develop. This occurs when one eye becomes dominant and the brain ignores messages from the other eye in order to avoid double vision.

Nystagmus is another eye condition in which there are abnormal eye movements. In this case, a jerky motion of the eyes occurs either in a cross-wise (horizontal), up and down (vertical), or circular manner. If you suspect that your child has either strabismus or nystagmus, you should discuss your concerns with your physician to determine if the child should be seen by an ophthalmologist.

Near-sightedness (myopia) and far-sightedness (hyperopia) are common conditions that usually can be corrected with eyeglasses. These conditions are caused by a deviation in length of the eyeball or changes

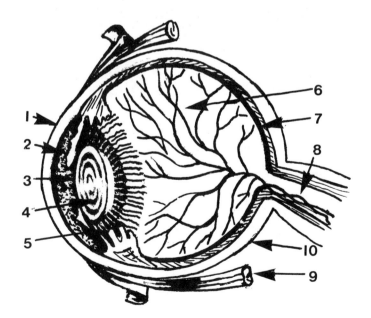

Figure 2.   Cross-sectional view of the eyeball, showing structures of the eye: 1, cornea; 2, anterior chamber; 3, pupil; 4, lens; 5, iris; 6, vitreous body; 7, retina; 8, optic nerve; 9, eye muscle; 10, sclera.

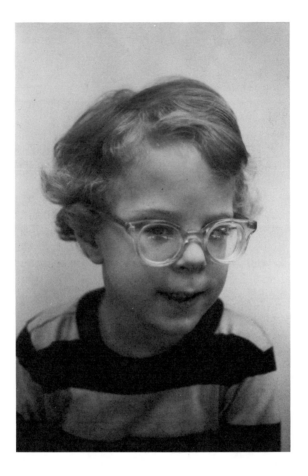

in the lens so that the light image is projected either a little in front of or a little behind the back of the eye.

Detection and Diagnosis

During infancy and early childhood, parents and pediatricians usually are the first to suspect that a child may have vision problems. If a child has difficulty coordinating eye movements, appears to hold objects very close to the face, or seems to have poor eye-hand coordination, there may be a vision problem. If you notice these problems, you should have your child examined by an ophthalmologist.

Visual acuity becomes easier to evaluate once a child develops basic skills such as following directions and naming pictures or letters of the alphabet. Visual acuity testing generally involves reading a chart of letters or pictures using the Snellen Eye Chart for an older child or an E

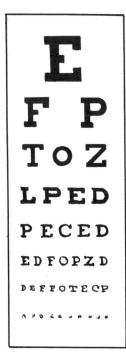 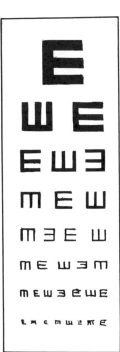 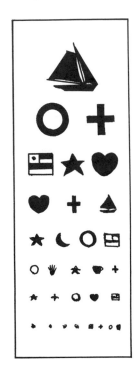

Figure 3.   The E Chart and the Picture Chart are used to assess a young child's ability to see.

Chart or Picture Chart (see Figure 3) for a younger child. For the latter two charts the child has to respond by pointing to the direction of the "legs" of the E on the E Chart or identifying the object on the Picture Chart.

Very young children or those with severe developmental delays are frequently difficult to test. If there is a question about whether or not a child can see, one procedure that can be used is a visual evoked potential examination. This involves recording the brain's response to visual stimulation similar to that of a brainwave test or an electroencephalogram. By placing electrodes on specific areas on the back of the head, the electrical activity received in the brain's vision center can be recorded. The pattern of responses is then compared to that of a youngster with normal vision.

Treatment and Prognosis

Many visual impairments can be corrected easily with eyeglasses. If amblyopia has been diagnosed, patching of one eye is frequently done to strengthen the "lazy eye." At times, eye surgery is performed to correct a muscle imbalance or remove a cataract. In general, the earlier the problem is detected and treatment is begun, the better the prognosis.

For blind children, the onset of blindness is an important factor. A child who is blind from birth will have more difficulties in certain developmental areas than a child who becomes blind after having had a few years of vision. For instance, a child blind from birth usually will have difficulty with spatial concepts such as large and small or how much liquid a container will hold. Motor skills also tend to develop more slowly in a blind child who cannot see the movements of others and thus does not learn by imitating. Because blind children cannot explore with their eyes, they have to rely on their other senses. The tactile (touching) sense becomes highly developed in many blind children. Caregivers should be aware of how important it is for the visually impaired child to touch objects. Fortunately, language development generally is not affected by a visual deficit.

HEARING IMPAIRMENT

Description

Hearing is a complex process involving the three major parts of the ear—the outer, middle, and inner ear as shown in Figure 4. Each part contains several components such as the tympanic membrane or eardrum, the ossicles or small bones in the middle ear that conduct the sound, and the auditory, or hearing, nerve, which carries sound messages to the brain.

Each component of the ear must work properly if a child is to hear normally. Hearing impairments may result from problems in any part of the ear or of the hearing center of the brain. There are three major types of hearing problems: conductive, sensorineural, and mixed hearing impairments. A conductive hearing loss indicates a problem in the outer or middle ear. A sensorineural hearing loss refers to problems of the inner ear such as the auditory nerve. When both conductive and sensorineural hearing problems are present, the impairment is referred to as a mixed type of hearing impairment.

Many youngsters have hearing problems in only one ear, called a unilateral hearing loss. If both ears are affected, it is a bilateral hearing loss.

The intensity of a hearing loss is determined by how loud a sound must be before it can be heard. Sound intensity is measured in decibels, abbreviated dB. People with normal hearing can detect a variety of sounds at 20 decibels or less.

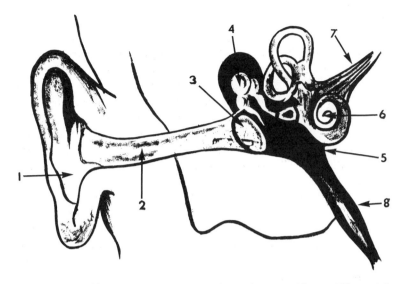

Figure 4. Structures of the ear: 1, outer ear; 2, ear canal; 3, eardrum; 4, ossicles; 5, middle ear; 6, inner ear; 7, hearing nerve; 8, Eustachian tube.

There are four levels of hearing impairment: A mild hearing loss means that sounds must be between 25 to 40 decibels and above before they can be heard. An individual with a mild hearing loss can hear and participate in conversations but may have difficulty hearing sounds and noises from a distance or whispered sounds. Even though children with mild hearing problems may be delayed in language development, speech and articulation generally are normal.

A moderate hearing impairment means that sounds cannot be heard until they reach 45 to 70 decibels and above. At this level, normal conversation is difficult to hear and articulation often is impaired. Language development in these children is usually delayed.

A severe hearing impairment means a hearing loss in the 70 to 90 decibels range. At this level, an individual generally cannot participate in normal conversations. Most of what is said will not be heard. Hearing aids can be very helpful to persons with both moderate and severe hearing impairments.

A profound hearing loss means that sounds must be 90 decibels or louder in order to be heard. Normal-sounding speech is not possible, and hearing aids are only partially beneficial. Profoundly deaf individuals generally learn an alternative system of communication such as sign language or use of a communication board.

Causes

Head injuries and infections are some of the most common causes of hearing problems in children. During the preschool years, many children are prone to frequent throat and middle ear infections (the latter is also called otitis media). Chronic middle ear infections may result in a mild to moderate conductive hearing loss. This type of hearing problem may be temporary, and also can fluctuate in intensity.

Another common problem in children that can cause a temporary hearing loss is the buildup of wax, or cerumen, in the ear canal. When the ear canal is totally blocked, sounds cannot reach the eardrum, and hearing is impaired.

Sensorineural hearing impairment can be caused in numerous ways. It may be inherited, in which case these children are often born deaf. A viral infection or the use of drugs during the early stages of pregnancy may cause damage to the unborn baby's hearing apparatus. A difficult birth causing a lack of oxygen to the baby also may result in a sensorineural hearing impairment. In infancy and childhood, a number of antibiotics such as streptomycin and certain serious illnesses such as bacterial meningitis may be associated with later sensorineural hearing problems.

Excessive noise in the environment sometimes causes mild to moderate sensorineural hearing impairments. These problems may be temporary. If the exposure to excessive noise continues, it can become permanent. For adolescents, a common source of excessive noise is listening to loud music or attending rock concerts. Some reports indicate that noise levels at rock concerts have reached 120 decibels, similar to the noise of a jet engine. Although numerous causes of hearing impairment have been discovered, many children suffer from a hearing loss the reason for which is unknown.

Incidence

Approximately 1 in every 1,000 children has a profound hearing loss and is considered deaf. Of these, it is estimated that 65 percent were deaf from birth. When mild, moderate, and severe degrees of hearing impairment are added to this statistic, estimates of affected children increase to 15 to 30 in 1,000. Hearing problems frequently occur along with other handicapping conditions. A survey of children in schools for individuals with hearing impairment found that 40 percent had an additional disability.[1]

---

[1]Batshaw, M.L., & Perret, Y.M. (1986). *Children with handicaps: A medical primer* (2nd ed.). Baltimore: Paul H. Brookes Publishing Co.

Detection and Diagnosis

During infancy and early childhood profound hearing losses usually are detected by parents and family members. They may notice that the baby does not react to loud sounds and voices and does not seem to know his name or understand any speech. Milder or fluctuating hearing problems are more difficult to detect. However, if a child has frequent ear infections, responds inconsistently to speech, or is slow to acquire language skills, a thorough hearing evaluation should be obtained.

Audiologists, or hearing specialists, have ways of testing hearing of children of all ages. Some of these methods are outlined in Chapter 22. Most audiometric tests involve presenting a variety of sounds of different intensity and frequency to each ear and having the youngster indicate when the sound is heard. Depending on the age and ability of the child, the audiologist may use headphones to present sounds or may observe the child's reactions to sounds in a testing room.

Audiologists also may test the flexibility and mobility of the eardrum using a procedure called impedance audiometry. For very young or difficult-to-test children, auditory evoked response (AER) (sometimes called brain stem evoked response, BSER) testing often is recommended. Further descriptions of these tests are provided in Chapter 22.

Treatment and Prognosis

Conductive hearing problems resulting from frequent ear infections or fluid in the middle ear space generally improve with medical treatment. Many children respond well to antibiotics, whereas others may require minor surgery in order to drain the fluid buildup. A common surgical procedure involves a myringotomy with tube insertion. In this procedure, under general anesthesia a tiny cut is made in the eardrum, and a small tube is placed in the middle ear to promote the drainage of fluid from this space.

Sensorineural hearing losses generally cannot be cured. In some cases, special implants have been attempted with moderate success. Hearing aids can be very useful for certain children with sensorineural impairments. Although they may not restore perfect hearing, they do make many sounds loud enough for the child to hear. The two most common types of hearing aids are the body-style and the behind-the-ear type, as illustrated in Figure 5.

Children with hearing impairments often are delayed in learning language. The more severe the hearing loss, the harder it is to acquire normal language. Some children never learn to speak, but do develop other ways to communicate such as through sign language or use of a communication board. Hearing impaired children who do speak often

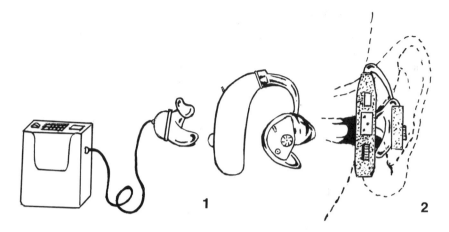

Figure 5. Body-style hearing aid at left is usually attached to straps or clothing. A behind-the-ear hearing aid is depicted on the right. Shown is a frontal view (1) and side view (2).

have articulation problems. The improper pronunciation reflects the child's inability to hear sounds accurately.

Special education services usually are required for hearing impaired children. Extra help from early intervention programs designed for hearing impaired children is particularly important during the preschool years. Some type of special help may be required throughout the school years for hearing impaired children.

LACK OF SENSATION

Description

Difficulty in feeling various sensations is common in handicapping conditions associated with paralysis or nerve damage such as spina bifida. Sensations include touch, as well as the ability to feel pain, temperature changes, vibration, and a sense of position in space. A loss or impairment of sensation may be partial or total as well as temporary or permanent.

Causes and Incidence

Any disease, injury, or handicap that affects the nerves and sensory receptors may affect the ability to feel sensation. Conditions such as cerebral palsy, which involves the motor system, may affect the ability to interpret sensations. There also is a rare condition known as congenital insensitivity to pain, in which children cannot feel pain.

Specific data on the number of children or adults with impaired sensation or a lack of sensation are not available.

Diagnosis and Detection

By observing a child's reactions to various sensations, you generally can tell if there is a specific concern. The pediatrician or neurologist can evaluate your child's sensory abilities more systematically to determine if there is a problem with sensation.

Treatment and Prognosis

The cause of the sensory problem will determine the type of treatment the child will receive. Temporary impairments caused by illnesses, for example, will generally disappear with the treatment of the illness. Youngsters with permanent disabilities may not be cured, but their ability to feel or interpret sensation can be improved with therapy.

In cases where the loss of sensation is total and no improvement is expected, children and parents are taught how to avoid injury to insensitive body parts. For example, paralyzed youngsters who spend hours at a time seated in wheelchairs learn to shift their positions to avoid skin sores.

ACKNOWLEDGMENTS

Contributions have been made to this chapter by Patricia S. Scola, M.D., M.P.H., and Janet L. Tobin, M.S.

◀ Chapter 9 ▶

Communication Disorders

Communication can be defined as a process of exchanging information, thoughts, and ideas. It encompasses the ability to interpret, transmit, and express messages. Communication not only involves the vowel and consonant sounds we use and the sentences we create but also the tone of our voice, rate of delivery, eye contact, facial expression, and body movement. Some of these communication skills are already present at birth. As infants develop, their ability to communicate expands to using and understanding spoken and written language.

DESCRIPTION

Communication disorder is a general term comprising any number of concerns affecting the development of language and communication skills. Communication disorders can be categorized into problems of articulation, voice disorders, stuttering, and language disorders resulting from damage to the brain such as expressive aphasia and apraxia (all of these terms are explained in this chapter). In addition, many youngsters have language processing disorders that sometimes are referred to as language-based learning disabilities.

ARTICULATION

Articulation refers to the ability to pronounce vowel and consonant sounds correctly. Appropriate coordination of movements of the lips, tongue, palate, and jaw are necessary for proper articulation. Development of this coordination begins in infancy with the process of sucking, chewing, and swallowing. As the child grows, drinking from a cup refines coordination of the muscles of the mouth and prepares the child for production of vowel and consonant sounds. Early speech usually is a poor approximation of actual words. However, as children learn to speak and practice pronunciation, articulation gradually improves. By the age of 6 to 7 years, most children have learned to produce all the sounds of their language correctly.

Articulation problems are likely to be present in youngsters who have physical problems causing interference with coordinated move-

ments of the lips, tongue, and other anatomical structures that take part in speech production. Children who have language delays (that is, who are late in acquiring their first words) or youngsters with structural defects such as cleft palate may have problems with articulation. Infants with swallowing or chewing difficulties or excessive drooling may also develop articulation problems.

VOICE DISORDERS

Voice disorders are less common in children than adults; however, they do occur. Voice disorders also are refered to as abnormal phonation.

Judgment about whether a child's voice sounds normal can be very subjective. However, conditions of excessive or prolonged hoarseness or a nasal or denasal voice (i.e., a voice that has a head cold quality) usually are identified readily by parents. If this unusual quality persists, parents may adapt to it so that it no longer sounds strange to them. Therefore, it is important to closely monitor any voice changes in the developing child. If changes persist over 2 to 4 weeks, an evaluation is indicated.

Hoarseness can be caused by chronic irritation of the throat, infection, allergy, and vocal abuse such as yelling or screaming. Hoarseness needs to be evaluated medically to determine the cause and to initiate treatment if indicated. Hypernasality exists when too much sound is passing through the nose; its opposite, hyponasality, refers to too little sound passing through the nose. Both conditions require medical evaluation. Blockage of the nasal passages, allergies, and chronic colds can cause hyponasality and may contribute to a speech pattern that is difficult to understand. Hypernasality occurs when the soft palate fails to close the nasal passages, thus allowing air to pass through the nose. Children with cleft palate often have this type of voice pattern due to insufficient palatal tissue.

STUTTERING

As the child progresses toward sentence production, occasional repetitions, hesitations, or long pauses can be heard in the child's speech. Often this is labeled stuttering or stammering. It is important to note that until the age of 5 or 6 years, this type of nonfluency is a normal part of language and speech development. The complicated process of learning to converse with others is not yet automatic and requires the ability not only to choose the correct words but to put them into the proper order while using correct grammar. It is understandable that a child might hesitate at times or repeat while attempting to respond verbally.

Distinguishing the just-described normal nonfluency from real stuttering is one of the jobs of a speech pathologist. If parents are concerned about the amount of nonfluency present in a child's speech, they should seek professional help. Nonfluency, often a part of both children's and adults' verbal expressive language, is not necessarily abnormal. Anxiety only increases stuttering and nonfluency, and therefore the less attention called to the speaker's hesitations or repetitions, the easier it will be for that individual to produce more fluent speech patterns.

LANGUAGE DISORDERS CAUSED BY
CENTRAL NERVOUS SYSTEM DEFECTS

In the development of speech and language the central nervous system and the nerves that control our senses and muscles play a vital role. In order to absorb information from the environment, children must see, hear, and feel what is going on around them.

If damage has occurred to any of these sensory systems, delays or disruption of the normal process of speech and language development can occur. It is important to recognize these problems early in order to aid the child in developing strategies to compensate for these deficiencies.

Two communication disorders caused by problems in the brain itself are *expressive aphasia* and *apraxia*. These terms refer to the inability to produce language due to problems in processing information and producing responses. These difficulties often are described as a short-circuit in the system of receiving and sending messages. Often inconsistencies in language abilities are seen in children with aphasia and apraxia. This suggests that the brain's system is working at times and failing at others. These youngsters often have echolalic speech; that is, they repeat or echo what is said to them. They also tend to be distractible, nonverbal, and easily frustrated by conversations they do not understand. On occasion, they can use words meaningfully. But if asked to repeat what they said, aphasic and apraxic children often are unable to respond correctly. Both these disorders require the assistance of professionals and a rehabilitation program.

LANGUAGE PROCESSING DISORDERS AND
LANGUAGE-BASED LEARNING DISABILITIES

The school-age child who begins having difficulty learning academic subjects may have problems in one or more of the following: understanding spoken or written language; expressing ideas either orally or in writing; finding the appropriate words; and processing or discriminating information through the senses of hearing, seeing, touching, or movement. The prevalence of this type of disorder is felt to be in anywhere from 40 percent to 60 percent of the learning disabled population.

Because the language-based learning disability is subtle and not easily recognized, it often is not detected in the preschool years. However, there are early signs that may indicate a language-based learning disability. For example, the family may observe the child having difficulty focusing on tasks, becoming confused easily by lengthy directions or conversations, having difficulty attending to and following stories read aloud, being unable to express ideas in an orderly fashion, and verbally rambling without actually communicating an idea. As these language problems usually affect a specific area of the total language process, they easily can be overlooked, unlike the child who fails to talk at an appropriate age or has difficulty pronouncing words.

The language-based learning disabilities include specific deficits such as difficulty using the correct words in a given situation; substituting an explanation for a specific object label; using nonspecific words— for example, "that thing," "this stuff"; inability to understand and express the how and whys of a situation; or difficulty making appropriate judgments in social situations. In the comprehension area youngsters sometimes misinterpret words that represent time or space concepts, such as *yesterday* or *tomorrow, near* or *far;* have difficulty understanding multiple meanings of words (*trunk*—a suitcase or part of an elephant);

or literally interpret figurative language (e.g., *she is a backseat driver, he is falling apart*).

These language disorders affect how the child reasons, reacts to family members and peers, and performs in the classroom. Without the abilities to understand and use language, many children fail to progress beyond routine repetitious learning. For example, they may be able to count, recite the alphabet in order, and memorize mathematic facts without understanding the concepts involved.

Evaluation of a child's language abilities and disabilities, together with an assessment of educational, cognitive, and social development, are necessary to identify the area or areas of difficulty. Once identified, appropriate treatment programs can be developed. It is the team process, professionals working together with family members, that is most important in determining the problems and piecing together all the components of an educational treatment program to help the child progress through the elementary and secondary school years.

CAUSES

The causes of communication disorders in children are as varied as the problems themselves. In many instances, the exact reason cannot always be determined. In the case of stuttering, a cause for the disorder has never been documented, although many theories have been proposed. Some researchers believe it is caused by emotional or psychological factors in the family environment or in the children themselves. Others attribute the problem to a malfunction of the central nervous system. Voice disorders in children frequently are caused by physical abnormalities or misuse of the voice mechanism. A physical examination by a physician, most often an ear, nose, and throat specialist (otolaryngologist), X ray studies of the voice box (larynx), and assessment of the oral mechanism often are needed to determine the presence of a structural defect that may be contributing to the child's unusual sounding voice. Articulation disorders may be due to a delay in maturation; imitation of another child with pronunciation problems; physical or structural abnormalities of the mouth, lips, tongue, jaw, or throat; or a neurological impairment.

INCIDENCE

The incidence of communication disorders is variable, depending upon the age of the population discussed and what disorders are included in the total number. It has been reported that approximately 6 percent of children age 6 to 18 years have problems in the area of voice, articulation, and stuttering. The study did not include those children with specific language disorders or language-based learning difficulties.

ASSESSMENT OF COMMUNICATION DISORDERS

The evaluation of communication disorders generally consists of four parts. When a parent or physician suspects a child to have a speech or language problem, the youngster may be sent to a speech and language pathologist for an evaluation. This professional examines the physical mechanisms for speech production, hearing ability, speech quality, voice and rhythm patterns, and comprehension and expression of verbal language. The pathologist first evaluates the oral mechanism, usually by looking at the structure of the mouth and observing the movements of the tongue, lips, and jaw during the production of speech. In addition, the examiner usually will ask the child to imitate various mouth movement patterns, sounds, and words. A referral to a physician may be necessary for a more complete assessment of the vocal mechanism if a physical problem is suspected.

Second, articulation or pronunciation usually is tested by asking the child to name a specific series of pictures or tell a story. It is important for the speech and language pathologist to hear how a child pronounces each consonant and vowel sound in isolation, single words, and in conversational speech. Pronunciation often seems better in a one-word response than in conversation. This is directly related to the amount of fine motor coordination that is involved in producing a long sentence as opposed to a single word. When sounds are mispronounced, the evaluator may ask the child to try to imitate the appropriate pronunciation to help determine if therapy is needed and the type of program that may be indicated.

The third aspect of assessment, that of the language process, probably is the most time-consuming of the evaluation. The speech and language pathologist usually administers a series of standardized tests to determine a child's ability to understand and use spoken language. The type of tests used varies, depending on the child's age, ability, and attention span. Most tests involve the use of pictures or toy objects. Comprehension or the ability to understand spoken language is usually evaluated by asking a child to point to the one picture in a group that has been named by the examiner or to follow a series of directions. The tests typically measure comprehension of nouns; action words; adjectives; concepts such as size, quality, and quantity; and grammar. Some of the more frequently used tests are the Test of Auditory Comprehension of Language, Zimmerman Pre-School Language Scale, Sequenced

Inventory of Communication Development, Tina Bangs Vocabulary Comprehension Scale, Bracken Basic Concept Scale, Test of Language Development, Clinical Evaluation of Language Function, and the Peabody Picture Vocabulary Test.

The evaluation of expressive language includes a child's use of vocabulary, sentence structure, thought sequence, ideas, and response to simple what, when, how, where, and why questions. The evaluation of language usage also involves the use of common pictures or toys. The youngster may be asked to imitate sentences produced by the evaluator. Specific questions are asked in order to assess how children formulate their thoughts and how well they can communicate these ideas to their listener. The examiner observes the body movements, gestures, and facial expressions that the child uses in addition to or in place of words. This becomes especially important when evaluating children who have difficulty expressing themselves verbally. Instruments used to evaluate all of these functions include the just-mentioned tests and the Word Test, Test of Problem Solving, Expressive One Word Picture Vocabulary Test, and Test of Language Competence.

Audiological evaluation makes up the fourth area of assessment, and is discussed in Chapter 8.

After testing, the scores and observations are compiled by the evaluator, and a judgment is made as to whether or not the child is functioning on par with other children of similar age. Further evaluation, which may include medical, educational or psychological testing, may be recommended at that time to determine the cause of the child's language problem.

TREATMENT

The type and severity of the communication disorder, as well as the child's age, will determine if specific language or speech therapy is needed. Very young children often require ongoing language stimulation activities to foster the development of communication skills. Such activities may be recommended by a language therapist or a professional in early child development, to be carried out by parents and family members. The activities are designed to aid the child in acquiring skills or in some cases to teach the child to compensate for a physical abnormality.

For school-age children, speech and language therapists may provide individual therapy or design programs to be carried out in the classroom. Again, the individual needs of the child determine the type of services to be provided.

COMMUNICATION AIDS

For many reasons, oral communication, or speech, is so difficult for some children that it is virtually impossible for them to make their needs known verbally. For these youngsters, one of the numerous communication aids available may enable them to express their needs to others.

Every day we use alternatives to speech to communicate. Facial expressions, gestures, and writing are common examples of nonverbal communication. Many deaf and hearing impaired people use sign language as the primary mode of communication. For developmentally disabled and physically handicapped children unable to speak, these and other alternatives are used if possible. Often simple picture, word, or object systems are devised specifically for the individual handicapped child. In other cases technologically sophisticated electronic aids with voice synthesizers or printers are used.

Communication Boards

The simplest type of communication aid is the communication board or book. Depending on the child's abilities, the board or book presents a display of pictures, drawings, words, or symbols. To communicate, the youngster simply points to or touches the items shown. A child who wants a snack may make his request by pointing to the words, "I want a cookie." A younger child might simply point to a picture of a cookie to make the same request. Children with severe cognitive deficits may use object boards to communicate, on which replicas or miniature objects are displayed. Because communication boards can be cumbersome to carry around, many children use communication books instead. The book, like the board, displays pictures, words, or symbols on the pages. Children are required to flip to the necessary page and then to point to the pictures or words that communicate their ideas.

Mechanical Aids

Mechanical aids refer to those that have moving parts but are not electronically operated. An old-fashioned nonelectric typewriter is an example of a mechanical communication aid. Many children with poor fine motor control are unable to write legibly but are able to press keys on a typewriter and thus to express their thoughts.

Electronic Aids

The effectiveness and the variety of available electronic communication aids have increased dramatically in recent years. The advantages of electronic aids are that they can provide a much larger vocabulary, can be connected to a digital display, monitor, or printer, and can be programmed or updated relatively easily. Some electronic aids have voice synthesizers that "speak" for the child. Many voice synthesizers have a monotone voice quality and resemble "robot" speech. However, the quality of speech of recently developed voice synthesizers is much improved. Some electronic communication aids are no bigger than a desktop calculator, whereas others look like small communication boards mounted on a briefcase. Other more sophisticated devices resemble small computers.

The variety of communication aids now available has opened up a world of social interactions and communication for many handicapped individuals who otherwise would be passive participants in social activities.

ACKNOWLEDGMENT

Contributions have been made to this chapter by Janet L. Tobin, M.S.

◀ # Chapter 10 ▶

Autism

DESCRIPTION

Autism is a rare developmental disorder. Children with autism are withdrawn and tend to avoid interacting with others. They also have severe language problems and often display ritualistic and self-stimulatory behaviors such as rocking, spinning, and finger flicking. Some severely affected children never learn to speak and engage in self-abusive behaviors such as head-banging or biting. Many autistic children also are mentally retarded. The word *autism* refers to the tendency to withdraw into oneself, ignoring much of what goes on in the environment.

CAUSES AND INCIDENCE

No one is really sure what causes autism. At one time, a poor relationship between mother and child was thought to be the cause. However, this has been proven false. Researchers now believe that autism is a specific neurological or brain disorder. What exactly is wrong with the brain and how it malfunctions in autistic youngsters is not yet known.

Autism occurs in about 2 to 4 of 10,000 children. Boys are affected approximately three times as often as girls. No one knows why this disorder is so much more common in boys.

DIAGNOSIS

For a child to be diagnosed as autistic, he or she must meet all the conditions listed in the section following. If a youngster does not show all the characteristics, the term *autistic-like* may be used to describe the child's problems.

Criteria for Autism

1. The condition appears before the age of 30 months.
2. The child is unresponsive to others. For example, in infancy autistic children often avoid making eye contact with others, may resist cuddling or other physical contact, and may not smile or laugh

appropriately. Older autistic youngsters may not develop cooperative play skills or make friends.

3. Language development is severely impaired. Many autistic children also lack nonverbal communication skills, such as the ability to use gestures. It is very common for autistic children who speak to repeat words and phrases they hear. This characteristic, called echolalia, can occur immediately after hearing a phrase or perhaps a short time later.

Another common characteristic of autistic speech is to mix up pronouns (using "I" for "you") or to use the wrong verb tenses ("will do" for "have done").

Some autistic children demonstrate excellent rote memory skills, which means they can memorize long lists of items, but are seldom able to use the information they have memorized. Although many autistic children learn to speak, problems with language generally continue into adulthood.

4. Unusual responses to the environment are observed. Autistic children often resist changes and insist on maintaining a sameness in many areas of their lives. They may show a strong interest in certain objects such as spinning toys, as well as in certain repetitive movements like rocking, twirling, and hand-gazing.

5. Children with autism usually have some mental handicaps and often are limited intellectually. The mental handicaps make it difficult for autistic children to understand relationships among people, objects, and events. Their thinking tends to be concrete, and most of them have difficulty using abstract symbols.

There are other handicapped children who may display autistic-like behaviors, such as avoiding eye contact, engaging in repetitive activities, and not using language to communicate. Yet, they do not have autism.

The diagnosis of autism and similar conditions is best done by a team of professionals who are thoroughly familiar with all developmental disabilities.

TREATMENT AND PROGNOSIS

Autistic children generally require specialized educational and behavioral treatments to learn basic skills. They usually do best in settings that are well-structured and consistent and where teaching occurs individually or in very small groups by highly skilled teachers. In terms of prognosis, about one-sixth of children diagnosed as having autism eventually make a reasonable social adjustment, although they may retain some weaknesses in their cognitive skills. Another one-sixth are reported to have a fair outcome. The remaining two-thirds are severely handicapped throughout life. However, with special training, supervision, and support, many autistic adults can live and work in the community.

ACKNOWLEDGMENT

Contributions have been made to this chapter by Ann S. Zartler, Ph.D.

◄ PART III ►

Inherited and Acquired Developmental Disabilities

In a book of this nature, it is impossible to include all the disabilities that have been identified. Instead, we have chosen to give an overview of the most common developmental disabilities as well as a few of the less frequently occurring disorders.

Specific disabilities may refer to problems in a single area of functioning or might represent a cluster of problems. When problems or symptoms occur in groups, they generally are referred to as a syndrome. A number of syndromes are included in this section.

For each topic, we define and describe the disability and provide information about the incidence; cause, if known; prognosis; and treatment. In addition, methods used to diagnose the disorder are mentioned.

A number of medical terms and some examples of professional jargon that you are likely to hear are included and explained. Familiarity with such terms will help you to improve your ability to communicate with the professionals you meet.

◄ Chapter 11 ►

Chromosome and Genetic Disorders

DESCRIPTION

Certain developmental disabilities are caused by either abnormal chromosomes or abnormal genes. Chromosomes are microscopic, rodlike structures that contain thousands of genes. Genes are the hereditary material that determine how we grow, our eye color, hair color, height, and how our body and brain work.

CHROMOSOME PROBLEMS

Human cells normally contain 46 chromosomes each, except for sperm and egg cells, which have 23 chromosomes each. At conception, when the sperm and the egg unite, the newly formed cell again has 46 chromosomes, as shown in Figure 1. Chromosomes are arranged in pairs. Twenty-two pairs are called autosomes. The remaining 23d pair contains the sex chromosomes, known as X and Y chromosomes. A person with two X chromosomes is female. A male has one X and one Y chromosome, as noted in Figure 2.

Occasionally, during the formation of the egg or sperm, an accident occurs with the chromosomes, causing an imbalance in the amount of chromosome material in egg or sperm. If there is too much or too little chromosome material in the egg or sperm that come together at conception, abnormalities in the developing individual may be observed. Most embryos with chromosome problems are miscarried. It has been estimated that between 8 to 10 percent of all embryos are miscarried.

There are three major types of chromosome disorders:

1. If there is an extra chromosome, the disorder is referred to as *trisomy*. One less chromosome is called *monosomy*. If a piece of chromosome is missing, it is called a *deletion*.
2. Some parents have two chromosomes attached to each other, a condition known as *translocation*. If this translocation is passed on to a child, he or she could develop physical and mental abnormalities.

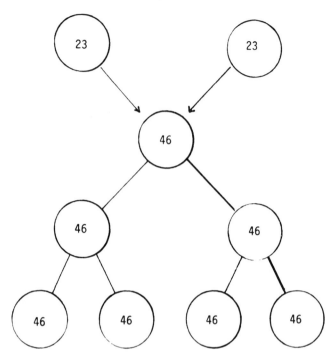

Figure 1. Twenty-three chromosomes derive from each germ cell. At the time of fertilization, the first cell has 46 chromosomes. Under "normal" circumstances, this cell will continue to divide, and in subsequent cell generations, each cell will have 46 chromosomes.

Translocations are also observed in some children whose parents have normal chromosomes.

3. Not all chromosome problems occur before conception. Some occur after conception and thus do not affect all the cells in the developing embryo. This condition, in which some cells are normal and some have a chromosome problem, is called *mosaicism*. When mosaicism occurs, the child may show typical features of the syndrome, though to a lesser degree. The extent of the problem depends on the percentage of abnormal cells present in the child's body.

Through analysis of chromosomes, the specific pair of chromosomes affected is identified by a number. For example, trisomy 21, observed in children with Down syndrome (see discussion later in this chapter), is caused by an extra chromosome in the 21st pair, as seen in Figure 3. Similarly, trisomy 13 refers to an extra #13 chromosome, and in trisomy 18, three #18 chromosomes are noted.

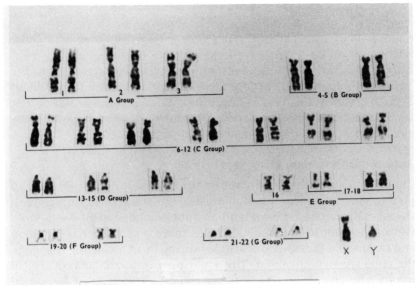

Figure 2.   Chromosomes (karyotype) of a normal female are shown on the left; karotype of a normal male is depicted on the right.

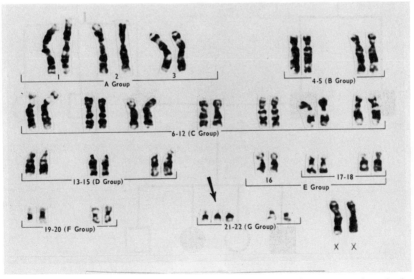

Figure 3.   Karyotype of a girl with Down syndrome. Note the extra #21 chromosome as shown by the arrow.

GENETIC PROBLEMS

Abnormalities in a parent's genes may cause a disorder in a child. Whether or not a youngster is affected depends on the pattern of inheritance of the disorder. Genetic disorders are classified according to the method of inheritance. The four basic categories, autosomal dominant disorders, autosomal recessive disorders, X-linked recessive disorders, and multifactorial disorders, are defined next. Some of the more common genetic disorders are described later in this chapter.

Autosomal Dominant Disorders

Children of an adult with an autosomal dominant disorder have a 50 percent chance of inheriting the disease, as demonstrated in Figure 4. Occasionally, a child is born with an autosomal dominant disease that was not present in the parents. This is called a spontaneous mutation and means that the disease developed owing to an accidental change in the child's genetic material. This child then has a 50 percent risk of passing the disease on to his or her children. Examples of autosomal

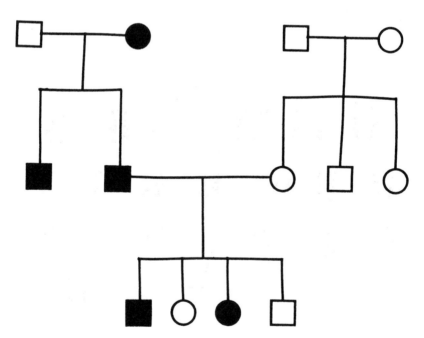

Figure 4.   In autosomal dominant inherited disorders, affected individuals are often observed in each generation, as noted in this pedigree. (square = male; circle = female; solid shading = affected individual.)

dominant disorders include achondroplasia (a form of dwarfism) and
Huntington disease (a disorder affecting the brain).

Autosomal Recessive Disorders

An individual affected by an autosomal recessive disorder inherits two
abnormal genes, one from each parent. If a child inherits only one
abnormal gene, the disease will not become evident. A person carrying
only one abnormal gene is known as a carrier. Carriers do not get the
disease, but can pass the gene on to their children. When parents who
are carriers for the same disease have children, each child born to that
couple will have a 25 percent chance of being affected, a 50 percent
chance of being affected, a 50 percent chance of being a carrier, and a 25
percent chance that the gene pair will be normal, as seen in Figure 5.
Autosomal recessive disorders are more likely to occur when an individual marries a close family member, because of the shared genetic
background. For example, phenylketonuria (PKU), a disorder caused by
a deficiency of the enzyme phenylalaninehydroxylase and causing profound mental retardation if not treated appropriately, is an autosomal
recessive disorder.

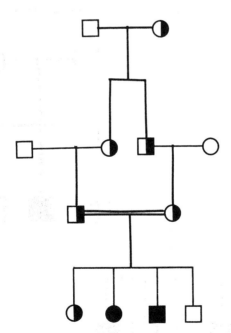

Figure 5. Example of autosomal recessive inheritance. The parents who are first-degree cousins are
heterozygotes; they have two affected children. (half-shading = carrier individuals.)

X-linked Recessive Diseases

X-linked recessive disorders are transmitted by genes on the X chromosome. They also are called sex-linked disorders. Common X-linked disorders are muscular dystrophy, hemophilia, and color blindness. The abnormal gene is carried by a mother on one of her two X chromosomes. The mother usually is not affected by the disorder but she can pass the gene on to her children, as noted in Figure 6. There is a 50 percent chance that a son will be affected. Daughters usually will not be affected, but they have a 50 percent chance of inheriting the abnormal gene and becoming carriers. (See generation 2 in Figure 6.) In the rare instance that an affected man marries a woman who is a carrier for the same disorder, there is a 50 percent chance that a daughter will be affected by the disorder. (See generation 4 in Figure 6.)

Multifactorial Disorders

Multifactorial disorders are those in which genes and environmental factors together seem to cause the disease. Simply having the affected genes or being exposed to an adverse environment will not cause the disorder. Examples of conditions that are inherited in a multifactorial manner include cleft lip and cleft palate, clubfoot, spina bifida (opening

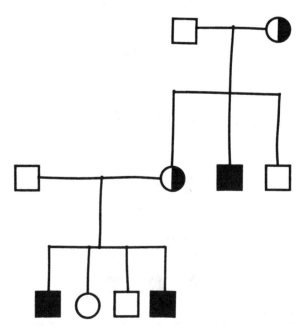

Figure 6.   Example of X-linked recessive inheritance where the mutant gene is carried by the female, but only males are affected.

at the spine), hip dislocation, and congenital heart disease. In a family with one affected child, the risk of another child of the family having the same defect is generally felt to be 2 percent to 5 percent.

CAUSES OF CHROMOSOME AND GENETIC DISORDERS

No one knows what causes most chromosome abnormalities, but most arise in the egg or sperm. Some scientists believe that viral infections, abnormal hormone levels, X rays, potent drugs, or a genetic predisposition may lead to chromosome problems. However, there is no definite proof that any of these conditions causes a chromosome problem in a particular child.

Some of the chromosome disorders seem to occur more frequently in older mothers. This is true of Down syndrome. The older the mother, the greater the chance that she may have a child with Down syndrome. There also is an increased risk of having a child with Down syndrome if the father is older than 50. We do not know what is responsible for changes in genes that may result in genetic disorders.

INCIDENCE

The incidence for specific chromosome and genetic disorders varies with each disability. In the chapters that follow, the incidence of individual disorders is listed, if known.

Once parents have had a child with a chromosome disorder, they wonder about the likelihood of having another child with the same problem. If neither parent has an abnormality in their chromosomes, their risk of having a second child with a chromosome disorder is considered small, about 1 percent. However, this is somewhat higher than the risk for the general population.

One way parents can learn more about their particular risk of having children with genetic or chromosome disorders is through genetic counseling. See Chapter 4 for a discussion of the role of a genetic counselor.

DETECTION AND DIAGNOSIS

If a chromosome disorder is suspected, a physician may order a special blood test to analyze the chromosomes. When the chromosomes are lined up according to size, a karyotype is constructed as shown in Figure 2. The karyotype shows the 23 pairs of chromosomes. The chromosomes are then examined for any abnormalities. If there are problems, such as an extra chromosome (trisomy), deletion, translocation, or other structural chromosome abnormalities, it will be revealed in the karyotype.

A chromosome analysis usually is done to confirm a doctor's clinical impression of a disorder. Many chromosome and genetic disorders are associated with specific physical features. Recognizing the presence of these features is the first step in making a diagnosis. For example, when a physician sees a newborn with the particular facial features associated with Down symdrome, he or she may order a chromosome analysis to confirm the clinical impression.

PROGNOSIS AND TREATMENT

The impact of a chromosome or genetic disorder on a child's life depends entirely on the specific disorder. Whereas some disorders are associated with mental retardation, health problems, and physical abnormalities, others may affect the individual's reproductive ability only. At this time, there is no effective medical treatment to correct chromosome disorders. However, many of the therapies discussed later in this book, such as early intervention, help these children to reach their fullest potential. Some of the more common chromosome disorders are described in the sections following.

DOWN SYNDROME

Perhaps the most familiar chromosome abnormality is Down syndrome. As stated earlier, individuals with Down syndrome or trisomy 21, have an extra 21st chromosome, giving them a total of three 21st chromosomes (see Figure 3). This means there are a total of 47 chromosomes in each cell instead of the normal 46. Down syndrome occurs in approximately 1 in every 800 to 1,000 births. There is quite a range of intellectual functioning in children with Down syndrome. The majority have mild to moderate mental retardation. There are some children with Down syndrome who are severely mentally retarded, as well as some who function in the borderline and low-average range of intelligence.

Children with Down syndrome have a number of similar physical characteristics that make them easily recognizable. The back of the head is often flattened, the eyes may be slightly slanted, skin folds at the inner corners of the eyes—called epicanthal folds—may be present, the bridge of the nose often is depressed, and the nose and ears are usually smaller than normal. A newborn baby with Down syndrome frequently has excess skin at the back of the neck. Typically, the hands and feet are small. Children with Down syndrome also have loose or lax ligaments, and during infancy their muscle strength and muscle tone are usually

diminished. About one-third of children with Down syndrome have congenital heart disease. Other defects may be present at birth, such as blockage of the bowel. There is a wide variation in physical features, mental ability, behavior, and developmental progress in children with Down syndrome. Many individuals with Down syndrome live well into their 50s and 60s.

CRI DU CHAT SYNDROME

Cri du chat (a French term meaning "cry of the cat") syndrome is a rare condition resulting from a loss of some genetic material from chromosome 5. Cri du chat syndrome occurs in approximately 1 in every 20,000 births. Children who have cri du chat syndrome may be so recognized at birth. They tend to be small and grow slowly. They typically have a distinct cry and may sound like a meowing cat. Children with cri du chat syndrome are mentally retarded. Most will learn to walk, but their language and their mental development are severely affected. The physical appearance of a child with cri du chat syndrome includes a small head with a round face, wide-set eyes, and small folds of skin over the inner corner of the eyes. These children often have strabismus, or cross-eyedness. The face may lack symmetry and the ears may be shaped abnormally. In addition to these features, congenital heart disease and other abnormalities may be present. Children with cri du chat syndrome usually survive into adulthood.

TRISOMY 18

Trisomy 18 is a disorder arising from the presence of an extra #18 chromosome. It occurs in approximately 2 to 3 in every 10,000 births. In general, these infants are small and have a weak cry at birth. Children with trisomy 18 have an unusually shaped head, abnormal ears, narrow eyelids, and a small mouth and chin. The hands are characteristically clenched, with overlapping fingers. The fingernails may be abnormally small. Many additional anomalies may be seen in these children. Children with trisomy 18 are usually feeble. They often have episodes where they fail to breath, called apnea. They may have limited sucking capability and may require feeding by tube. Only 10 percent of these children survive the first year of life, and those who do are severely or profoundly mentally retarded.

TRISOMY 13

Trisomy 13 is another extremely serious chromosome disorder. It occurs on the average of 1 in every 10,000 births. As the name implies, there is an extra #13 chromosome present. The brain is malformed, with incomplete nerves for sight and smell. Children with this syndrome have severe mental defects and may develop seizures. In addition, many have a cleft lip and cleft palate, congenital heart disease, and other abnormalities. Less than 10 percent survive the first year of life. The survivors have seizures, fail to grow normally, and are often profoundly mentally retarded.

TURNER SYNDROME

Children with Turner syndrome are females who most often have only one X chromosome instead of the normal two. Their appearance is characterized by some swelling of the back of the hands and feet at birth, a low hairline at the back of the neck giving the appearance of a short neck, and a broad chest with widely spaced nipples. They also may have heart disease, most commonly a narrowing of the aorta, which is the major vessel coming from the heart. As these children develop, the swelling of hands and feet diminishes. Their growth is slow and usually their stature is short, often less than 5 feet. Their ovaries are underdeveloped, and to mature sexually, these individuals require hormone treatment starting in adolescence. The vast majority of these women are infertile. Individuals with Turner syndrome are usually of average or low-average intelligence. The incidence of this rare syndrome is estimated at 1 in every 10,000 births.

NOONAN SYNDROME

Noonan syndrome may affect males or females. Individuals with Noonan syndrome are similar in appearance to those with Turner syndrome. Noonan syndrome most often is inherited as a dominant disorder. Unlike Turner syndrome, no chromosome abnormality has been identified in these children. Noonan syndrome is more common than Turner syndrome, occurring in approximately 1 in every 1,000 births. These children often have congenital heart disease that is somewhat more severe than that found in Turner syndrome. In addition, children with Noonan syndrome may be mildly mentally retarded or have learning disabilities.

FRAGILE-X SYNDROME

Fragile-X syndrome is a disorder that runs in families. It is sex-linked inherited and is marked by the presence of some X chromosomes with weak- or fragile-looking areas at their lower part. This is seen only when a special chromosome analysis is done in the laboratory. Males who have fragile-X syndrome are mildly to severely mentally retarded. Abnormal facial features and large testes in adults also have been described. Some females with fragile-X syndrome are mildly mentally retarded or have borderline intellectual functioning.

ACKNOWLEDGMENTS

Contributions have been made to this chapter by Patricia S. Scola, M.D., M.P.H., Karen E. Senft, M.D., and Siegfried M. Pueschel, M.D., Ph.D., M.P.H.

◀ **Chapter 12** ▶

Environmental Events

INFECTIONS

Over the past several decades, much has been learned about the cause, treatment, and prevention of infections. Numerous childhood deaths and ill-effects from infections such as whooping cough (pertussis), diphtheria, lockjaw (tetanus), polio, and measles have been prevented by immunizations. Naturally, the serious physical and intellectual damage that sometimes accompanied these infections do not occur in children who are properly immunized. Unfortunately, there are other infections for which immunizations are not available, and infections that can affect babies before they are born.

Description

Serious developmental problems can be caused by certain infections that affect children in the prenatal (before birth), perinatal (shortly before, at, and after birth) or postnatal (after birth) periods. Prenatal infections are transmitted to an unborn baby by an infected mother. Any serious bacterial, viral, or parasitic infection in a pregnant woman may harm the unborn baby. The effect of prenatal infections on the fetus varies, depending on the type of infection and the time during pregnancy in which it occurred. Perinatal infections occur around the time of delivery, and postnatal infections can be observed any time after birth.

Toxoplasmosis, German measles or rubella, and cytomegalic inclusion disease are some of the infections that can prenatally infect an unborn baby. Herpes simplex in the birth canal can infect the baby perinatally. In the postnatal period, meningitis and encephalitis pose the most serious risks to children. These infections, their incidence, and possible effects on the child are described in the sections following.

Toxoplasmosis *Toxoplasmosis gondii* is a parasite found throughout the world. Cats serve as the major host for the parasite. The transmission of the parasite is caused primarily by contact with infected cat feces or with contaminated, improperly cooked meat. A toxoplasmosis infection transmitted to the fetus in the womb can result in premature birth or an infant who is small for gestational age. In addition, early infant death, mental retardation, and visual problems including blindness may occur in infected children. The child's head may be unusually large or unusually small. Approximately 0.5 to 1.0 per 1,000 live born infants are infected with toxoplasmosis, 25 percent of whom have symptoms.

German Measles   German measles or rubella usually is acquired from other infected humans through their cough or moist expired air. An infant, infected prenatally, may be smaller than expected at birth. The baby also may be deaf, have congenital heart disease, and have visual problems due to cataracts and inflammation of the retina. The baby may have a small head and be mentally retarded. Because almost all females in the reproductive age have been immunized against German measles, congenital rubella syndrome is rarely seen.

Cytomegalic Inclusion Disease   Cytomegalovirus is a common virus found throughout the world. Most infants infected in the womb do not have signs and symptoms at birth, but may be at risk for a hearing loss detected at a later age. Some infants who had been infected with cytomegalovirus in the womb have symptoms at birth. These babies may be smaller than expected, have blood spots on the skin (petechiae), jaundice or a yellow cast to the skin, a small head or microcephaly, delayed development, and various degrees of mental retardation. It has been estimated that about 0.2 percent to 2 percent of newborns are infected with cytomegalovirus, and only a few of these children display symptoms as described here.

Herpes Simplex   Herpes simplex virus infections are caused by one of two types: type 1 is known as oral herpes; type 2 is genital herpes, which is spread by sexual contact. A newborn infant, however, may contract type 2 herpes simplex by passage through an infected birth canal. Pregnant women may be without symptoms, yet still be able to infect the baby. An affected baby usually shows signs of the infection during the first month of life. The symptoms range from skin problems to the involvement of any organs, including the brain. Mental retardation or even death may occur. Approximately 0.1 to 0.5 of 1,000 live born newborns are infected with herpes simplex virus, more than 95 percent of whom become symptomatic.

Meningitis   Meningitis is an infection of the membranes covering the brain and spinal cord and the adjacent neural tissue. Many kinds of bacteria can cause meningitis, and specific names are applied to the diagnosis—for example, *pneumococcal meningitis* or *Hemophilus influenzae meningitis*. The age of the child, the type of germ causing the infection, the severity of the infection, and the effectiveness of the specific treatment determine the outcome that results. Some children recover completely after an episode of meningitis, whereas others may survive with major handicaps such as blindness, deafness, paralysis, seizures, or mental retardation.

Encephalitis   Encephalitis usually is caused by a virus. *Encephalitis* refers to an inflammation of brain tissue, whereas *encephalomyelitis* indicates involvement of both brain and spinal cord, and *meningoencephalitis* is an infection of both the brain and its covering membranes. When a prolonged coma is a symptom associated with such an infection, the term *sleeping sickness* has been used. The type of virus, the age of the child, and the severity of the infection determine the individual outcome and whether or not a developmental disability develops. Certain childhood illnesses, including German measles and mumps, may lead to encephalitis. Also, the herpes simplex virus and many others can cause encephalitis. The subsequent brain damage may lead to mental retardation and behavior disturbances.

The immunizations used to prevent childhood illnesses may themselves cause encephalitis, although this is extremely rare. The risk of such a postimmunization encephalitis is far less than the risk of complications from the childhood diseases.

Causes

Certain drugs, alcohol, cigarette smoke, bacteria, viruses, and other harmful substances that cause an unborn baby to develop abnormally are called teratogens (see section on "Drugs, Alcohol, and Smoking," later in this chapter). Why certain infectious agents act as teratogens when contracted prenatally is not completely understood. What is known is that at critical stages of fetal development, infections can have serious, long-lasting effects.

During the first trimester of pregnancy, when the basic structures including the brain are formed, the embryo or fetus is particularly vulnerable to infections. During birth and the postnatal period, certain infections, especially those that attack the brain and nervous system, also can cause brain damage and developmental disabilities.

Diagnosis

When a newborn baby is suspected to have been infected prenatally, various tests can be done in an attempt to determine whether or not an infection occurred and if so, what kind of infection. Some physicians then ask that a TORCH titer be done. This test requires a blood sample from both mother and baby, which is then examined for antibodies against TORCH organisms, whereby T stands for toxoplasmosis, O for other germs, R for rubella or German measles, C for cytomegalic inclusion disease, and H for herpes simplex. If a very high antibody titer against one of the organisms is found, then there is a real possibility that a prenatal infection had taken place.

If meningitis or encephalitis is suspected in a child, the doctor most often will do a lumbar puncture or spinal tap. The physician will place a needle between the spinal cord and its membranes and withdraw some spinal fluid. The spinal fluid is then examined for bacteria or viruses. Also, certain chemical tests can be done on spinal fluid, which will help to make the diagnosis.

Treatment and Prognosis

The type of treatment a youngster receives and the effects of the illness depend on the particular infection and the severity of the disease. Antibiotics are given immediately if meningitis has been diagnosed. The type of antibiotic used will depend on the specific bacteria found and their sensitivity to various antibiotics. For instance, for a baby who has been infected prenatally by German measles or cytomegalovirus, no specific medical therapy is indicated, because most of the damage has been done. If a child contracts encephalitis after birth, new antiviral drugs are now available for treatment.

DRUGS, ALCOHOL, AND SMOKING

During pregnancy there may be times when the mother needs to take prescription drugs or over-the-counter medicines. Unfortunately, medicines that help the mother sometimes harm the unborn baby. A number of medicines, illicit drugs, and other substances have caused abnormalities in fetal development. One of the most publicized catastrophies in medicine occurred 25 years ago in Europe and involved the use of the drug thalidomide during pregnancy. Women who took the drug as a sleeping pill during the first few months of pregnancy gave birth to children with shortened or absent limbs. This cluster of abnormalities led to studies that pinpointed the drug responsible and caused it to be taken off the market.

Description and Incidence

Serious medical conditions such as seizure disorders, cancer, infections, and blood diseases may necessitate a mother's use of medicine during pregnancy. Drugs commonly used to treat such conditions, but that can damage the baby, are described next.

Seizure Medications   Seizure medications, or anticonvulsant drugs, must be given with utmost care during pregnancy, since they are potentially dangerous to the unborn baby. These medications should be administered by a physician aware of the potential effects on the fetus.

Dilantin   Dilantin (hydantoin) causes congenital anomalies in about 43 percent of infants exposed to it in the womb. Thirty-three

percent are mildly affected, and the remaining 10 percent have the so-called fetal hydantoin syndrome. These children have unusual facial features with wide-set eyes, short nose, and small fingernails and toenails. Occasionally, these youngsters are mildly mentally retarded.

Trimethadione Trimethadione (Tridione) is an anticonvulsant medication known to cause abnormalities in over two-thirds of the children exposed to it in the womb. The affected children generally have characteristic facial features such as a short, upturned nose, a broad and low nasal bridge, a prominent forehead, abnormal genitalia, congenital heart disease, and mental deficiency.

Depakene Recent studies have indicated that spina bifida or meningomyelocele occurs in approximately 1 percent of children exposed to a newer anticonvulsant medication, Depakene (valproic acid), in the womb.

Anticlotting Medications

Coumadin Anticlotting, or anticoagulant, medications are occasionally necessary in the pregnant mother. When Coumadin, a common anticoagulant, is taken during pregnancy, affected children may have numerous congenital anomalies including short fingers, low birth weight, a small nose, and unusual facial features. Five of 16 reported children have shown significant mental retardation. Approximately two-thirds of exposed infants will be normal, and one-third will show bodily effects and brain abnormalities, or will be aborted spontaneously.

Anticancer Drugs Women who develop cancer during pregnancy and who are in need of life-saving but toxic medications will require careful medical management by both their obstetrician and their oncologist (physician who treats cancer). In order to save her life, the mother may need to take many drugs that may be harmful to the unborn baby.

Other Medications Many drugs are marketed each year, and careful surveillance is necessary to identify those that may be harmful to the fetus if taken during pregnancy. An example of a new drug found to be harmful if taken during pregnancy is the new acne medication *Acutane* (cis-retinoic acid). This medication is given for severe acne. Women who have taken the drug during pregnancy have had children with brain malformations.

The list of drugs known to be hazardous to the unborn child undoubtedly will be expanded as more studies are done and more drugs are released on the market. During pregnancy it is wise to use only those drugs that are absolutely essential. Even drugs that can be purchased without a prescription may be dangerous and should not be taken without your obstetrician's knowledge.

Alcohol Besides heeding the hazards of medications, pregnant women have a responsibility to their unborn children to avoid consuming other products known to damage the fetus. The best-known such substance is alcohol. Women taking 2 drinks per day throughout pregnancy may have small children. Those taking 4 to 6 drinks per day may have children with subtle findings of fetal alcohol syndrome. Eight to 10 drinks or more per day may result in children with the full-blown fetal alcohol syndrome. Children with this syndrome are small, they may be mildly retarded, often are irritable during infancy, and frequently are hyperactive later on in childhood. They usually have characteristic facial features including narrow eyelids. Congenital heart disease also may be present. The risk of a child of an alcoholic woman being affected is 30 percent to 50 percent. To date, the question of whether binge drinking in pregnancy is harmful has not been answered. Studies are ongoing, but until this question is answered, it would be wise for pregnant women to totally avoid alcohol.

Smoking Many women who smoke continue to do so during pregnancy. There are numerous studies on the effects of smoking on the fetus. Some studies have shown an increased rate of spontaneous abortion and death in the newborn period. Most studies show that children born to smoking mothers tend to be smaller than those born to non-smoking mothers.

Cause

Like other teratogens, when drugs, alcohol, and tobacco are taken by a pregnant woman, they can cross the placenta and affect the baby. They are particularly dangerous during the early stages of development. Yet, the manner in which these substances interfere with the embryo's or fetus's development is not fully understood.

Diagnosis

Diagnosis of a developmental disability caused by substance abuse is made primarily by a detailed medical history and a thorough physical examination of the baby. Reports of the mother's use of alcohol or drugs or of smoking during pregnancy, coupled with unusual physical features in the baby, and of the infant's slow growth and development, suggest that such substances may have had harmful effects.

Treatment and Prognosis

As with other causes of developmental disabilities, the severity of a child's problems will determine the amount and type of treatment needed. The long-term effects on the baby of teratogenic substances consumed by the mother during pregnancy depends to a large extent on the substance, the amount taken, and the time range during pregnancy when it was consumed. As mentioned in the descriptions of specific substances, the effects range from mild anomalies to severe deformities and mental retardation.

ACKNOWLEDGMENTS

Contributions have been made to this chapter by Patricia S. Scola, M.D., M.P.H., Karen E. Senft, M.D., and Siegfried M. Pueschel, M.D., Ph.D., M.P.H.

Chapter 13

Birth Defects

ABNORMAL DEVELOPMENT OF THE BRAIN AND SPINAL CORD

The formation and development of a human being is a complex process. What begins at conception as a single cell starts dividing, differentiating, developing, and maturing to finally form a complete human being. Within 2 weeks after conception, the primitive central nervous system, called the neural plate, already is present. By about 3 weeks, after further differentiation, the neural plate develops into what is called the neural tube and the primitive brain. Over the next several weeks and months, the complete formation of the nervous system occurs.

At birth, the brain is nearly fully developed. This complex organ has a number of areas of specialized functions. Some of these functions direct movements of the body and limbs, while others are responsible for vision, language, memory, thinking, hearing, feeling, and many other important functions. Deep inside the brain are hollow spaces called ventricles, which contain fluid. This fluid also cushions and bathes the brain on its outer layer. In the lower part of the brain are the midbrain and brain stem, which direct basic functions such as sucking, swallowing, and breathing. Another part, called the cerebellum, which controls refinement of movement, is located in the back of the brain. Finally, there is the spinal cord, which runs down through the bones of the spine and contains nerves that carry impulses to the muscles. In order for a child to function adequately, a well-formed nervous system is needed. If there are disruptions in brain development that may lead to permanent malformations, serious disabilities may become apparent.

Description

Common birth defects involving malformations of the brain or spinal cord are described in this section. Two conditions, hydrocephalus and spina bifida, are covered in greater detail because of their more frequent occurrence.

Anencephaly

A child with anencephaly has major parts of the brain missing because the neural tube does not close during early development. As a result, the brain and skull do not form properly. These children may have enough brain stem function at birth to breathe and suck initially. However, these infants do not show any appreciable developmental progress, and they almost invariably die of infection or respiratory complications in the newborn period. Anencephaly is estimated to occur in 0.1 to 6.7 per 1,000 live births.

Once a mother has had a child with anencephaly, there is a 2 percent to 4 percent chance of recurrence in a future pregnancy. However, prenatal tests are available to detect anencephaly and related disorders during pregnancy (see Chapter 22 for a description of prenatal diagnosis).

Hydranencephaly

In this malformation, the skull is intact and usually of normal size or larger. However, the space inside the skull, which should contain brain tissue, primarily is filled with fluid. In hydranencephaly, the brain stem may be functioning, allowing the child to suck and breathe for a short period of time. Most children born with hydranencephaly do not have the potential for intellectual growth, and most die in the first few months of life.

Holoprosencephaly

Holoprosencephaly is another problem of early brain development. During the third week of pregnancy, when the basic structures are being formed, the cells that are destined to become the person's face as well as the front of the brain fail to develop correctly. As a result, the brain forms abnormally and cannot function properly. In addition, the face shows abnormalities in that the eyes are very close together and the nose is extremely small or almost nonexistent. A large cleft palate is often present. The most severely affected children usually die in the newborn period. Other slightly less affected children may live beyond infancy, but their capacity for intellectual achievement is poor. Some youngsters have uncontrollable seizures originating in the abnormal brain. Holoprosencephaly is seen in some children with trisomy 13 and occasionally in other chromosome anomalies, but often no specific cause can be found.

Hydrocephalus

Hydrocephalus (also called water on the brain) refers to increased fluid in the hollow spaces, or ventricles, of the brain. As the ventricles fill and enlarge, two effects will be observed: the head will be expanded and the brain tissue will be compressed, which, if not treated promptly, eventually will result in brain damage.

Causes and Incidence   Hydrocephalus can be caused by overproduction of fluid in the brain, a blockage in one of the passages that drains fluid from the ventricles, or severe bleeding into the ventricles in the newborn period. Hydrocephalus occurs in approximately 0.8 to 1.6 of 1,000 live births.

Treatment and Prognosis   The prognosis of children with hydrocephalus depends on many things including the cause, the severity of the condition, and how quickly treatment is provided. Children who have hydrocephalus because the brain is severely deformed are less likely to do well than youngsters whose hydrocephalus results from blockage of the drainage system. Children with long-standing hydrocephalus more often have brain damage than those who are treated early in the development of their disease.

In some families, hydrocephalus is inherited as an X-linked recessive trait (for a description of recessive inheritance pattern, see Chapter 11, on "Chromosome and Genetic Disorders"). In another very small group of families, hydrocephalus recurs in subsequent offspring, but in most instances, hydrocephalus is not hereditary and the risk to future pregnancies is small.

An effective treatment of hydrocephalus is the placement of a plastic tube into the fluid spaces of the brain, which drains the excessive fluid into the abdomen (for a description of the procedure, see Chapter 25). Sometimes special medicines that reduce fluid production can be used.

Recently, exciting advances in the treatment of children with hydrocephalus have been made. Ultrasound techniques now are available that permit physicians to visualize the baby in the womb before birth. This technique, which is described in more detail in Chapter 22, can show the size of the head as well as the brain's fluid spaces. If repeated ultrasound images indicate that the ventricles are getting larger and hydrocephalus is diagnosed, the obstetrician may elect to deliver the baby early so that an operation (shunt placement) can be done before too much of the brain is damaged. When the hydrocephalus is detected and it is too early for the child to be delivered safely and to survive outside the uterus, an operation can be performed while the baby is in the uterus that drains the excess fluid of the baby's ventricles into the surrounding amniotic fluid. Although this type of surgery remains risky and experimental at present, it offers a great deal of hope for the future.

Spina Bifida

Spina bifida, or meningomyelocele, is a defect of the spinal cord and spinal column (see Figure 1). It occurs during the first few weeks of pregnancy when the spinal canal is being formed. In the process, the

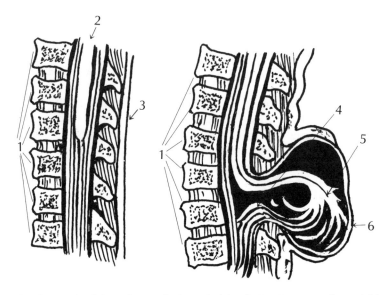

Figure 1. Cross-sectional views of a normal spine on the left and spine of a person with spina bifida on the right. In the drawing of spina bifida, note the opening at the spine and the protrusion of the spinal cord and its nerves through the back. Shown are: 1, bones of the spine; 2, normal spinal cord; 3, normal skin covering; 4, opening of the spine; 5, damaged spinal nerves; 6, sack with spinal fluid and nerve tissue.

spinal canal does not close completely, and the spinal cord, the surrounding tissue, and the membranes covering the spinal cord bulge out through the back of the spine. The delicate nerves in the spinal cord that protrude are damaged, leaving the child paralyzed in the lower part of the body. The severity of paralysis depends on where the nerves protrude through the spine. When the opening is high up on the back, paralysis is the greatest, and children usually will be wheelchair bound. Children with lesions in the midback area also may have to use a wheelchair, although they may be able to stand, and some may walk for short periods with appropriate bracing. Lower-back lesions generally permit walking some distance with braces and crutches. Children with even lower lesions may walk with light-weight ankle braces or without any assistance at all.

Because the nerves have been damaged, many children will have numbness of the feet, legs, and buttocks. The extent of the numbness depends on the level of the spinal cord lesion. The damage to the nerves also affects the child's bowel and bladder control. Children with severe nerve damage cannot feel the urge to pass urine or stool, and they lack the muscle control to do so voluntarily. In addition, urinary tract infections are common, as many of these children develop reflux, a backing up of urine from the bladder into the kidneys. Over 90 percent of children with meningomyelocele also have hydrocephalus.

Cause and Incidence   The exact cause of spina bifida is unknown; however, both genetic and environmental factors are thought to play a role. Estimates of the incidence of spina bifida, one of the most common birth defects, are 1 in every 1,000 births. Once a woman has a child with spina bifida, the chances of having a second affected child are approximately 2 percent to 4 percent. Today prenatal tests are available to detect meningomyelocele (see Chapter 22 for a description of the alpha-fetoprotein blood test for spina bifida).

Treatment   Because meningomyelocele involves so many areas of functioning, a team approach to treatment is recommended. With such an approach, children can receive appropriate counseling, medical care, and educational services. Medical treatment is necessary immediately after birth. Infants usually are transferred to a special care nursery. The defect in the back is then closed surgically, and a shunt operation is performed if development of hydrocephalus is noted. If these operations are carried out promptly, and if there are no complications such as infections or shunt malfunction, then the outlook for the child's cognitive abilities is good. In fact, the greatest danger to the newborn with spina bifida is an infection of the fluid spaces in the brain, called ventriculitis. If this can be prevented, it is likely that the child will have normal or near-normal intellectual development.

Urinary problems caused by nerve damage may be dealt with in many ways. If a child has a very large bladder that does not empty on its own, it can be emptied manually by applying pressure over the bladder. This procedure is called Credé method. Until recently, many children with meningomyelocele underwent surgery for an ileal loop, whereby the ureters or tubes coming from the kidneys are brought to the surface of the abdomen (Figure 2) (see also Chapter 25 on surgery). The child then wears a bag attached to the stoma (opening in the abdominal wall) to collect urine (Figure 3). Today, a nonsurgical approach is used most often, called intermittent catheterization. This involves placing a small plastic tube into the bladder for drainage of the urine, and must be done several times a day. Bowel continence can be encouraged with regularity of timing of bowel movements, diet, and laxatives or suppositories as needed. Most children find the best program for themselves through experimentation.

As mentioned before, damage to the nerves causes numbness of certain parts of the skin. Skin that is numb may break down, and sores develop easily. Therefore, meticulous skin care is very important.

Adaptive equipment and physical therapy is essential for children with spina bifida. Professionals can help these youngsters achieve as

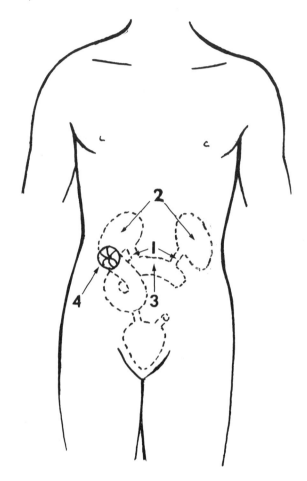

Figure 2. An ileostomy. The ureters (1) of the damaged kidneys (2) are connected to a part of the bowel (3), which is brought to the stoma (4) at the abdomen.

much independence as possible with proper equipment and practice. The type of equipment needed will depend on the level of the lesion and the degree of paralysis (see also Chapter 23).

CLEFT PALATE AND CLEFT LIP

Cleft palate is a birth defect in which the two halves of the palate (roof of the mouth) fail to join properly. This leaves an opening (a cleft) at both the hard and soft palates and sometimes the lip. When the development is interrupted during the early stages, the result may be a cleft in the lip only. The cause of the interruption in development is not always

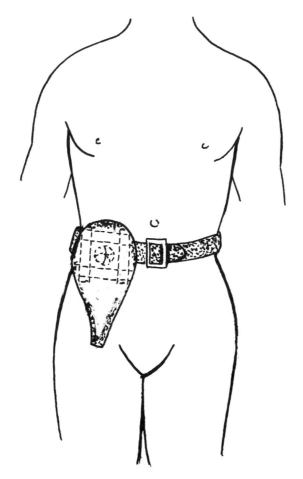

Figure 3.   Plastic bag worn over the stoma to collect urine.

known. Certain environmental events such as use of drugs, German measles, and vitamin deficiencies have been associated with clefts. Cleft lip and cleft palate are also often associated with specific syndromes such as trisomy 13. In other instances, there seems to be a genetic predisposition for the development of a cleft. Cleft lip and cleft palate are multifactorially inherited disorders (see Chapter 11), with a recurrence risk of approximately 2 percent to 4 percent.

Clefts are known to occur at different rates in various racial groups. Reports list the incidence of clefts in Caucasians as one in every 550 live births. The incidence among blacks is much lower, approximately one in every 2,500 live births.

A child with a cleft lip and cleft palate will have immediate feeding problems, as normal sucking will not be possible. Specialized feeders are utilized, and instructions for home feeding are given to the parents before the baby is discharged from the nursery. To correct the palate and lip defect, a series of surgical procedures are performed, usually within the first year and a half of life. A child with cleft palate may or may not have speech problems, depending on the size of the cleft and the success of surgical repair. In addition to oral surgery, the child's dental development often requires monitoring by both a dentist and orthodontist, as missing, malformed, or malpositioned teeth occasionally are observed.

Ear infections and conductive hearing loss are common in this group of children. Therefore, careful follow-up of the youngsters' hearing is needed. Special attention should be given to these conditions so that they do not interfere with language, speech, and cognitive developments.

CONGENITAL HEART DISEASE

To understand birth defects of the cardiovascular system, it helps to know how the normal heart and blood vessels are structured and how they function. The following is a brief description of the components of the heart and how they work together to pump blood throughout the body. The various types of heart defects are then explained.

The Normal Heart

The heart is a muscular organ that acts as a pump and circulates blood to the body and all its organs. The heart has four chambers—right and left upper chambers known as atria, and right and left lower chambers called ventricles. The right and left atria and right and left ventricles are separated from each other by a wall of muscle called the septum. Blood from the right atrium flows into the right ventricle through a valve known as the tricuspid valve. The left atrium connects to the left venticle by the mitral valve, as shown in Figure 4.

Under normal circumstances, blood is pumped from the left ventricle through arteries to all parts of the body. After flowing through the capillaries, where the cells receive oxygen and nutrients from the blood, the blood returns to the heart through the veins. The blood then enters the right atrium and subsequently flows to the right ventricle. From there it is pumped to the lungs through the pulmonary artery, where the blood is enriched with oxygen. The oxygen-rich blood returns to the left atrium of the heart, flows to the left ventricle, and then again is pumped to all parts of the body.

In the unborn baby, the blood follows a slightly different path. Some of the blood that arrives at the right atrium is directed through a

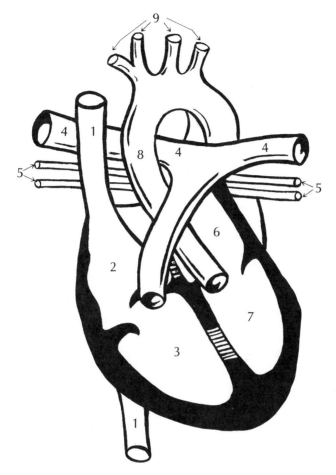

Figure 4. The human heart. The blood enters through the veins (1) into the right atrium (2). From there it flows into the right ventricle (3) and then enters the lungs through the pulmonary arteries (4). The blood returns from the lungs through the pulmonary veins (5) into the left atrium (6), and then continues into the left ventricle (7). From there, blood is pumped into the body through the aorta (8) and the entire arterial system (9).

hole, called the foramen ovale cordis, to the left atrium. In addition, most of the blood that is pumped from the right ventricle through the pulmonary artery is shunted to the main artery from the heart, or aorta, through a special vessel called the ductus arteriosus.

Defects of the Heart

In most infants the ductus arteriosus closes within hours after birth. In a condition known as *patent ductus arteriosus,* or *PDA,* the ductus arteriosus remains open and part of the blood going to the aorta is pushed into the pulmonary artery. This increase in blood flow to the lungs may cause heart and lung problems. Like the ductus arteriosus, the hole between the upper chambers or foramen ovale cordis usually closes shortly after birth as the pressure in the left atrium increases. There are occasions when it does not close spontaneously.

Congenital heart defects can be differentiated into those that cause cyanosis (blue discoloration of the skin, lips, and tongue), indicating a low level of oxygen in the blood, and those that are not cyanotic. Cyanotic heart disease usually is detected in the first few days of life. Any structural abnormality of the heart that inhibits blood flow to the lungs, where blood is oxygenated, or that causes a mixing of oxygenated and unoxygenated blood will produce cyanosis. Another way of looking at congenital heart disease is to consider the ways that structural defects obstruct or create abnormal blood flow through the heart and lungs.

In *transposition of the great vessels,* the arteries that leave the heart— the aorta and the pulmonary artery—are reversed; this means the right ventricle is connected to the aorta instead of to the pulmonary artery, and the left ventricle is attached to the pulmonary artery instead of to the aorta. In this situation, oxygen-poor blood is not returned to the lungs to get oxygen. Rather, it is pumped directly into the body's circulation, causing cyanosis.

Tetralogy of Fallot is a cyanosis-producing, congenital heart defect in which both obstruction of blood flow to the lungs and mixing of oxygenated and unoxygenated blood occurs. In tetralogy of Fallot, there are four defects: a narrowed passage between the right ventricle and the pulmonary artery; a thickening of the walls of the right ventricle, because of obstruction to blood flow; a defect of the wall between the two lower chambers; and a misplacement of the root of the aorta.

Endocardial cushion defect, or *atrioventricular canal,* occurs frequently in children with Down syndrome. This type of heart defect usually involves holes between the right and left atria and right and left ventricles. Often a defect of the mitral valve is present as well. This complex heart defect can range in degree from mild to severe.

A *ventricular septal defect,* or VSD, is an abnormal opening in the wall that separates the right and left ventricles. As a solitary defect (not grouped with others), ventricular septal defects rarely produce cyanosis. It accounts for approximately 20 percent of congenital heart disease. Ordinarily, the pressure in the left ventricle is greater than that in the right ventricle. When a ventricular septal defect is present, the unequal pressure in the chambers causes blood to be shunted from the left ventricle into the right ventricle. This increases the blood flow to the lungs, which ultimately increases the volume of blood delivered from the lungs to the left ventricle. Because of the increased blood volume, the left ventricle has to work harder to pump blood throughout the body. Small ventricular septal defects often close spontaneously. Complications of large ventricular septal defects include recurrent pneumonias, poor growth, and congestive heart failure.

Atrial septal defects, or ASDs, are of two types. When the hole in the wall separating the right and left atria is high near the foramen ovale cordis, it is called an *ostium secundum defect.* When the hole in the septum is low, it is called an *ostium primum defect.* Again, because of pressure differences in the two upper chambers, blood tends to flow across an atrial septal defect from the left atrium into the right atrium. In turn, an increased volume of blood is delivered to the right ventricle, which may lead to thickening of the walls of the right ventricle, called right ventricular hypertrophy. In an ostium primum atrial septal defect, frequently one of the valves between the upper and lower chambers, usually the mitral valve, also is defective. This may lead to mitral insufficiency, a condition in which blood in the left ventricle flows back into the left atrium when the left ventricle contracts, instead of flowing out through the aorta. This condition may lead to congestive heart failure.

Obstruction of circulation through the heart and lungs can occur at any of the valves in the heart. *Pulmonic stenosis* refers to a narrowing of the valve between the right ventricle and the pulmonary artery. *Aortic stenosis* is a narrowing of the valve between the left ventricle and the aorta. The degree of obstruction affects the amount of work the ventricle must do to push blood past the obstruction. The greater the obstruction, the harder the ventricles must work. Over time, the ventricles adjust to the obstruction by developing thickened muscular walls. But there is a limit to the effectiveness of this thickening. Heart failure may develop when the heart becomes overtaxed.

Another form of circulatory obstruction is *coarctation of the aorta.* This is a defect in which part of the aorta is narrowed or absent, and blood flow must be diverted through small branches, or collateral vessels, of the aorta.

A discussion of the assessment of congenital heart defects is provided in Chapter 22. Operations to correct these defects are described in Chapter 25.

ACKNOWLEDGMENTS

Contributions have been made to this chapter by Karen E. Senft, M.D., Katherine C. Castree, M.D., and Siegfried M. Pueschel, M.D., Ph.D., M.P.H.

◀　　Chapter 14　　▶

Problems in
the Newborn Period

Expectant parents may feel various intense emotions during pregnancy. There is excitement and anticipation over the ensuing birth. However, pregnancy also may cause anxiety as the delivery approaches and the reality of the baby settles in. In addition, many parents worry about the possibility that their child might have a handicap.

In today's modern health system, prenatal care is available to ensure the health of both expectant mothers and their future children. During prenatal checkups the baby's growth is followed closely and the mother's condition is monitored carefully for any potential problems. During labor, fetal monitoring may be used to check on the baby's heartbeat. If changes in the heartbeat, signaling stress, are detected, prompt delivery by cesarean section (incision through the walls of the abdomen and uterus; also called a C-section) may be life-saving for the baby.

Immediately after birth, a newborn's condition is evaluated and given a numerical rating from 0 to 10, called the Apgar Score (see also Chapter 2). Apgar Scores are assigned by delivery room personnel at 1 and 5 minutes after the birth of the baby. Five characteristics—the baby's color, respiratory effort, muscle tone, reflex activity, and heart rate—are evaluated, and each one is given a 0, 1, or 2 rating. The Apgar Score thus reflects the condition of the baby within the first few minutes of birth. A high score of 7 to 10 indicates that the baby is in good shape, whereas a low score of 0 to 4 may mean that the baby has serious difficulties and requires immediate attention.

Despite today's sophisticated health care, complications can develop during pregnancy, labor, or delivery that may affect the baby's future well-being. In this chapter, some of the common problems observed in the newborn period that may lead to developmental disabilities are discussed. For example, problems noted in some premature infants such as respiratory distress syndrome, retrolental fibroplasia, necrotizing enterocolitis, and intraventricular hemorrhage are highlighted, as are

other problems that also may occur in full-term infants following a difficult birth.

PROBLEMS OF PREMATURE INFANTS

Normally it takes about 280 days from the time of conception to the birth of the child. This period is referred to as gestation. During this time, children are growing and developing so that at birth they will be ready for life outside the womb. If a child is born prematurely and thus is underdeveloped, he or she may have difficulty surviving. *Prematurity* is defined as delivery before the 36th week of gestation.

Causes of Prematurity

Prematurity has many causes. For example, the membranes, or bag of water (amniotic sac) may break early, in which case labor pains often begin. An infection, especially of the mother's kidney or bladder, may also irritate the womb and cause contractions leading to early labor and birth. In addition, premature birth is also more likely to occur in adolescent mothers, in women who have had many babies, and in twin pregnancies. Some women have a weakness in the cervix (the narrow, outer end of the uterus), called incompetent cervix, which may lead to early labor. In addition, when there are serious complications in pregnancy, birth sometimes is induced early by the obstetrician to avoid endangering the life of the baby and/or the mother. Toxemia of pregnancy and high blood pressure, for example, are conditions that can be life-threatening if the pregnancy is allowed to continue. Also, placenta previa is a condition whereby the placenta is implanted over the inner part of the cervix, instead of in the wall of the uterus. In this condition, onset of labor may lead to serious bleeding, requiring bed rest and transfusions and, occasionally, necessitating premature delivery. Abruptio placenta, or the premature separation of the placenta from the wall of the uterus, is life-threatening for the child because the blood supply from the mother is interrupted. This may necessitate immediate delivery to save the baby's life.

Incidence

Estimates of the number of pregnancies ending prematurely are between 8 percent to 10 percent.

Treatment

Premature babies typically require treatment in an intensive care nursery in the hospital. In this setting, their conditions can be monitored closely and necessary treatment can be provided. The type of treatment a premature baby will need depends primarily on how early the baby is born, the baby's size, neurological problems, metabolic concerns, and respiratory activity. The subsections following "Prognosis" describe specific complications resulting from prematurity.

Prognosis

In general, the earlier a baby is born and the smaller and less developed he or she is, the greater the chances that there may be problems. With recent medical advances, babies as small as 1 to 2 pounds at birth and born as early as the 26th week of gestation now are surviving. Over 10 years ago these infants would have had little chance of living. However, many of these infants who now survive have problems in the newborn period that may result in long-term developmental disabilities.

SPECIFIC COMPLICATIONS OF PREMATURITY

Respiratory Distress Syndrome

A severe breathing problem that affects many premature infants is respiratory distress syndrome (RDS), also referred to as hyaline membrane disease. Respiratory distress syndrome may develop within a few hours or days of birth and is characterized by grunting respirations. Babies with respiratory distress syndrome have to expend a great deal of effort to breathe. Approximately 20 percent of premature infants develop respiratory distress syndrome. It is most common in babies born before the 32nd week of gestation.

Respiratory distress syndrome is caused by an inability to produce a chemical substance in the premature baby's lungs. Normally, after the first few breaths, the air sacs in the lungs are kept open by a substance called surfactant. Babies begin to develop surfactant between the 32nd to around the 36th week of gestation. Thus, a baby born before 32 to 36 weeks will be at risk for developing respiratory distress syndrome because of lack of surfactant.

The severity of respiratory distress syndrome will determine the type of treatment a premature infant receives. Children with a mild condition may need oxygen by mask. If the disease is more severe, an endotracheal tube may have to be placed in the windpipe, or trachea, to help them breathe. This tube is connected to a respirator, which assists the baby with breathing or actually takes over breathing by pumping air and oxygen into the lungs. Children with mild respiratory distress syndrome usually recover rapidly as their lungs mature.

Bronchopulmonary Dysplasia

A few babies, usually those who are very premature, may develop damage to the lungs leading to a condition known as bronchopulmonary dysplasia (BPD). Bronchopulmonary dysplasia is a serious complication of prematurity. Children with this disease may require oxygen for months to years. They also may have heart problems and may be more susceptible to colds and pneumonia than other children. Fortunately, bronchopulmonary dysplasia improves with age and with the growth of new lung tissue. Most children eventually will overcome their breathing problems.

Retrolental Fibroplasia

Retrolental fibroplasia, a serious eye problem, is another complication of prematurity. It is due to the overgrowth of blood vessels in the tissue of the back of the eye or retina. It occurs primarily in very premature infants who have required a great deal of oxygen in early life. Retrolental fibroplasia may cause nearsightedness. In some instances, it may lead to blindness. Modern neonatal care with careful monitoring of blood gases to determine the amount of oxygen in the blood decreases the frequency of retrolental fibroplasia, but is unable to eliminate it completely.

Necrotizing Enterocolitis

Necrotizing enterocolitis is a serious bowel disorder that occurs often in very small premature infants. In this condition, part of the bowel does not work and may die owing to lack of oxygen. The causes of necrotizing enterocolitis are not completely understood, but are currently under investigation. Children with mild necrotizing enterocolitis may recover when regular feedings are withheld and when nutrients are given directly into a blood vessel (hyperalimentation). Severely affected babies are at risk for developing a hole in the bowel, called a perforation, and may require surgery.

Intraventricular Hemorrhage

Intraventricular hemorrhage (IVH), or bleeding into brain tissue and fluid spaces within the brain (ventricles), is another major problem in very premature infants. In this condition, blood leaks from the vessels around the edges of the ventricles. Intraventricular hemorrhage is graded by severity: from Grade I, which is a slight leaking of blood, to Grade IV, indicating severe bleeding into the ventricles and seepage into the surrounding brain tissue. Children with Grade IV hemorrhage sometimes develop a blockage in the brain's drainage system that leads to marked enlargement of the fluid spaces (hydrocephalus). Hydrocephalus, also known as water on the brain, may require surgical intervention in which a tube is placed in the ventricles of the brain to drain the extra fluid. The tube goes from the brain to the abdomen, where the excess fluid is drained. This so-called ventricular-peritoneal shunt is described in more detail in Chapter 25 on surgery.

PROBLEMS OF FULL-TERM INFANTS

Description

When a child is born at full term, as most children are, chances are very good that everything will go well and that the baby will be normal and healthy. However, even with excellent prenatal care and appropriate monitoring, things occasionally go wrong and the baby is born with or develops a disability.

Full-term infants, like premature babies, may develop brain damage from injuries, diseases, or events that prevent enough oxygen from reaching the brain. Many of these children may show signs of cerebral palsy during the first few years of life. Problems of the mother during pregnancy, such as diabetes or malnourishment, can affect the baby. The use of drugs and alcohol during pregnancy, or infections, also may put the unborn baby at greater risk (see also Chapter 12). Because all these problems can cause developmental disabilities, each is discussed in greater detail in the following sections.

Causes

Events that cause oxygen insufficiency during birth in full-term infants are similar to those for premature infants and include early separation of the placenta, fetal distress, a difficult delivery in which the baby's head becomes lodged in the birth canal for a time, and the umbilical cord becoming tightly wrapped around the baby's neck.

Other less common problems may occur during pregnancy. For example, diabetic mothers are at risk for delivering large infants. These large infants—known as large for gestational age, or LGA, babies—have difficulty maintaining their blood sugar levels in the newborn period. If not closely monitored, low blood sugar, or hypoglycemia, may develop, which can result in brain damage. In addition, if the mother's diabetes has not been well controlled during pregnancy, the baby may be born with congenital anomalies (abnormalities).

If a mother has been ill or poorly nourished or if her placenta does not deliver sufficient nutrients to the fetus, a small and underweight infant may be born. These children are known as small for gestational age, or SGA, infants. This means that the child is smaller, although born after a full-term gestation. Once born, small for gestational age children may have trouble adapting to life outside the womb. Often, however, the mother of a small for gestational age infant had an uneventful pregnancy, and the reason for the poor fetal growth is not known.

Mothers who use unnecessary medications or drugs during pregnancy may put their children at risk for developmental disabilities. Tranquilizers, narcotics, barbiturates, and street drugs can cause addiction in the fetus before birth. After birth, the child then is abruptly deprived of the drug and suffers withdrawal. The baby may become very irritable, have tremors, and may even develop seizures. In addition, it has been found that infants of mothers who use strong narcotics, such as heroin, during pregnancy have a much greater risk of dying from crib death during the early months of life.

Children are also susceptible to many different kinds of infections before, during, and immediately after birth. When the infection occurs in the brain, it may lead to brain damage. This was discussed in detail in Chapter 12.

Incidence

The number of full-term infants who develop disabilities following complicated pregnancies, difficult deliveries, infections, or exposure to drugs or alcohol during fetal development is estimated to be 0.5 percent to 1.5

percent. In addition to these known risk factors, a certain percentage of apparently healthy full-term infants develop problems or disabilities during childhood.

Treatment and Prognosis

The treatment needed for full-term infants experiencing problems after birth depends on the type and severity of the disorder. Infants who suffer brain damage from a lack of oxygen during or after birth may require treatment in the hospital's intensive care nursery. The extent of the brain damage will determine how severely the baby is impaired. As mentioned earlier, babies of diabetic mothers may have difficulty regulating their blood sugar levels. Brain damage may be prevented with careful monitoring of the baby's blood sugar. Provision of intravenous glucose may be necessary for a period of time to control the baby's blood sugar level. Babies born with drug addiction often are treated with gradually decreasing doses of the medication the mother had been taking.

Meticulous prenatal care, careful monitoring during delivery with appropriate intervention if problems occur, and the development of special care nurseries staffed by experts in the care of sick newborns have decreased infant deaths in the prenatal period as well as the rate of serious disease.

ACKNOWLEDGMENT

Contributions have been made to this chapter by Karen E. Senft, M.D.

◀   **Chapter 15**   ▶

Cerebral Palsy

DESCRIPTION

Cerebral palsy, also called CP, is a general term used to describe disorders of movement that result from damage to the brain. Basically, cerebral palsy is a problem of muscle coordination. The muscles themselves are normal, but the brain is unable to send the appropriate signals necessary to instruct the muscles when to contract and when to relax.

There are three major types of cerebral palsy. Within each category, there are many degrees of severity. The type of cerebral palsy is determined by the location of the brain damage, and the severity is based on the amount of damage that has occurred.

1. *Spastic cerebral palsy* is found in more than half of all children with cerebral palsy. Spasticity means increased muscle tone. Children with spasticity will have tight or sometimes rigid muscles and are unable to move the involved limbs well. The limbs may be drawn into abnormal positions by overactive muscles pulling against weak muscles. This imbalance and the increased muscle tone may be slight and appear as clumsiness, or it may be severe, so that the child is unable to move voluntarily with good control. If one limb is involved, the palsy is called *monoplegia;* if two limbs are affected with either both arms or both legs involved it is known as *diplegia;* if one side of the body is compromised, the child has *hemiplegia;* and if all four limbs are affected, the palsy is called *quadriplegia.* The term *paraplegia* also is used to describe involvement of the legs only.
2. *Choreoathetoid cerebral palsy* is a term used when children have abrupt involuntary movements of the arms and legs. For individuals with this type of cerebral palsy, controlling the extremities to carry out activities is extremely difficult. At one time, choreoathetoid cerebral palsy was common, as it was the result of brain damage caused by complications from Rh incompatibility of mother's and baby's blood. Now that RhoGAM, a type of vaccine, is available to Rh-negative mothers who deliver Rh-positive children, choreoathetoid cerebral palsy is decreasing in frequency.

3. *Mixed-type cerebral palsy* describes patients with a mixture of spasticity and choreoathetoid movement.

Many children with cerebral palsy also are affected by other developmental disabilities. About 60 percent of youngsters with cerebral palsy have mental retardation, 40 percent are affected with visual problems, 35 percent may develop seizures, and 20 percent have language and hearing difficulties. Many youngsters with cerebral palsy, particularly those with mild conditions, are of normal intelligence and do not have any other disabilities.

CAUSES

Cerebral palsy is caused by brain damage, which may result from too little oxygen reaching the brain around the time of birth. A variety of events may lead to a lack of oxygen, such as a difficult labor causing fetal distress, separation of the placenta too early in labor, a stroke during fetal development, or severe respiratory distress syndrome during the early days of life. In addition, severe intraventricular hemorrhage or head injury can cause damage to brain cells. Genetic conditions, disorders of pregnancy, and diseases such as meningitis during infancy also may result in cerebral palsy. Although many causes of cerebral palsy have been identified, for approximately 40 percent of all children with cerebral palsy, the cause remains unknown.

INCIDENCE

Estimates of the number of persons with cerebral palsy vary considerably. A frequently cited figure is 1.5 to 2 per 1,000 live births. Of these, approximately 60 percent have spastic cerebral palsy, 20 percent choreoathetoid, and another 20 percent mixed-type cerebral palsy.

DIAGNOSIS

There is no specific test for cerebral palsy. Rather, it is diagnosed after the doctor has obtained a detailed medical history, examined the child, and observed the child's movements. Signs of cerebral palsy can include delayed development of motor skills, unusual patterns of movement, abnormal reflexes, and increased muscle tone. Cerebral palsy usually is not diagnosed until the baby begins to move and abnormal patterns of movement are noted. Most children with cerebral palsy are detected between 12 to 18 months of age. Often, a physician will see the child several times before making a definite diagnosis. It may take time to

determine if the problems in motor skills are the result of cerebral palsy or simply due to late developing motor skills.

TREATMENT

Although there is no cure for cerebral palsy, there are many ways to help persons with cerebral palsy improve their abilities and independence. Because of the complexities of the problems associated with cerebral palsy, an interdisciplinary treatment approach often is needed. Physical therapy programs provide exercises to keep muscles stretched and supple and to overcome imbalanced muscles. An occupational therapist can teach the child independence and self-sufficiency in skills such as dressing and feeding. Orthopaedic care can prevent contractures, permanent deformities, and limitations of joints due to very tight muscles through a prescription of exercises, braces, other adaptive equipment, and occasionally through surgery. Provision of braces and other needed special equipment can make the child more independent and able to participate in a wide variety of activities (see also Chapter 23 on "Adaptive Equipment"). Also, speech and language therapists can monitor language development, provide speech therapy, or devise alternative communication systems should they be needed.

PROGNOSIS

Because cerebral palsy is the result of brain damage, it is permanent and will be present throughout the person's life. With appropriate assistance and optimal treatment, many youngsters achieve some control of their muscles and are able to carry out many daily activities. Many individuals with cerebral palsy are well-accomplished professionals.

Of course, the more severe the cerebral palsy, the more difficult it is for the child to develop muscle control. Individuals with severe cases may never become ambulatory and may require assistance in basic skills throughout their lives.

ACKNOWLEDGMENT

Contributions have been made to this chapter by Karen E. Senft, M.D.

Chapter 16

Seizure Disorders

DESCRIPTION

Seizures may occur in children with developmental disorders. A child with a seizure disorder, however, may not be developmentally delayed and, in fact, may be normal in all other aspects. The terms *seizures* and *convulsions* are used interchangeably here.

To comprehend what a seizure is, it is necessary to understand that electrical activity is present in the living brain. This activity can be recorded by means of a brainwave test, also called an electroencephalogram or EEG. A seizure is the result of abnormal electrical discharges which often, but not always, can be detected by a brainwave test. In many instances, different types of seizures show specific patterns of the brainwaves.

The terms used to describe seizures and the method of classifying seizure disorders are not well standardized. Some common terms used to characterize seizures are *tonic, clonic,* and *atonic.* Tonic means the muscles are in a rigid state. Clonic refers to fast, jerky movements of the muscles. A combination of tonic-clonic seizures is often observed in children with grand mal convulsion. An atonic or drop seizure describes a loss of normal muscle tone that causes the patient to fall. The duration of the abnormal movements and the loss of consciousness that often accompanies a seizure are important in differentiating the types of seizures. Although watching someone have a seizure can be frightening, it is helpful to the doctor if parents or others note the various characteristics of the seizure.

A child with a seizure disorder may experience a warning sign just prior to the seizure such as an unusual odor, strange feeling, or a brief motor movement. The seizure itself is called the ictal stage and is followed by a postictal period, during which the person may be drowsy or may sleep.

SIMPLE FEBRILE CONVULSIONS

One common type of seizure that is not considered epilepsy is a simple febrile convulsion. A simple febrile convulsion usually occurs for the first time between the ages of 6 months and 6 years. The seizure is associated with a sudden rise in temperature and usually is brief and generalized. Children who have had a simple febrile convulsion are at no greater risk of developing epilepsy than anyone else, although they may have a repeat febrile convulsion if a high fever recurs.

GRAND MAL SEIZURES

Of those seizures that are grouped together under the term *epilepsy*, the type most commonly known is the grand mal or major motor seizure. This type of seizure disorder may develop anytime from infancy to adulthood. The seizures are generalized with tonic-clonic movements and loss of consciousness. In addition, there may be a temporary loss of bladder control.

PETIT MAL SEIZURES

Mainly children are affected by petit mal epilepsy. These seizures are rarely seen in infants and adults. Petit mal seizures are brief in duration, often less than 30 seconds, and may happen anywhere from a few to 100 times a day. Frequently, they consist only of brief staring spells, but motor signs such as twitching of the eyelids also may be seen. A specific brainwave pattern is a characteristic of petit mal epilepsy.

TEMPORAL LOBE SEIZURES

Temporal lobe or psychomotor epilepsy usually occurs in later childhood and in early adult life. Signs of temporal lobe seizures include inappropriate movements and behavioral patterns. Although some features such as staring spells or repetitious movements may be common to both petit mal and temporal lobe seizures, the duration of the seizure is longer in temporal lobe epilepsy. In addition, the findings on brainwave tests are different. In temporal lobe epilepsy, abnormal electrical discharges are confined to the temporal area of the brain.

MYOCLONIC SEIZURES

Myoclonic epilepsy includes several forms, such as minor motor seizures, infantile spasms, and massive myoclonic jerks. Myoclonic seizures are characterized by sudden flexion or bending of the body and neck while the arms are outstretched. Children who develop myoclonic seizures before 2 years of age usually have developmental delays and continue to have a poorer outlook than children whose seizures develop

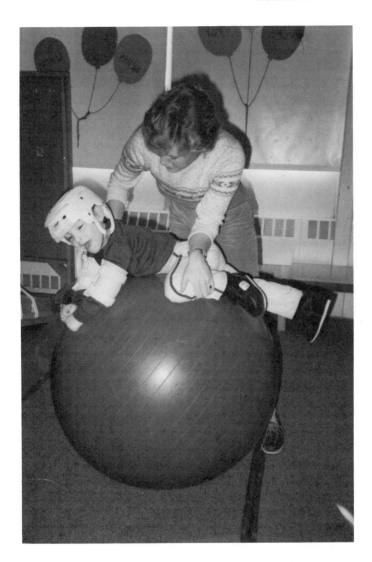

later in childhood. A disorganized electrical pattern of the brainwave, known as hypsarrhythmia, is characteristically seen in young infants with the seizure disorder.

The use of specific seizure medications and monitoring of drug dosage by means of blood levels have been of great assistance in controlling seizures. Continued public education and elimination of misinformation about seizure disorders are equally important to allow the child with seizures to participate in all life experiences.

CAUSES AND INCIDENCE

Many causes of seizure disorders have been discovered, although in most cases the reason why the seizure disorder develops remains unknown. Known causes of seizures include genetic factors, brain injuries, infections, lack of oxygen, and brain hemorrhage. It is estimated that seizure disorders affect approximately 1 percent of the general population. The number of developmentally disabled youngsters who have seizures is reported to be between 5 percent and 10 percent.

TREATMENT AND PROGNOSIS

Children with seizures usually are treated with one or more anticonvulsant medications. Medications are used to prevent or reduce abnormal electrical activity of the brain that characterizes seizures. For a detailed description, see Chapter 24 on medications.

Many youngsters with seizure disorders are well controlled with proper medication. For some, however, the severity of the disorder makes control of seizures difficult. Some cases of epilepsy diminish as children grow older. Often, these youngsters can be taken off medication and then remain seizure free. Others may need to take medication throughout their lives.

ACKNOWLEDGMENT

Contributions have been made to this chapter by Patricia S. Scola, M.D., M.P.H.

Chapter 17

Neurological Disorders with Associated Skin Findings

There is a group of serious diseases of the brain and nervous system that can be diagnosed because there are associated skin abormalities. As a class, these are known as neurocutaneous syndromes, or phakomatoses. This chapter describes the common neurocutaneous disorders.

TUBEROUS SCLEROSIS

Tuberous sclerosis is a dominantly inherited neurological disorder that affects the brain and the skin. Children with this disorder often have seizures, mental retardation, and an overgrowth of certain brain cells, causing small tumors to develop. Calcium deposits in certain parts of the brain also are common. Specific skin lesions of tuberous sclerosis include: adenoma sebaceum, an acnelike skin condition on the cheeks, nose, and chin; shagreen patches, thickened areas of skin that have an orange peel texture; and ash-leaf marks, pale areas of the skin that are seen more easily when ultraviolet light is held close to the skin. Other manifestations of this disease include tumorous growths in many parts of the body. In the back of the eye a tumor known as a mulberry lesion may develop. Tumors also may be found in the kidneys, bones, lungs, and on the skin. Problems with endocrine glands also are associated with tuberous sclerosis.

Cause and Incidence

Tuberous sclerosis is a genetic disorder with an autosomal dominant inheritance pattern. However, approximately 80 percent of all cases are new mutations. The incidence of tuberous sclerosis is reported to be 1 in every 100,000 births. If a parent has tuberous sclerosis, there is a 50 percent chance in each pregnancy that the child may have the disease.

Treatment and Prognosis

Specific therapy to treat tuberous sclerosis is not available at this time. However, affected children who have seizures should be treated for the seizure disorder. Occasionally surgical intervention is necessary to remove tumors. Special education is indicated for youngsters functioning in the mentally retarded range. The course of tuberous sclerosis is variable. In many cases, the neurological progression of the disease shortens the life span of affected individuals.

NEUROFIBROMATOSIS

In neurofibromatosis, brain, nerves, bones, muscles, skin, and glands may be affected. Two common skin findings are observed: café-au-lait spots or light brownish marks; and tumors along the nerve fibers, called neurofibromata. Café-au-lait spots generally resemble very large freckles. Neurofibromatosis may range from a mild problem to a very serious and debilitating disorder.

Years after café-au-lait spots are noted, neurofibromata of various sizes may appear beneath the skin. Symptoms depend on where these tumors appear. Tumors of the nerves of ears and eyes may affect hearing and sight. There may be multiple tumors appearing beneath the skin, resulting in deformity. Tumors of the bone may lead to fractures and skeletal changes such as scoliosis or curvature of the spine. Ten percent to 25 percent of those affected with neurofibromatosis have mental retardation, although most of these children function in the mildly retarded range. Seizures and hypertension or high blood pressure also are common.

Cause and Incidence

Neurofibromatosis is an inherited disorder with an autosomal dominant pattern of inheritance (see Chapter 11 on "Chromosome and Genetic Disorders," for discussion of inheritance patterns). The incidence rate is approximately 3 in every 10,000 live births.

Treatment and Prognosis

There is no definitive treatment available for neurofibromatosis. At times, surgical removal of tumors may be indicated. Seizures should be treated with appropriate medications, in the same manner as any other seizure disorder. Progressive monitoring is recommended for scoliosis and hypertension, and when these conditions are present, appropriate treatment should be initiated. The severity of the disease varies widely. The bodily difficulties experienced by affected individuals may range from minimal to severe.

STURGE-WEBER SYNDROME

Sturge-Weber syndrome is characterized by a large, dark, red birthmark called a port-wine stain most often seen over the forehead and cheek on

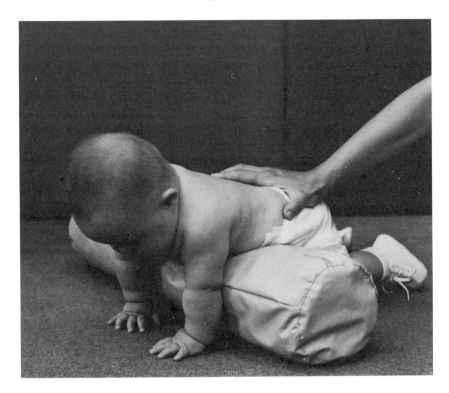

one side of the face. The lip, nose, and eyelid on the involved side may appear swollen. It is a neurological disorder in which the brain may have a blood vessel abnormality similar to that seen on the skin that causes seizures in 90 percent of the patients. Mental retardation occurs in 30 percent of affected individuals and may be accompanied by personality problems. About half of the patients will have one-sided paralysis or hemiplegia. This disease is not genetic, and therefore, recurrence is unlikely.

ATAXIA-TELANGIECTASIA

Ataxia-telangiectasia is a familial disorder (occurs in more members of a family than expected by chance alone), characterized by progressive ataxia, or uncoordinated movements, and choreoathetosis, or involuntary movements. An affected child may start to walk normally and later gradually develop increasing unsteadiness. The involuntary jerky movements also may start earlier. As the muscles around the mouth are involved, the youngster's speech may become progressively more difficult to understand. As children become older, they may lose the ability to sense where their bodies are in space. At about 5 to 6 years of age, spidery dilated blood vessels, known as telangiectasia, become apparent in the white of the eyes and later on the face and neck. The children's mental functioning decreases gradually. Many patients with ataxia-telangiectasia also have defective immune systems and have difficulty fighting infections. There may be multiple bouts of pneumonia and sinusitis, which can lead to progressive permanent lung damage or bronchiectasis and eventual respiratory failure. There is no specific treatment available for ataxia-telangiectasia at this time. Antibiotics are used vigorously to control infections. This disease is inherited in an autosomal recessive way (see Chapter 11 on "Chromosome and Genetic Disorders").

ACKNOWLEDGMENT

Contributions have been made to this chapter by Karen E. Senft, M.D.

◀ Chapter 18 ▶

Diseases of Muscles and Bones

Well-coordinated body movements are the result of nerve impulses that travel from the brain and through the spinal cord, to connect with nerves that carry messages to the muscles. These nerve impulses tell the muscles when to relax, when to tighten, and how to move the limbs. For smooth, coordinated movements, bone joint structures must be normal, and the muscles must be attached to the bones properly. If one of these parts is not working well or is defective, normal muscle function and well-coordinated movements will not be possible.

This chapter describes a number of developmental disabilities in which the primary areas affected are the muscles and bones. In each case, problems with movement and coordination are the primary disabilities.

FRIEDREICH ATAXIA

Friedreich ataxia, or spinal cerebellar degeneration, is a progressive disorder involving degeneration of nerves in the spinal cord. Individuals with this disease show unsteadiness and loss of coordinated movement. Affected persons lose their ability to know where their arms and legs are in space and become increasingly disabled. The muscles of the heart also may be involved, and sometimes intellectual limitations are noted. This disease usually has its onset in the first 20 years of life.

SPINAL MUSCULAR ATROPHY

Spinal muscular atrophy is an inherited disease that involves severe wasting of muscle. The actual defect is in the nerve cells of the spinal cord that ordinarily convey messages from the spinal cord to the muscles. Because the impulses cannot travel down the nerve, the muscles cannot work, and gradually waste away.

There are three subgroups of this disease, each of which has a different level of severity. The most severe form, known as Werdnig-

Hoffmann disease, is recognized at or shortly after birth. These children have very weak muscles, will later experience difficulty swallowing, and have frequent respiratory infections. These children usually do not survive the first year of life. Children affected by the intermediate form of spinal muscular atrophy have a somewhat better survival rate. Intensive physical therapy and appropriate orthopaedic intervention may allow some of these youngsters to walk. Kugelberg-Welander disease is the mildest form of spinal muscular atrophy. Again, physical therapy and orthopaedic care can help these children develop motor skills.

The spinal muscular atrophies are autosomal recessive disorders. That means both parents must be carriers of the gene for the disease in order to have an affected child (see Chapter 11 for a discussion of inheritance patterns).

CHARCOT-MARIE-TOOTH DISEASE

Charcot-Marie-Tooth disease also is known as peroneal muscular atrophy. Youngsters with this disease lose function in their peripheral nerves. The earliest symptoms usually occur by ten years of age, and include foot deformities such as a high arch and curled toes, as well as gait abnormalities. The disease progresses slowly and as it develops, weakness and wasting of foot muscles occurs. Later, the hand muscles may be involved. This disease is inherited in an autosomal dominant fashion (see Chapter 11 for a discussion of inheritance patterns).

ROUSSY-LÉVY SYNDROME

Roussy-Lévy syndrome is similar to Charcot-Marie-Tooth disease, but affected individuals may have more disabilities. In addition, they usually have tremors. These individuals also may develop diabetes mellitus.

MYOTONIC DYSTROPHY

Myotonic dystrophy is a disease of the muscles. The basic problem is an inability to relax muscles. For example, after shaking hands, the affected person will have difficulty letting go. This disorder may be passed on in either an autosomal dominant or autosomal recessive manner.

MUSCULAR DYSTROPHIES

The muscular dystrophies are a group of inherited disorders characterized by progressive degeneration of muscle tissue. There are several forms of muscular dystrophy.

Duchenne Muscular Dystrophy

Duchenne muscular dystrophy is the most common of the muscular dystrophies. It is an X-linked recessive disease and therefore affects boys almost exclusively. The onset is usually in the first few years of life. An abnormal gait typically is the first symptom noticed. Parents also report that the child falls frequently, has difficulty climbing stairs, and seems to be developing muscle weakness. The gait often is described as waddling and wide-based, which is a result of weakness in the pelvic and hip muscles. There is a relentless deterioration in muscular dystrophy, with children becoming wheelchair bound early in their second decade. Weakness is most noticeable in the muscles closest to the body's center, such as the trunk, shoulder, and hip muscles. The calf sometimes appears larger, a condition called pseudohypertrophy. However, larger in this case does not mean stronger. The heart muscle also can be affected. Once an individual loses the ability to walk, probably in the early teens, scoliosis or curvature of the spine may develop. As the disease progresses, the muscles used for breathing become weaker, which may lead to frequent colds and pneumonia.

Becker Muscular Dystrophy

Becker muscular dystrophy is similar to Duchenne muscular dystrophy, although it is a milder form. People with Becker muscular dystrophy generally are able to walk, and maintain this ability into adolescence and perhaps into early adulthood.

Limb Girdle Muscular Dystrophy

In limb girdle muscular dystrophy, there is a predominant weakness in the musculature of the pelvic region. The prognosis varies greatly and must be assessed individually. Inheritance of this form of muscular dystrophy is autosomal recessive.

Facioscapulohumeral Muscular Dystrophy

Facioscapulohumeral muscular dystrophy affects mainly the shoulder and facial muscles. The disease usually is relatively mild with slow progression, but more severe forms do occur. Inheritance is autosomal dominant.

OSTEOGENESIS IMPERFECTA

Osteogenesis imperfecta, or brittle bone disease, is a disorder in which the bones break easily. In the most severe form, many bone fractures are present at birth. In these cases, the infants might not survive the newborn period. In milder forms, fractures are frequent and may cause some degree of dwarfism. The effects of osteogenesis imperfecta on individuals vary greatly. In some children, fractures rarely occur, whereas in others even normal movements can cause fractures. Affected individuals also may have deficiencies of tooth enamel, as well as a hearing impairment. The whites of the eyes, or sclera, may appear blue. The basic abnormality in osteogenesis imperfecta is a defect in formation of connective tissues. This disease is inherited in an autosomal dominant manner. It also may occur as a new mutation. There is no specific treatment available, but meticulous orthopaedic management and preventive care will minimize deformity.

ACHONDROPLASIA

Achondroplasia is a term that describes the failure of bones to grow normally. It causes extreme shortness of the arms and legs. As a result, affected individuals are dwarfed. The head of individuals with achondroplasia often is enlarged. Youngsters with achondroplasia usually are of normal intelligence. Achondroplasia is an autosomal dominant inherited disorder, which means the risk of recurrence is 50 percent. This disorder occurs in approximately 1 of every 10,000 births.

CAUSE AND TREATMENT

The diseases discussed in this chapter are genetic in origin. A definitive cure is not available for any of these disorders, but supportive treatment can help. The principles of treatment include physical therapy and appropriate orthopaedic management to prevent deformity and to increase and maintain function for as long as possible.

ACKNOWLEDGMENT

Contributions have been made to this chapter by Karen E. Senft, M.D.

◄   Chapter 19   ►

Metabolic Disorders

The biochemical processes of the human body are extremely complex. Often many steps are needed to break down or build up bodily materials. Specific proteins called enzymes regulate many of the metabolic processes in the human body. Defective or absent enzymes can lead to dangerous excesses of some biochemical products and deficiencies of other chemicals the body needs to function properly. The excesses and deficiencies of certain chemical products can cause serious disabilities. The degree of disability varies with the specific chemical process that is disturbed, the type of chemicals that are deficient or produced in excess, and the availability and efficacy of treatment.

Metabolic diseases usually are categorized by the chemical product that is affected, such as parts of protein, fat or lipid, and sugar or carbohydrate. If the metabolic product associated with the disease is detected in the blood, a term ending in *emia* is used. When the product is detected in the urine, the descriptive term ends in *uria*. Thus, hyperphenylalaninemia indicates there is too much of a specific part of the protein or amino acid called phenylalanine in the blood, while phenylketonuria indicates the presence of certain chemicals called phenylketones in the urine.

DESCRIPTION

This chapter describes three major types of metabolic disorders. Each section includes information on the cause, incidence, and treatment of the disorder. The chapter concludes with a brief mention of lysosomal storage diseases.

DISORDERS OF AMINO ACID METABOLISM

Amino acids are chemicals that when linked together form proteins. Amino acids frequently are called the building blocks of protein. The most common amino acid disorder is *phenylketonuria*, often abbreviated PKU. This disorder is caused by the lack of a specific enzyme known as phenylalanine hydroxylase. This enzyme is needed to change the amino

acid phenylalanine into another amino acid, tyrosine. If phenylalanine is not broken down and an excess of this chemical builds up in the body, severe mental retardation can result. Since most protein foods contain phenylalanine, it is important to detect and treat children with phenylketonuria as early as possible. Otherwise, phenylalanine will begin to accumulate in infants with phenylketonuria, causing serious disabilities. Untreated infants may become irritable, vomit, develop a skin rash, have a distinctive odor described as musty, be developmentally delayed, and become mentally retarded. Fortunately, phenylketonuria can be detected in the newborn period, and all newborn babies born in the United States and many other countries are screened for phenylketonuria. Infants found to have phenylketonuria can be treated with a special diet that has limited amounts of phenylalanine. Early treatment can prevent mental retardation. Most children with phenylketonuria who are treated in infancy and throughout childhood are of normal intelligence.

Phenylketonuria, like most metabolic disorders, is inherited as an autosomal recessive trait. That means parents who have a child with phenylketonuria have a 25 percent chance of having another affected child in each future pregnancy. Phenylketonuria, the most common of the metabolic disorders, is actually quite rare and occurs in about 1 in every 14,000 births.

Another example of an amino acid disorder is *maple syrup urine disease,* so called because the urine of affected children smells like maple syrup. The defect involves a group of amino acids called branched chain amino acids. Maple syrup urine disease is much rarer than phenylketonuria, occurring in approximately 1 in every 120,000 births. This disorder also can be detected in the newborn period, and children can be treated with a special diet. When undetected and thus untreated, many infants die within the first 2 weeks of life. Dietary treatment has saved the lives of many infants with this disease.

Numerous amino acid disorders have been discovered in the past decades, but not all of them are amenable to treatment. Many of the amino acid disorders cause irritability, feeding problems, seizures, and other neurological problems in the newborn period. Mental retardation and growth failure also are common features in many of these disorders if left untreated or if no treatment is available.

DISORDERS OF LIPID METABOLISM

In disorders of lipid metabolism, abnormal amounts of fat are stored in body tissue. This group of metabolic diseases is called sphingolipidoses. There are subgroups of this disease group that are classified by the particular fat or sphingolipid involved and the respective enzyme defect.

Tay Sachs disease is perhaps the best-known example of this group of disorders. Tay Sachs is a degenerative disease resulting from a deficiency of the enzyme hexosaminidase A, which causes an accumulation of a sphingolipid called ganglioside GM_2. Infants with Tay Sachs disease appear normal at birth, but as the sphingolipid accumulates in the nervous system, muscle weakness, failure to thrive, blindness, and developmental regression leading to severe mental retardation are observed. Most children with the disease die between 3 and 5 years of age.

Tay Sachs disease is a recessively inherited disorder (see Chapter 11 for a discussion of inheritance patterns). It occurs in approximately 1 in every 3,000 births in people of Jewish background. There is a 25 percent chance in each future pregnancy that a family with an affected child will have another youngster with the disease. Carrier detection and prenatal diagnosis now are available for this disorder.

Other sphingolipidoses include *metachromatic leukodystrophy, Gaucher disease,* and *Niemann-Pick disease.* Since the onset of symptoms and the eventual outcome of the different sphingolipidoses vary with the specific biochemical defect, it is important to establish the diagnosis by means of specific laboratory studies and to provide appropriate counseling to the family.

DISORDERS OF CARBOHYDRATE METABOLISM

A group of metabolic diseases in which complex sugars or carbohydrates accumulate in the urine is called mucopolysaccharidoses. Their classification has been complicated by the fact that they were recognized as diseases long before biochemical tests were available to differentiate them. Thus, they were initially labeled *Hurler, Hunter, Sanfilippo, Maroteaux-Lamy,* and *Scheie* syndromes, to name a few.

Hunter syndrome is a sex-linked disorder, while the other mucopolysaccharidoses are autosomal recessively inherited. Hurler syndrome is the most severe of these disorders. It is caused by an accumulation of chemical products in the bones and other organs of the body, including the brain. As a result, affected children deteriorate physically. Marked changes are seen in the shape of the face, hands, joints, and spine. Enlargement of liver and spleen are observed. Mental retardation as well as visual and hearing impairments accompany the disease. At present, no effective treatment has been devised for this disorder. It affects approximately 1 in 100,000 children, and most die in early childhood.

Galactosemia is another disorder of carbohydrate metabolism in which a specific sugar called galactose cannot be metabolized or broken down because the body lacks an essential enzyme called galactose-1-phosphate uridyl transferase. In galactosemia, symptoms begin in infancy when the baby is given milk, and include vomiting and other gastrointestinal symptoms followed by listlessness and poor muscle tone. Jaundice and liver problems also may be present. If untreated infants survive, they often develop cataracts and become mentally retarded. Galactosemia occurs in about 1 in 40,000 newborns. Dietary treatment, in which galactose is eliminated from the diet, should be started as early as possible to prevent both physical and mental retardation or early death.

LYSOSOMAL STORAGE DISEASES

In addition to classifying diseases by the type of biochemical and enzymatic defects, it is now possible to determine where in the cell the biochemical problem is situated. For example, there are certain small structures within a cell called lysosomes. These are enzyme-containing particles that ordinarily break down certain chemicals. If a lysosomal enzyme is defective, then the material to be metabolized may be stored within the lysosomes, instead of being broken down. The diseases that result are called lysosomal storage diseases. This category includes some of the sphingolipidoses, mucopolysaccharidoses, mucolipidoses, and other similar disorders. A great deal of research now is being carried out in the area of metabolic diseases, since abnormalities of metabolism can result in severe disabilities.

ACKNOWLEDGMENTS

Contributions have been made to this chapter by Patricia S. Scola, M.D., M.P.H., and Siegfried M. Pueschel, M.D., Ph.D., M.P.H.

◀   **Chapter 20**   ▶

Endocrine Disorders

Endocrine glands produce hormones that regulate many functions of the body. For example, hormones control water balance, blood sugar level, growth, sexual maturation, and many other bodily functions. Although the lack of these hormones may cause devastating effects, most are not directly related to developmental disabilities. There is one notable exception, however, in which deficient thyroid hormone activity leads to hypothyroidism, previously known as cretinism.

HYPOTHYROIDISM

Description

At birth, children with hypothyroidism may appear normal, although they may have a greater than average birth weight. In the newborn period, constipation, lethargy, prolonged jaundice, poor feeding, and low body temperature may be present. If hypothyroidism is not treated with thyroid hormone, the child eventually will develop a puffy face, a dull appearance, a protruding tongue, and a prominent abdomen with umbilical hernia, and the child may become severely mentally retarded.

Cause and Incidence

Congenital hypothyroidism results from lack of thyroid hormone or is caused by an absent thyroid gland. About 1 in 4,000 infants is born with this disorder.

Detection and Treatment

Today, most infants born in the United States and other countries are screened for hypothyroidism before they are discharged from the hospital nursery. If the screening test is positive, the child's physician is notified, and treatment with thyroid hormone is begun immediately if the diagnosis of hypothyroidism is confirmed.

Prognosis

With early treatment, the prognosis is good. If a child with hypothyroidism is not identified and treatment is delayed, then the child may be-

come intellectually handicapped. Thus, the time at which treatment is started plays an important role in the outcome.

ACKNOWLEDGMENT

Contributions have been made to this chapter by Karen E. Senft, M.D.

◄ PART IV ►

Special Care for Your Child

Procedures, Appliances, and Medical and Surgical Treatments

◄ Chapter 21 ►

Strategies for Helping Your Child

Once a child is found to have a developmental delay or another handicapping condition, most parents and families are anxious to begin helping their child in any way possible. Depending on the child's particular problem, a number of strategies may be useful. This chapter briefly outlines the various types of strategies and interventions that generally have proven helpful for children with developmental disabilities. As you read the description of each intervention, keep in mind that not all children require all types of services. Your child's individual needs, which have been identified during the evaluation process, will determine the specific kind of interventions that are necessary. Also, remember that the various treatments, therapies, and interventions described here do not necessarily cure children of their disability. In many cases, the interventions help the youngsters to become more lively participants in everyday activities. In other instances, the assistance or therapy may enable children to learn or improve basic skills such as feeding and dressing.

Some strategies are primarily educational in nature and may be provided in a public school or special center. The program may focus on developing the child's thinking and language skills through special instruction with carefully designed materials and specially trained teachers. Whatever the intervention, the aim is to help the child and family in those areas in which assistance is needed.

The process for selecting the appropriate intervention begins with developmental and diagnostic evaluations (see also Chapters 22 and 27 on "Tests and Procedures" and "Assessing Developmental Disabilities," respectively). During such an in-depth assessment, professionals will determine a child's strengths and weaknesses and find out whether a developmental disability exists. This is the first step in planning an appropriate intervention. Obviously, a treatment program cannot be developed until the child's needs have been identified. The more thorough the assessment, the more specific and comprehensive the recommendations for treatment can be.

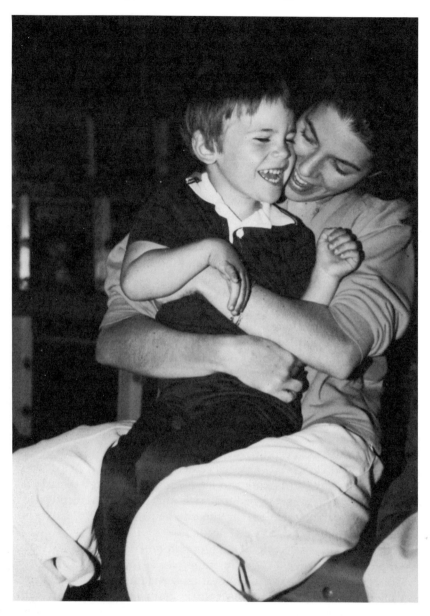

After an initial evaluation, children with developmental disabilities may need to return for repeated evaluations each year or every few years. Reassessment may be necessary because the child has matured physically and developmentally. Growth of the child may mean that certain tests can now be performed that were difficult to carry out previously. Moreover, the child's specific needs change as he or she grows and develops. For example, an adolescent will have different concerns than a preteenager. In addition, recently acquired knowledge of a particular disorder might suggest new directions for care and management. Thus, assessment must be considered an ongoing process. The results of each reevaluation or new test may affect the type of treatment given. Therefore, it is important that the appropriateness of current interventions be carefully monitored and that changes be made whenever new information indicates that they are necessary.

It is also essential that the effectiveness of the intervention program be studied. If the planned program is not meeting the child's needs, or if new knowledge is obtained, additional assessment may be necessary to determine how the program can be improved.

Various kinds of intervention strategies are summarized in the sections following. They are grouped in categories for ease of discussion.

MEDICAL AND SURGICAL INTERVENTIONS

Many children with developmental disabilities have health problems resulting from a birth defect, injury, or other causes that require medical or surgical intervention. The term *medical intervention* simply means that the child's health problems need to be taken care of by a physician. This could be the family doctor, the child's pediatrician, or a specialist such as a neurologist, orthopaedist, or cardiologist. At times, a child with a specific disorder such as spina bifida will need to be followed in a clinic where children with such problems are treated by a number of specialists. The specific treatment or intervention provided to a child may consist of frequent visits to the doctor or other health care provider, such as a physical or occupational therapist; careful monitoring; or taking medications regularly. It also could include using special equipment at home or a stay in the hospital. A child with multiple problems might need a variety of treatments combined into a special regimen to be followed daily. For example, a child with cerebral palsy and a seizure disorder might have to take medications as well as participate in a regular physical therapy program.

Surgical interventions may require an operation to correct or alleviate certain problems. Although many minor operative procedures such as hernia operations or tonsillectomies are now often performed on an outpatient basis, major operations usually require a stay in the hospital. Decisions to operate are made carefully. A number of factors will need to be taken into consideration by the doctor and family, such as the severity of the child's problem, and the child's size, weight, and general health, before electing to perform an operation. Surgeons want their patients to be in the best physical condition possible prior to an operation to reduce the chance of complications and improve the likelihood of a speedy recovery. However, there are situations when surgery must be performed on an emergency basis to save the life of the patient.

For children who are facing hospitalization, further information on preparation and aftercare is found in Chapter 26. Operations that are frequently performed on children with various kinds of developmental disabilities are described in more detail in Chapter 25 on surgery.

NUTRITIONAL INTERVENTIONS

Many parents of children with developmental disabilities may require the assistance of a nutritionist, dietitian, nurse, physician, or other professional to ensure that their child receives the proper kind and the right amount of food. Proper nutrition involves getting adequate amounts of proteins, carbohydrates, fats, minerals, and vitamins that the body needs to grow and develop normally. For children with feeding problems, food allergies, or food intolerances, a nutritional evaluation may be necessary in order for them to eat and develop properly. Nutritional strategies may focus on what, how much, or how often a child eats. Parents might have to increase or decrease the total number of calories fed to a child in a day, change the number of meals provided, or give the child a special food supplement. A nutritional evaluation may be concerned with how or in what position a child is fed. For example, a child who has trouble swallowing may need to be fed with a tube, or a child who is unable to chew may stay on strained or pureed foods while efforts are made to develop necessary feeding skills such as proper swallowing or chewing.

Nutritional intervention may be part of an overall treatment plan. Whenever a treatment is prescribed, it is very important that the instructions be followed carefully. In this way the doctor, nutritionist, or other professional involved can evaluate whether or not the treatment is working. This is particularly important, because if the expected improvements do not occur, the treatment plan may have to be adjusted or changed. Therefore, before a change is made, you and the professionals will want to be sure that it was the treatment that was ineffective rather than a failure to correctly implement a good plan.

Special dietary treatment plans or nutritional interventions are essential for children who have certain metabolic disorders. The words *metabolic* and *metabolism* refer to the way the body digests, processes, and breaks down the foods we eat. Some metabolic disorders are caused when a child is born without a certain essential body chemical (enzyme) needed to break down foods. A well-known example of a metabolic disorder requiring nutritional intervention is phenylketonuria, or PKU. Children with phenylketonuria are born without a specific enzyme needed to metabolize a building block of protein called phenylalanine, which is necessary for growth. When children with phenylketonuria eat foods containing phenylalanine, most of the phenylalanine remains unused and builds up in the body and the brain. This buildup can be harmful and can cause brain damage and mental retardation. Fortunately, children with phenylketonuria can be treated by providing them with a special diet. The diet consists of avoiding foods containing large amounts of phenylalanine and taking a special formula that has just enough phenylalanine to ensure proper growth and development. The earlier the treatment for phenylketonuria begins, the greater the chance that the child will grow and develop normally. Because early treatment is so important in preventing brain damage and mental retardation, all children born in the United States are screened routinely for phenylketonuria before they leave the newborn nursery. (See also discussion of PKU in Chapter 19.)

Babies who are having difficulty gaining weight and growing are likely to need a nutritional intervention. This condition is often referred to as failure-to-thrive or failure-to-gain-weight. Depending on the cause of the individual child's problem, part of the plan may involve giving the baby a special fortified formula that will add extra calories and nutrients to the diet. Parents may have to increase the number of feedings offered to the baby each day and carefully monitor how much is actually consumed.

However, increased weight gain and obesity can also necessitate nutritional intervention. In our culture many children are overfed and become overweight from an early age on. It is important that parents be provided with information on a balanced diet for their children containing an appropriate amount of calories. It is easier to prevent increased weight gain than to treat obesity.

EDUCATIONAL INTERVENTIONS

Throughout the United States special education services are available to help developmentally disabled children. A major purpose of special education is to ensure appropriate educational programming for those children who need special assistance in order to be able to learn. Depending on the particular child, the help required may be a small part of the overall educational plan, or it may involve all aspects of the program. For example, the only assistance a youngster of normal intelligence with a mild form of cerebral palsy may need is regular physical therapy to improve walking skills. Such assistance easily could be provided within a regular education program. Multiply handicapped children who demonstrate significant delays in all areas of development will need special assistance in all facets of their educational program. Such services can be delivered best in a special education classroom where the child can get the quality and quantity of the services needed. At times, the child's need may be so great that the child will require a prolonged school program (about 230 days) instead of the usual 180-day program.

The passage in 1975 of Public Law 94-142, the Education for All Handicapped Children Act, guaranteed that all school-aged children who qualify for special education services can receive a free and appropriate education in the least restrictive environment. The phrase "least restrictive environment" means that handicapped children must receive their special assistance in as normal an educational setting as possible. Thanks to Public Law 94-142 many handicapped youngsters now spend some of their school days in a regular education classroom. They may need to go to a resource room or therapy for several periods of the day for their special treatment, but they spend a significant amount of time with their peers. For additional information on the schooling process and Public Law 94-142, see Chapter 29.

The ages at which services become available for handicapped children vary from state to state. Some states provide special education services beginning from birth on, whereas others begin at ages 3 or 5. Public Law 94-142 indicates that services must begin by age 5. However, the newest Public Law, 99-457 (Education of the Handicapped Amendments of 1986), expands upon Public Law 94-142 and mandates that services begin at 3 years of age. This law is designed to assist every state in extending services to this age group by 1990, and encourages them to begin services at birth.

At present, those states where special education does not start at birth offer other programs available to help children with handicaps or developmental delays. Such programs are called early intervention programs. A detailed description of the various types of early intervention programs can be found in Chapter 28.

Early intervention is a form of educational program for infants, toddlers, and preschoolers. Because early intervention is for babies and very young children, program goals emphasize developing basic skills. For this reason, the term *developmental program* is often used to describe early intervention programs. This term emphasizes that children are encouraged to achieve skills in the normal developmental sequence such as crawling, pulling to stand, walking, babbling, using words, exploring and manipulating toys, and so on. Unlike special education programs, which are provided in a school or special center, early intervention programs can be home-based or center-based as well as parent-

or child-oriented. Many programs offer a combination of service formats. If more than one type of early intervention program is available, investigating the types of services offered, the level of parent involvement expected, whether the program is center-based or home-based, and exploring other relevant questions will help families select the program that best suits their child's needs and the family's life-style.

THERAPEUTIC INTERVENTIONS

Many developmentally disabled children require one form or another of special therapy at some point during their lives. The most common forms of treatment are physical therapy, occupational therapy, speech and language therapy, respiratory therapy, and specific psychological services. Each type has a unique purpose.

Physical Therapy

Physical therapy, commonly called PT, attempts to help children develop their gross motor abilities. Gross motor skills involve the use of the large muscles of the body. Examples of gross motor skills include walking, running, crawling, and jumping. Physical therapists may work with infants, toddlers, and young children as well as teenagers and adults. A baby may receive therapy to develop basic skills that will be needed before complex skills like walking can be learned. For example, one baby might need assistance in improving head control or rolling from front to back, whereas another child might need help learning how to get into the sitting position and maintaining balance. An older youngster's therapy program might concentrate on improving walking skills or helping the child learn to use special equipment such as a wheelchair or walker.

Many physical therapists are trained specifically to work with children. These pediatric physical therapists have learned special ways to handle children. Techniques used with babies and small children include proper positioning and motivating the child to move by using toys. Other activities performed by the therapist include stretching tight muscles or increasing the range of motion of limbs. Such passive activities may be an important part of a therapy program, but generally should not constitute the entire treatment plan. Many therapists today strive to have the children actively participate in the therapy program. Active participation is the best way for children to learn what they must do in order to move in a desired way.

Individual physical therapy sessions may last anywhere from 15 or 20 minutes to an hour. The duration of the treatment depends on the individual's needs and tolerance. Some children require therapy several times a week, whereas other youngsters need only to be seen once every month or so.

Usually, physical therapists work closely with the child's parents or other family members. In the case of a school-based physical therapy program, the therapist would also consult with a child's classroom teacher. By keeping in close contact with parents and teachers, the therapist can demonstrate and review methods used to encourage development of the child's gross motor skills. Families are expected to continue working with the child on some of the exercises and activities at home as well. This is essential if improvements are to be made. Without carryover of the program to home and school, where children spend most of their time, the effects of weekly or even monthly therapy sessions would be lost quickly. By working with a therapist, many parents have become excellent cotherapists for their children.

The physical therapist also can be instrumental in helping parents learn to use adaptive equipment, braces, splints, or other special devices that have been prescribed for their children (for details on this subject see Chapter 23 on "Adaptive Equipment").

Occupational Therapy

Many people are confused by the idea of occupational therapy, particularly when it is recommended for young children. The term *occupational therapy,* or *OT,* originally was referred to as a form of treatment for handicapped adults, who, because of injury or deformity, were unable to participate in activities of daily living. These patients, who had difficulty using their hands to complete everyday tasks, were helped by therapists to improve their occupational skills.

Occupational therapy for young children refers to a form of treatment that will enhance their fine motor skills and control of the smaller muscles of the body. This includes muscles of the arms and hands needed for reaching, grasping, and holding objects. It also involves muscles of the face and mouth that are important for chewing, swallowing, and maintaining lip closure. In addition to improving control of particular muscles, an occupational therapist is concerned with improving the way different muscles work together, such as in eye-hand coordination. Some types of occupational therapy can be useful to children who are overly sensitive to touch or whose touch perceptions appear distorted. These children often experience difficulty interpreting information received through their senses, and benefit from a form of occupational therapy called sensory integration.

Like the physical therapist, the occupational therapist will want to work closely with parents, teaching them how to incorporate the necessary exercises into daily routines. The occupational therapist also can advise parents on the use of special equipment, the application and use of hand splints, and other types of bracing devices. Many occupational therapists have been trained to construct hand and arm splints. For a detailed description of the various kinds of appliances, see Chapter 23.

Speech and Language Therapy

Professionals who specialize in the treatment of language problems and speech disorders are called speech pathologists or speech and language therapists. Children who show a significant language delay or hearing loss, or who are having difficulty producing speech sounds, may benefit from speech and language therapy. Depending on the individual's problems, speech therapy may be provided in a small-group setting or on an individual basis. For very young children, who have not yet begun to talk, therapy may consist of language stimulation activities, sound imitation training, and activities to encourage babbling and to make other sounds. Older children may need articulation training or speech therapy to help them produce clearer sounds. For a hearing impaired child, language therapy may consist of hearing training and development of a communication system using sounds, gestures, and hand signals. Speech therapy, like other therapies already discussed, is more successful when parents and other family members continue with the recommended exercises and activities at home.

Speech therapists share a concern with occupational therapists about the function of the muscles of the face, mouth, and throat, since these muscles are primarily responsible for speech production. If a child has marked problems with muscles around the mouth so that speech is severely impaired, the therapist and the child's family may decide to develop alternate means of communication. Alternative forms of communication range from sign language and communication boards (with pictures and/or words) to sophisticated computerized speech synthesizers. The type of alternative communication device depends on the child's age and cognitive abilities. In order to use a communication board with pictures or words, the child has to recognize names of objects, understand that pictures are representations of objects, and comprehend that written words refer to specific things. Implementing an alternative system of communication generally takes considerable time for both planning and training. However, the efforts can be very rewarding, as the system enables a child to communicate with others.

Respiratory Therapy

Children with medical or physical conditions that impair their breathing may require respiratory therapy to prevent lung infections and to improve breathing efficiency. Chest percussion is a form of treatment for respiratory problems, which consists of pounding the child's chest in order to loosen the secretions of the bronchial tubes so that the mucous can be coughed up. This type of therapy may be needed several times a day in order to keep the lungs clear. Other forms of respiratory therapy involve the use of mechanical devices that aid breathing, such as a respirator, a mist tent, or an oxygen mask or tent. Respiratory therapy is often provided while a child is hospitalized. Children with certain diseases such as cystic fibrosis who have problems with chronic lung infection and congestion may also need regular chest therapy at home. For these children, teaching the parents or caregivers the treatment procedures is essential to the child's well-being.

Psychological Services

A psychologist can help children with developmental disabilities and their families in a number of different ways. Often, the initial contact with the psychologist occurs during the evaluation process. The psychologist may have tested the child to determine if developmental delays or behavioral problems are present. Beyond evaluation, the range of psychological services also includes individual therapy for the child, counseling or therapy for parents together, family therapy where all members including sisters and brothers are seen together, and consultations on specific problems such as discipline, behavior problems, learning, and emotional disorders. Many parents seek help because they are having difficulty coping with the stresses of everyday life. These problems may have originated long before their handicapped youngster was born. It is not unusual for the birth of a handicapped child to reactivate previously existing problems.

For many individuals, a psychologist can be of most assistance by helping parents and family members learn more about their child's problems and understand the impact on their own and their child's lives. Talking to a psychologist or trained counselor frequently helps people sort out their feelings and come to terms with problems that may have seemed insurmountable. Psychologists also may be consulted by teachers, therapists, and/or other professionals working with handicapped children about behavior problems, unusual social interactions, learning difficulties, and discipline strategies. Psychological assistance may consist of suggestions of ways to manage behavior problems by working directly with the child and family on behavior management programs. In the case of an emotional problem or unusual social behavior, a psychologist may decide to see the child on a regular basis for individual therapy. The type of therapy provided would depend on the child's specific problem. Techniques that are commonly used for treatment include play therapy, behavior modification techniques, group therapy, and family therapy.

Social Service Intervention

It is not unusual for families of handicapped children to feel overwhelmed at times because of the numerous demands and problems presented by caring for their disabled child. All parents face crises with their children at one time or another, but parents of handicapped or mentally retarded children tend to face a never-ending succession of both major and minor crises as their child grows. Whether or not each crisis is handled successfully or results in enormous stress on the family depends on many factors such as the severity of the problem, parents' coping ability, and resources available to the family including financial, professional, and emotional support from others. Issues that frequently are the focus of family crises can range from acute health or medical problems of the child, decisions about therapeutic or surgical interventions that have been recommended, concerns about financial resources needed to obtain optimum care, unusual time demands required of the parents, and worries about their child's future. Parents also may be bewildered by the number of agencies and professionals involved in their child's care and confused about the types of services each offers. Other potential sources of stress are the parents' own feelings and emotional responses to their child and to the handicap, and their experience with friends, neighbors, other family members, and strangers. To help solve some of these problems and relieve the feelings of stress, people often turn to a social worker for assistance. Many social workers are trained in psychotherapy and counseling skills and are knowledgeable regarding community agencies available to families. They can be extremely helpful in directing parents to the appropriate agency for assistance.

The amount and type of assistance a social worker provides vary from family to family. The assistance also may vary from clinic to clinic, as the social worker's role may be different in various settings. Many parents simply need to be pointed in the right direction and then are able to obtain help on their own. Often, these are the families that have an extended support network already available to them and who are coping fairly well with their child's handicap. Other families, where the problems are more extensive, may benefit from regular counseling.

Various social service interventions available to aid people with handicapping conditions differ from state to state. To learn more about what is available in your area, you will need to contact your state social service or welfare agency for information, the nearest branch of the

Association for Retarded Citizens-U.S., local chapters of various associations for different disabilities (e.g., Muscular Dystrophy Association, United Cerebral Palsy, Spina Bifida Association, National Down Syndrome Congress), or diagnostic centers offering services to mentally retarded and handicapped children. Most areas have agencies that can assist parents in their efforts to care for their disabled children. Sometimes, helping families means finding a way to give parents a break from the demanding responsibilities their child presents. These breaks, or respites, can be anywhere from an occasional afternoon to 1- or 2-week vacations, temporary foster care, or placement in a group home if necessary.

As parents find they are having trouble managing the care of the child alone, they may begin to think about alternative arrangements. In these situations, talking to a social worker can be extremely helpful. Social workers may help families to find appropriate programs that are geared primarily to enriching the handicapped individual's life. Many localities in the United States offer extensive recreational and vocational programs for their retarded citizens. Most readers probably are familiar with the Special Olympics program, which has grown considerably in the past two decades. This program has probably done more nationwide for the self-image of the persons who participate in it than any other individual program. In addition to helping its participants, Special Olympics has brought national attention to the needs and rights of persons with mental retardation and other disabilities in our country.

Thus, the social worker is often a resource broker, that is, a person who may help you to discover what services are available to you and your developmentally disabled child.

ACKNOWLEDGMENT

Contributions have been made to this chapter by Leslie E. Weidenman, Ph. D.

◀ **Chapter 22** ▶

Tests and Procedures

Over the past several decades, some of the most dramatic advances in medicine have been made possible because of the development of numerous medical tests and special procedures. Today, the human body can be studied in many ways not even envisioned 20 or 30 years ago. More and more physicians are relying on technologically sophisticated tools such as ultrasound, computerized tomography, and magnetic resonance imaging to diagnose and treat difficult medical conditions. This chapter describes these techniques and other commonly used tests and procedures, and shows how they may be applied to various medical disorders and developmental disabilities. A number of these procedures have been briefly described in previous chapters of this book. Cross-references are included to guide your reading.

PRENATAL DIAGNOSIS

As genetic counseling has become more effective, greater emphasis has been placed on diagnosing certain handicapping conditions before birth. Through the use of various prenatal studies and tests, many chromosome disorders and genetic diseases can be diagnosed during pregnancy (see also Chapter 11).

Ultrasonography

Ultrasound or ultrasonography is a noninvasive procedure during which sound waves are sent into the womb. These sound waves bounce off the various fetal structures and provide a picturelike image of the unborn baby. This procedure most often is used to obtain an objective assessment of the baby's size and development, which in turn allows the physician to estimate the approximate due date. In addition, certain structural abnormalities can be diagnosed with ultrasonography such as spina bifida, hydrocephalus, certain skeletal disorders, congenital heart disease, and others.

Amniocentesis

The most widely used test for prenatal diagnosis is amniocentesis. Amniocentesis usually is performed between the 15th and 17th week of pregnancy. This procedure ordinarily is done on an outpatient basis. It involves introducing a needle through the abdomen into the womb and withdrawing some of the liquid, called amniotic fluid, which surrounds the unborn baby. This amniotic fluid then can be studied for various metabolic problems, chromosome disorders, and alpha-fetoprotein. Cells—called fibroblasts—obtained from the amniotic fluid need to be grown in a laboratory. After about 2 to 3 weeks in culture, these cells can be examined for chromosome problems and for certain biochemical disorders.

The risks associated with amniocentesis are very small, especially when the procedure is carried out by experienced obstetricians guided by ultrasonography. However, like any surgical procedure, amniocentesis carries a slight risk of infection, and there is a slight increase of spontaneous abortion. These risks must be weighed against the benefits of the procedure. There may be some discomfort when the needle is pushed through the skin into the womb.

Amniocentesis is usually recommended for women who are 35 years and older, for families who already have a child with a chromosome or genetic disorder, if one of the parents is a translocation carrier, or if a metabolic problem in the fetus is suspected.

Chorionic Villus Sampling

During the past few years, a new technique for prenatal diagnosis during the first trimester of pregnancy has been developed. It is called chorionic villus biopsy, or chorionic villus sampling (CVS). The *chorion* refers to the part of the placenta that is near the unborn baby. In this procedure, a small sample of the chorion is obtained for diagnostic studies.

This technique has not been evaluated fully. At present, it is performed only at certain large university centers. Chorionic villus sampling requires a trained professional in ultrasonography and a skilled obstetrician. Ultrasound is needed to localize the placenta from which the obstetrician can obtain a tissue sample.

The advantages of chorionic villus sampling over amniocentesis are: first, a chromosome analysis can be performed immediately, with results made available in a few hours; and second, chorionic villus biopsy can be performed at an earlier time in pregnancy, usually during the 3rd month of gestation. In addition to chromosome analysis, the tissue sample can be used for biochemical studies and DNA analysis.

As with any procedure, there are advantages and disadvantages as well as technical difficulties. Future investigations will determine whether chorionic villus biopsy is a safe procedure yielding accurate results.

Fetoscopy

A more invasive diagnostic test used in the prenatal period is fetoscopy, which uses fiber optics. During this procedure, a tube is placed into the womb, through which the fetus can be visualized and blood can be obtained. This procedure is performed only if the baby is suspected to have a specific blood disorder that cannot be diagnosed through amniocentesis. Because fetoscopy poses a risk to mother and baby and the rate of complications is somewhat higher than other procedures, it is used only on a very limited basis. Fetoscopy is being replaced by sophisticated level II sonography.

DNA Analysis

A new diagnostic method involves the use of deoxyribonucleic acid (DNA) analysis. This test can provide information about the actual genetic makeup of the fetus. It is used to detect a wide variety of blood disorders in the fetus such as thalassemia and sickle cell disease, as well as other genetic disorders.

To do the test, small blood samples are needed from each parent and their affected child. A fetal sample can be obtained by amniocentesis, chorionic villus sampling, or fetoscopy. The samples are then sent to a special laboratory that is equipped to carry out the DNA analysis. The results are usually available in 2 to 3 weeks.

Alpha-fetoprotein

To determine if an unborn baby has spina bifida, a birth defect in which the spine fails to form properly, maternal blood can be analyzed for alpha-fetoprotein. Alpha-fetoprotein is a substance produced by the unborn baby. From there it enters the amniotic fluid and then passes into the mother's blood. If the alpha-fetoprotein level obtained from blood samples between the 16th and 18th weeks of the pregnancy is abnormally high, ultrasonography is done to rule out other conditions that could result in high alpha-fetoprotein levels. For example, a twin pregnancy or intrauterine death may result in high levels of alpha-fetoprotein. Also, if the date of the expected birth has been miscalculated, the alpha-fetoprotein level could be elevated. If such conditions have been ruled out, an abnormally high alpha-fetoprotein level could mean that the baby has spina bifida. In such instances, amniocentesis and/or ultrasonography are recommended to enable a more definite diagnosis.

During recent years, it has been observed that many women who gave birth to children with Down syndrome had very low alpha-fetoprotein levels. Therefore, an increasing number of alpha-fetoprotein screening programs recommend amniocentesis and subsequent chromosome analysis if the alpha-fetoprotein level is significantly decreased and if there is a high risk that the mother may carry a fetus with Down syndrome or any other chromosome problem.

NEWBORN SCREENING

Metabolic disorders refer to problems of the body's chemicals. For many years, tests for a variety of metabolic disorders have been performed routinely, using samples of blood, urine, amniotic fluid, and other tissues. During the past two decades, for example, nearly all newborn babies in the United States and other countries have had blood tests for certain metabolic conditions such as phenylketonuria and hypothyroidism (see Chapters 19 and 20, on metabolic and endocrine disorders, respectively). Many states also screen for other rare metabolic diseases such as maple syrup urine disease (see Chapter 19), homocystinuria (liver enzyme [cystathionine synthase] deficiency), and galactosemia (hereditary disorder of galactose metabolism). Throughout the United States, different states test for different metabolic disorders.

During screening, a few drops of the baby's blood are collected on a filter paper within the first few days of life and sent to a laboratory for testing. In some states, a sample of the baby's urine also is obtained to test for specific metabolic disorders. If a child is identified to have a metabolic disorder, appropriate treatment can be started immediately. Treatment for metabolic disorders may mean giving the baby a special diet or administering medications. With early detection and treatment of certain metabolic disorders, mental retardation and other physical problems can be prevented in many children who otherwise would have had serious handicaps.

Various biochemical tests also are carried out in older children who are suspected to have a metabolic problem. For example, a urine specimen can be examined for the presence of increased amounts of amino acids or organic acids that, if found, may suggest a specific metabolic disorder. Cells obtained from blood and skin can be checked for certain enzyme deficiencies, as in Tay Sachs disease, Hurler syndrome, and others (see Chapter 19 on "Metabolic Disorders").

SWEAT TEST

A sweat test, or iontopheresis, is used to diagnose cystic fibrosis, a relatively common inherited disease affecting the intestinal and respiratory systems. A sweat test measures the concentration of sodium and chloride in the child's sweat. In most cases, an excess of sodium and chloride in the sweat is an indicator of cystic fibrosis. It is important to identify children with cystic fibrosis as early as possible because supportive care, administration of intestinal enzymes, and antibiotic therapy for respiratory infections will improve the prognosis of these children.

CHROMOSOME ANALYSIS

Chromosome analysis is used to diagnose a number of chromosome disorders such as Down syndrome, Turner syndrome, and Klinefelter syndrome. This procedure usually involves taking a blood sample from the child. Also cells from skin, amniotic fluid, and other tissues can be used for chromosome analysis. The cells are incubated in a laboratory for about 3 days. Then the cells are placed on a glass slide, stained, and specially prepared so that the chromosomes can be examined under a microscope. The number and the structure of the chromosomes are then analyzed.

Various chromosome abnormalities can be detected, such as the presence of an extra chromosome in one of the pairs (called *trisomy*), the attachment of one chromosome to another (called a *translocation*), a missing part of a chromosome (referred to as a *deletion*), or a portion of a chromosome upside down (called an *inversion*) (see Chapter 11 on "Chromosome and Genetic Disorders").

It is important for a physician to know if a child has a chromosome abnormality. Once detected, appropriate genetic counseling can be provided to the parents.

TESTS FOR NEUROLOGICAL DISORDERS

Electroencephalogram

For many years neurological disorders, or problems with the body's nervous system, have been studied using various tests and procedures. One of the most frequently used tests is the electroencephalogram, or EEG, commonly known as a brainwave test. During an electroencephalogram, a child will have 16 small electrodes placed on various locations of the scalp. These electrodes are connected to the electroencephalogram machine, which then records the electrical activity generated by the child's brain cells on a paper strip. The recording shows the individual pattern of the brain's electrical activity, which is interpreted by a neurologist.

Electroencephalograms of children with grand mal, petit mal, or other seizure disorders often show characteristic patterns of electrical activity (see also discussion of seizure disorders in Chapter 16). Information obtained from the electroencephalogram, together with the child's medical history, helps the physician diagnose and treat various seizure disorders. In addition to seizure disorders, abnormal electroencephalograms may indicate space-occupying lesions such as tumors, abscesses, and other abnormalities of the brain. Other tests will be needed, however, to make an accurate diagnosis of such conditions.

Computerized Tomography and Magnetic Resonance Imaging

Over the past 10 years, the diagnosis of neurological problems has been revolutionized by the development of two new procedures: computerized tomography, also known as CAT scan or CT scan, and magnetic resonance imaging, commonly referred to as MRI. A CT scan is a sophisticated three-dimensional X ray printed out by a computer in two dimensions. Magnetic resonance imaging involves the magnetic sensing of the atoms of the brain to create an image of brain structures. The pictures obtained from the CT scan and MRI allow the physician to see the fine structures of the brain. Previously only invasive procedures were available, such as the injection of dye into an artery or air into the ventricular system. These procedures often were painful, riskier, and provided less information about brain structures than the new imaging techniques. Both CT scan and MRI are extremely helpful in diagnosing tumors, hydrocephalus, abnormal blood vessels, bleeding in the brain, and other structural problems of the brain and the rest of the body.

Anticonvulsant Blood Levels

Children with seizures who are treated with anticonvulsant medications will have a small amount of blood drawn at regular intervals to measure the concentration of the seizure medication in the blood stream. These measurements or blood levels tell the physician whether the child is getting enough medication to control seizures. Medications must be in sufficient quantity in the child's body for their benefits to be felt. The blood levels also will reveal if a child has too much medicine in the body. Medication levels that are too high may cause side effects or toxic symptoms (see also Chapter 24 on medication).

PROCEDURES TO DIAGNOSE NEUROMUSCULAR DISORDERS

Neuromuscular disorders, including Duchenne muscular dystrophy, spinal muscular atrophy, and others, can be assessed in various ways, including blood tests for muscle enzymes, studies of muscle contractions and nerve conduction, and muscle biopsies.

Muscle Enzyme Test

The presence of high levels of certain muscle enzymes may mean that the muscles are abnormal or diseased. For example, testing for the enzyme creatine kinase, sometimes referred to as CK or CPK, will help a physician diagnose specific muscle diseases such as Duchenne muscular dystrophy. The procedure for muscle enzyme testing involves obtaining a blood sample and sending it to a laboratory for examination.

Electromyography

The electrical conductivity of nerves going to the muscles and muscle contractions can be studied by a procedure called electromyography, or EMG. During this procedure, a very small needle is inserted directly into the muscle and the electrical activity during a muscle contraction is recorded. Normal muscles have specific patterns, whereas diseased muscles show abnormal recordings.

Nerve Conduction Studies

Nerve conduction studies involve placing electrodes at two sites on the same nerve. The electrodes must be separated by several inches. A small electrical charge is sent through the nerve at one end and recorded at the other end. Normal nerves conduct electrical charges at a specific speed, and the readings show distinct patterns. Diseased nerves, however, show abnormal patterns of electrical conductivity.

Both electromyography and nerve conduction studies can assist in determining whether the affected child has a primary muscle disease or whether the nerve tissue is compromised.

Muscle Biopsy

Muscle biopsy involves the surgical removal of a small portion of muscle and examining it under both a light microscope and an electron microscope. Before the tissue is examined, it is prepared with special stains and chemicals. These procedures are most helpful in diagnosing several forms of muscular dystrophy and other neuromuscular disorders.

PROCEDURES TO DIAGNOSE SENSORY DISORDERS

Audiogram

An audiogram or hearing test can indicate whether or not a child has a hearing impairment. A child who has delayed language development or who fails to respond normally to sounds should have a hearing assessment (a detailed discussion about hearing impairment is provided in

Chapter 8, on "Sensory Disorders"). The techniques used during the hearing examination may vary according to the child's age, cooperation, and cognitive abilities. If the child is under 6 months of age, the audiologist will observe the child's responses to sounds of controlled intensities and frequencies. The child may respond to sounds by turning the head, blinking, startling, widening of the eyes, or cessation of sucking. In a somewhat older child, visual reinforcement audiometry often is used, which means an animated toy or a flashing light reinforces a localization response to sounds. For children from 2 to 6 years old, conditioned play and audiometry frequently is employed, whereby children engage in play activities, such as putting a toy into a box, each time a sound is heard. In older children, pure tone audiometry may be used, during which a tone is presented at different intensities and frequencies. If a hearing loss is present, the audiogram can tell the degree of the hearing impairment and whether the ability to hear high- or low-pitched sounds is affected.

Tympanometry

Tympanometry involves placing a seal over the outer ear canal and gently injecting small amounts of air through the seal into the ear canal. The normal eardrum, also called tympanic membrane, will move back and forth slightly against the tiny jet of air. This movement can be measured and compared to established norms. If this movement is markedly reduced, the middle ear may be filled with fluid or the eardrum itself could be stiffened. The lack of flexibility of the eardrum observed in various conditions often will compromise the child's hearing significantly.

Brain Stem Evoked Response

Direct measurements of electrical conductivity along the nerves that carry sound impulses into the brain can be made using a procedure called brain stem evoked response (BSER), or auditory evoked potential. This procedure is quite similar to an electroencephalogram, described earlier. The child is placed in a quiet environment and measured sounds are presented to each ear. Electrodes placed over certain portions of the scalp then measure the rate of conduction of the sound through the auditory nerve to the brain. A slower than the expected rate of conduction or lack of response may indicate a serious hearing problem. Small children often need to be sedated for this test.

Visual Evoked Potential

A process similar to the brain stem evoked response, called visual evoked potential, is available for studying visual abilities. In this test, visual stimuli are given instead of auditory stimuli, and recordings of the nerve conduction of the visual information are made from different portions of the brain.

EVALUATION OF RESPIRATORY DISORDERS

Chest X Ray

Respiratory disorders such as pneumonia, asthma, and lung problems in cystic fibrosis are best diagnosed with the help of a chest X ray. The chest X ray is one of the most reliable tools available to the physician, since it allows the physician to locate and identify the respiratory problem.

Taking X rays is like taking a photograph. The X-ray pictures are obtained in a special room with lead walls so that no radiation can leave the room. The child's chest is placed against a photographic plate, the child is asked to take a deep breath, and then the picture is taken with special rays that can "see through" the body. Usually the amount of radiation is quite small and will not harm the child. Once the chest X ray has been taken, it will need to be developed like any other photograph. Following this, a radiologist will interpret the X-ray picture. For example, the doctor, usually a radiologist, can determine whether the child has pneumonia, bronchitis, an overinflated lung, collapsed lung, tumor, or an abnormal collection of fluid in the chest cavity. The X ray also reveals which part of the lungs is involved.

Pulmonary Function Tests

During pulmonary function tests, a child breathes into a machine that measures the amount of air that moves in and out of the child's lungs. In certain lung diseases, the volume of air moving in and out of the lungs may be significantly reduced. In addition, pulmonary function tests can measure the concentration of specific gases in the expired air. These tests usually are given to children who have cystic fibrosis, muscular dystrophy, or other disorders that affect the lungs. Through pulmonary function studies, a physician can determine the extent of a child's lung disease and whether there is improvement with treatment or whether it is getting progressively worse.

ASSESSMENT OF CARDIAC DISEASES

Cardiac diseases can be studied through combined use of chest X ray, electrocardiogram, echocardiogram, and cardiac catheterization. In addition, chest X rays allow the radiologist to find out whether the heart chambers are enlarged.

Electrocardiogram

The electrocardiogram, or EKG, provides a direct measurement of electrical activity produced by the nerves in the heart. This procedure is much like the brainwave test described earlier, but here the electrodes are placed on the limbs and across the chest. By analyzing the patterns of the electrical activity shown on the electrocardiogram, the physician can determine whether the heart rhythm is normal, whether the heart chambers are enlarged or damaged, whether heart muscle is stressed or pumping too hard, and whether the heart's nerve conduction system is working appropriately.

Echocardiogram

The echocardiogram is a noninvasive procedure in which sound waves are sent into the chest and the waves then "echo" or bounce off the structures of the heart to a recording membrane. From the pattern of the echoed sound waves, information can be obtained about the structures of the heart chambers, heart muscles, blood vessels leading to the heart, and valves that regulate the blood flow. The echocardiogram is an excellent tool for looking at certain congenital heart defects such as holes between the heart chambers, known as septal defects, and abnormal structures of the large blood vessels. The echocardiogram is similar to ultrasound procedures used in prenatal diagnosis.

Cardiac Catheterization

During cardiac catheterization, a dye is injected into the heart chambers through plastic tubing that has been threaded through either veins or arteries to the heart. Once the dye is in the heart, a series of X-ray pictures is obtained in rapid succession. This allows the cardiologist to visualize the inside of the heart as it pumps. In addition, this procedure enables the oxygen content and the pressure in both the heart chambers and adjacent vessels to be measured. Cardiac catheterization involves certain risks, which should be discussed with the cardiologist. The risk of catheterization often is outweighed by the information gained about the functioning of the heart. Since the child is slightly anesthetized, no real discomfort is felt during this procedure.

DIAGNOSTIC PROCEDURES USED IN INTESTINAL DISEASES

Intestinal disorders such as colitis and ileitis (inflammation of the bowels) and ulcers can be studied using direct visualization through endoscopy, rectoscopy, sigmoidoscopy, and colonoscopy, and with X-ray procedures such as barium swallow or barium enema.

Endoscopy, Rectoscopy, Sigmoidoscopy, Colonoscopy

During endoscopy, a long, narrow, flexible tube is inserted into the stomach through the mouth and the esophagus. The procedure allows the inside wall of the stomach to be examined. Ulcers, tumors, and bleeding are among the most commonly diagnosed problems using endoscopy.

Rectoscopy, sigmoidoscopy, and colonoscopy use a similar but longer tube to study diseases of the rectum and colon, or large bowel. Inflammatory bowel disease such as ileitis or colitis, polyps, diverticulosis, or cancer can be diagnosed this way, since the physician can visualize any changes or abnormalities on the inside of the bowel. At the same time, a specimen of suspicious bowel tissue can be obtained during colonoscopy, sigmoidoscopy, or rectoscopy for microscopic studies. These procedures can be done either on an inpatient or an outpatient basis. Although these procedures usually are not painful, there may be some discomfort when the instrument is inserted into the rectum.

Barium Swallow

X-ray studies, including a barium swallow and an upper GI (gastrointestinal) series, can give a picture of the lining of the esophagus, stomach, and the intestinal tract. These procedures involve swallowing a small amount of barium, a whitish chalky material that can be seen on an X-ray film. The barium is followed through the esophagus into the stomach and then through the upper portion of the small bowel. X rays are taken at specific times during this process. Usually no pain or discomfort is associated with these procedures.

Barium Enema

A barium enema is similar to the barium swallow. In this case, the barium is introduced into the rectum and sigmoid, which is the lower part of the large bowel. Again, the radiologist can examine the progression of the barium through the colon and take X-ray pictures of various parts of the large bowel.

UROLOGICAL DISORDERS

Urological disorders likewise are studied by using a combination of direct inspection with the cystoscope and indirect visualization with X-ray techniques. The most common X-ray studies of the kidneys and bladder are the intravenous pyelogram and the voiding cystourethrogram.

Intravenous Pyelogram

The intravenous pyelogram, also known as IVP, involves injecting a dye into one of the veins in the forearm. The dye is carried through the blood stream and then passes through the kidneys, ureters, and bladder. X rays are taken of these structures at various times after the injection of dye. By looking at the flow of the dye through the kidneys and ureters into the bladder, the radiologist can determine whether or not there are any problems such as kidney stones, tumors, kidney damage, areas of narrowing or widening of the tube system, or bladder problems.

Voiding Cystourethrogram

A voiding cystourethrogram, called VCUG, involves the injection of dye into the bladder. A tube is inserted through the urethra, which is the passageway from the bladder to the outside, into the bladder. The dye then is passed through the tube into the bladder. Subsequently, X-ray pictures are taken, which may show abnormal structures inside the bladder, and which also reveal whether there is a problem with reflux. Reflux occurs when urine from the bladder is backing up into the ureters and kidneys. Normally, a one-way valve in the bladder prevents reflux, but in certain conditions, such as repeated urinary tract infections or abnormal ureters, reflux may occur. Placement of the tube through the urethra into the bladder may be associated with some discomfort, particularly in boys.

Cystoscopy

Direct visualization of the bladder can be accomplished by cystoscopy. During this procedure, a metal tube is passed through the urethra into the bladder. With the cystoscope, the urologist can see whether inflammation, tumors, bleeding, stones, or abscesses are present. During cystoscopy, the urologist also can measure the pressure in the bladder.

PHYSICIAN'S RESPONSIBILITY

There are, of course, numerous other tests and procedures applicable to children with developmental disabilities. However, they cannot all be detailed in this book.

It is the responsibility of the physician ordering the tests and procedures to explain to the child and the child's family why the tests and procedures are necessary, what the benefits of the procedures are, the degree of risk and discomfort involved, and the possible course to be followed once the test results are obtained.

ACKNOWLEDGMENTS

Contributions have been made to this chapter by Edward A. Sassaman, M.D., and Siegfried M. Pueschel, M.D., Ph.D., M.P.H.

◀ Chapter 23 ▶

Adaptive Equipment

EQUIPMENT FOR CHILDREN WITH DEVELOPMENTAL DELAYS

Why Is Adaptive Equipment Needed?

Participation in daily routines of family and community activities may be difficult or nearly impossible for developmentally disabled children who have significant physical handicapping conditions. Yet, while a handicapped child's abilities may differ from those of his or her playmates or siblings, the child's curiosity and desire to participate may be quite similar. All children can benefit from a variety of experiences, and all children should have opportunities to be involved in enjoyable events.

Physically disabled children can delight in their achievements and independence, but achieving success often takes considerably more effort and persistence than most nondisabled people realize. Adaptive equipment can help handicapped youngsters improve control of their body movements, increase self-reliance, and make their daily routine easier. It also can improve the quality of the child's life by expanding opportunities for growth, satisfaction, and learning.

What Is Adaptive Equipment?

The term *adaptive equipment* refers to devices that help challenge people to overcome in some way the limitations caused by their handicaps. Adaptive equipment may be used for a variety of activities, or for just one specific task. Use of adaptive equipment always should be coordinated with other goals for a child's development. This is important because equipment used to improve skills in one area may disrupt the development of other essential skills. For example, if a headrest needed for head control at mealtimes is used throughout the day, it actually could prevent the child from developing good head control.

There are a number of types of adaptive equipment, including:

Positioning devices such as bolsters, wedges, and modified types of furniture
Mobility aids such as scooter boards, walkers, and wheelchairs
Transportation aids such as car seats and travel chairs

Items to facilitate daily care such as bath seats, lifts, and adaptive clothing
Communication devices such as scanners, pointers, nonoral communication systems, and artificial voices
Individualized seating systems
Modified tools, utensils, and work surfaces

In addition, many excellent adaptive devices have been made by modifying standard infant accessories—such as walkers, high chairs, swings, jumpers, and infant seats—with ordinary household materials.

This chapter familiarizes you with the problems of children who require adaptive equipment and the benefits they derive from using it. Various kinds of devices are discussed, including how, when, and why to use specific types. Guidelines are provided to help you select, measure, fit, and assess the effectiveness of the equipment. Important information on how to use various items properly also is provided.

ADAPTIVE EQUIPMENT FOR BODY CONTROL: POSTURE, MOVEMENT, AND BALANCE

Children with problems that involve the central nervous system (brain and spinal cord) and the musculoskeletal system (bones, muscles, and joints) often need special appliances to improve posture, stability, balance, and movement for many daily activities. Such devices help a child to be more independent. The following sections describe the various problems of developmentally disabled children and how equipment can be used to compensate for them.

Problems involving the Nervous System

The central nervous system controls all of our body's movement and posture by sending messages via the nerves to specific parts of the body. Specific areas of the brain are responsible for control of particular body parts. Certain areas of the brain also determine muscle tone. Muscle tone refers to the way muscles feel—for example, hard, stiff, and firm; or soft and floppy. Muscle tone also refers to how muscles react to the brain's signal to work. Muscles that react well move freely in coordination with one another and adjust readily to changes in movement or posture. Brain damage as well as abnormalities in brain structures can produce abnormal muscle tone and control, resulting in problems with coordination, posture, and balance. Children with cerebral palsy (motor disease due to damage to the brain), hydrocephalus (increased fluid in the brain), spinal muscular atrophy, brain malformations or masses, and degenerative neurological conditions often have these problems. Sometimes the nerves themselves or the spinal cord are damaged, preventing the brain's messages from reaching the muscles. This is the case in children with spina bifida or those who have had a traumatic injury to the spinal cord. These children generally have some degree of paralysis.

Problems involving the Muscles

Muscles contract and relax in various combinations and degrees, enabling us to maintain stability or move individual body parts. Certain diseases attack the muscle cells themselves, causing degeneration, which leads to muscle wasting and weakness. This is what happens in muscular dystrophy, an inherited muscle disease. Another cause of muscle weakness and wasting is abnormal formation or composition of the muscle fibers. Muscular problems contribute to poor posture, balance, and coordination, and can lead to abnormal or restricted patterns of movement.

Problems involving Bones and Joints

Abnormal bone and joint formations can cause limitations in movements of the joints. Muscles attached to the deformed bones may be held in abnormal alignment, which then limits their ability to produce normal joint motion, maintain body symmetry, and balance. This is the case in children with club feet, congenital scoliosis, congenital hip dislocation, arthrogryposis (persistent flexure or contracture of a joint), and many other conditions.

Temporary Muscle Problems

Injuries to bone and muscles often result in temporary limitations of movement. For example, casts or traction following a fracture or surgical procedure may be essential for healing, but at the same time will prevent exercise of the muscles or joints. The lack of activity can cause temporary stiffness in joints and a loss of some flexibility and strength in the muscles.

WHEN TO CONSIDER ADAPTIVE EQUIPMENT FOR YOUR CHILD

If your child has a disabling condition that causes problems in body control and effective, independent movement, you may find that many daily activities are too difficult for him or her to master alone. However, with your support and assistance, you will notice that your child is able to perform more capably. In this situation, you may be able to substitute adaptive equipment for your physical assistance, which allows the child to be more independent. Although you will need a professional's help in selecting, prescribing, and fitting the proper equipment, some general guidelines for determining when your child is ready for adaptive equipment are outlined here.

First, consider your child's age. An appliance should not be used to position children before they have reached the age when most children gain independence in that particular position. This is the time when youngsters are ready to use the new position to explore their environment and develop skills in other areas of functioning. For example, most children begin to prop themselves up and sit alone by 6 to 8 months of age. Thus, adaptive equipment to help a baby sit alone and play should not be considered before this age. If a child is unable to sit at the appropriate age, a special sitting device can be designed to help him or her develop fine motor skills and achieve more independence in social activities and other daily living skills.

A second point to consider is the sequence in which a child gains motor control. Infants first develop motor control lying on their backs (supine), then lying on their stomachs (prone). From there they progress to rolling, belly-crawling, sitting, propping up on hands and knees, creeping, standing, and eventually walking. Motor control generally develops gradually from head to toe and from large muscle groups of the trunk, shoulders, and hips to the smaller muscle groups of the hands and feet. Gaining control in basic areas enables a child to begin to practice more advanced skills. For example, children must be able to prop on their forearms before they can start to belly-crawl. Propping up on forearms allows the baby to practice shifting weight from arm to arm, an essential component of belly-crawling. If adaptive devices are needed, make sure the ones chosen encourage development of skills in a normal sequence. Each new skill becomes a building block for the next, and skipping over intermediate skills only makes it more difficult for a child to use the equipment designed for a more complex skill to his or her best advantage.

By providing appropriate equipment as soon as your child seems ready, you may help to prevent bad posture and movement habits. If, for instance, your child has difficulty sitting up properly during daily activities like meals or play, an appropriate chair can be devised to provide the necessary supports. By using the special chair, slumping over or slouching, which can lead to spinal deformity, can be prevented.

ADAPTIVE EQUIPMENT CAN IMPROVE
YOUR CHILD'S ATTITUDE AND INTEREST

A child's ability to enjoy activities and succeed at new tasks is also an important consideration in the use of adaptive equipment. Many parents find that the new independence fostered by adaptive equipment helps their children develop positive attitudes toward themselves. Building a positive attitude can have far-reaching effects on your youngster's enthusiasm and willingness to persist in challenging situations.

Think about adaptive equipment when your child's development seems to be at a standstill. This may be a clue that the next developmental step is too difficult to attain without additional assistance. Help in the form of a piece of special equipment or an appliance may be all your child needs to continue progressing in the normal sequence of development. Also, think about adaptive equipment when your child shows a strong interest in a particular skill, but is unable to master it, despite repeated tries over an extended period of time. In such situations, you may want to discuss your concerns with the professionals involved in your child's care. They can guide you toward appropriate devices to foster goals within your child's reach.

WHAT KIND OF EQUIPMENT DO YOU NEED?

As mentioned, before selecting equipment it is important to define the goal for which it is used. Deciding on a goal is often a natural extension of identifying a particular problem that disrupts performance and new skill acquisition.

As parents of a child with special needs, you are intimately aware of your child's strengths and weaknesses, successes and failures. You probably cannot help but compare your child's development to that of other children such as cousins, nieces, and playmates. By carefully noting what seems to be different about the way your child tries to sit, reach, creep, or accomplish other motor tasks, you may identify areas in which help is needed. For instance, if your child seems to fall over backwards in sitting, a firm, high-back chair may be necessary, while if he or she tends to fall forward, a tray or harness may prove more useful.

Not all adaptive equipment must be specially ordered from an appliance shop. Many useful devices can be created with household materials such as rolled towels, cardboard boxes, stuffed animals, and belts or straps temporarily added to the furniture and equipment you already use. Together, you and your child's therapist can fashion equipment with the features best suited for your child's needs.

If equipment must be ordered, it is wise to see whether you can rent or borrow the item. Appliance shops often rent or loan equipment for you to try prior to purchase. In addition, some organizations—for example, Muscular Dystrophy Association, Easter Seal Society, United Cerebral Palsy, Spina Bifida Association, to name a few—often have equipment that can be borrowed. If your child receives regular physical therapy, ask the therapist about borrowing a piece of equipment to try at home.

Further Considerations before Purchasing Equipment

Before you decide to buy a piece of equipment, you should consider several other factors. First, think about how the piece of equipment will fit into your family's life-style. If, for example, you are an active family, you will want to know if the equipment is portable, how much it weighs, how big it is, and how often it should be used. Often, several manufacturers make similar products with slightly different features. You might find one item designed to fold for convenience, while a comparable model is more rigid and requires more space. Or one device may be heavier than others. An on-the-go family will appreciate a light-weight model. Living conditions also can affect your choice of equipment. If you have to contend with stairs, small living space, and narrow doorways, or if you rely on public transportation, you will want to select a device that can be used easily and conveniently.

The length of time your child needs to use the equipment should also be considered. If you anticipate that an item will be necessary for only a brief period, you will not need to worry about making adjustments as your child grows. However, if long-term usage is anticipated, the adaptability or availability of accessories that can modify the equipment becomes much more important. A short period of usage is also more reason to endeavor to rent or borrow the equipment, rather than spending extra money to purchase it.

What is required to keep the equipment clean and in proper working condition also should be investigated. If you are considering an upholstered piece, find out if it is designed to resist staining, odor, and deterioration from exposure to urine or saliva. It also pays to check on the warranty. Ask the salesman about repairs or a service contract. Find out if replacement parts are readily available.

Consider your child's comfort and safety. Is the upholstery designed to "breathe" on hot days? Is the padding adequate on the back, seat, and armrest? Are cushions needed at bony prominences such as the spine and hip bone, to prevent skin breakdown? Comfort factors become more critical if the equipment is to be used for long periods of time. Check to see if harnesses and seat belts are secure and comfortably placed. Be sure the brakes of a wheelchair are easy to operate. Examine the equipment for any sharp edges, loose pieces, or other safety hazards.

Do not forget to consider how the equipment looks. Your child is likely to experience more acceptance from peers if the equipment looks like ordinary furniture and is attractively painted and nicely finished. Be sure to ask your child if he or she feels comfortable in the equipment and if he or she likes it.

Lastly, keep in mind that other parents can be an excellent source of information about adaptive equipment. From their experience, they can advise you on what equipment lasts the longest, and which devices are easiest to use, to keep clean, and to repair.

Being Realistic—What Else to Expect from Adaptive Equipment

It is important to be realistic about the effect that any piece of adaptive equipment can have on your child and family. Try to understand that expecting too much from adaptive equipment can lead to frustration. Realistic expectations will make the experience more positive for all involved and will increase your chances for success.

A piece of equipment is not likely to be the perfect solution to all your needs. If the equipment brings some improvement, but does not do everything you expected, consider it a good start. Even with the best possible equipment, adjustments and new accessories often are needed. Do not give up because you do not see immediate improvement. Be sure to allow enough time to give the device a fair trial. The more successful pieces of adaptive equipment generally are the result of small improvements made specifically for the individual owners. With modifications, many devices are "custom-fit" to the child. If you find the equipment simply does not meet your needs, try switching to a new device or perhaps consider a different approach to using the device.

When problems arise as your child grows and changes, it is important to make necessary modifications one at a time. If you make several adjustments at once, you will not be able to tell which one made the difference. Many ingenious solutions have been discovered by parents approaching the problems in an orderly way.

Periodically, as your child grows and gains skills, expect to reassess the need for equipment. Every so often you may want to check how well your child performs a particular skill when the amount of help provided by the equipment is reduced. If performance is unchanged with less support, your youngster may have outgrown the need for the amount of support given. You then can modify your child's equipment accordingly. If more help than needed is given when the equipment is used, it becomes less effective. That is, it actually will hinder the development of skills. On the other hand, your child could need more assistance and accessories as time goes by, as is the case with certain progressive and degenerative diseases.

HOW TO OBTAIN AND FINANCE ADAPTIVE EQUIPMENT

Before reading this section, be aware that procedures for obtaining and financing adaptive equipment differ from state to state. What is funded in one region may not be in another. Because of the complexities of funding, many of the people who prescribe or sell equipment can help complete or actually do much of the necessary paperwork for you. This can be extremely helpful to parents whose youngsters need equipment, but who do not require ongoing medical treatment or physical therapy and, thus, do not have easy access to professionals who can assist them in obtaining equipment.

First, find out whether a doctor's prescription is necessary to obtain the equipment and whether it is covered by your medical insurance. Most orthopaedic appliances (splints, braces, and others) require a special prescription, as do many large pieces of adaptive equipment or special accessories. Also, sometimes a prescription is needed only if you want an insurance policy or government-subsidized program to cover the cost. Many items are available without this.

If your child's needs are short-term, consider the advantages of making the equipment yourself, borrowing it from a friend, or renting it from an appliance store. Books are available with simple plans for homemade equipment. Your child's therapist may be able to provide you with plans or books, or put you in touch with parents willing to loan equipment. To find out which alternative is best, compare the cost of each with the expected period of use. If you decide to purchase an appliance, ask your child's therapist and physician for advice and assistance. The physical therapist is usually the most knowledgeable about where to obtain equipment in your area. In some instances, therapists may be willing to do the ordering for you, as they are familiar with the process and the paperwork involved. If you do not have regular contact with a therapist, try consulting one at your child's school or clinic.

Equipment always can be obtained through local surgical supply companies, but the brands and models they carry may vary markedly. To know what is available, it is best to check ahead of time. Some of these companies will send a representative to your home, if you wish, to discuss the product and ordering as well as to take care of any necessary details such as measuring or fitting. These companies usually deliver the equipment you purchase and make any adjustments your child needs. The representative also can teach you about proper use and maintenance of the equipment.

Some items can be ordered directly from the manufacturer. While you may pay some additional shipping and handling charges when ordering directly, the initial cost of the equipment may be a bit lower. Vendors or retailers may need to charge somewhat higher prices to cover their costs in shipping, as well as the cost of the extra services they provide. It may be worthwhile to compare prices from the manufacturer with those of several vendors, just as you would comparison shop for any major purchase. Remember that when you order directly from a manufacturer, you must know the size, model, and accessories you need. You also will have to make any adjustments on your own, or make arrangements for a therapist to see your child for a fitting.

Once the equipment is ordered, ask how long it will take to be delivered. Many vendors keep popular items in stock and can deliver them promptly. Frequently, individualized items require a wait, as they are purchased by special order only. Vendors often require prior consent from your insurance carrier or other payment source before they will process your order, and this can cause more delay in delivery.

Ordering accessories that you anticipate your child will need later at the time of the original purchase sometimes can lower the cost, and will ensure that you have everything you need to provide the proper help. Companies may offer options packages at a discount, similar to those for new cars. Also, insurance companies often cover the cost of accessories at the time of the original purchase, if detailed on the prescription, but may refuse to pay for items ordered separately. Call your insurance representative if you have any questions. The same procedures also hold for government assistance programs such as Supplemental Security Income (SSI), Title 19 Waiver, the Medicaid Program, and others. If you are unsure about the necessity or worth of some equipment options, it probably is better to order only what you need. That way, you will not be burdened with unnecessary trappings.

Whenever possible, use your medical insurance to cover the costs of your child's appliances. Insurance policies vary considerably. If your policy has Major Medical–type coverage, it may cover up to 80 percent of the cost of the equipment. You will be responsible for the standard deductible and the balance that is not covered by your policy. To avoid any unpleasant surprises, check with your insurance carrier for details. You may find that your insurance company stipulates a limit on the dollar amount of purchases for what they refer to as "durable medical equipment" in a given period of time.

Governmental assistance programs are another source of help for obtaining equipment. The Federal Supplemental Security Income Program sponsors a disabled children's program, which may cover the costs of such items. There are also special waivers, and the federal Medicaid Program—which states may choose to participate in—makes certain children eligible for many services. Some states have their own programs for developmentally disabled persons as well. All of these programs have their own eligibility limit requirements. Sometimes there is a limit to the amount of assistance you can receive over a specified time. Ask the social worker at your child's clinic or school, or the local Medicaid office, for specific details on eligibility and the application process.

Support groups like the Spina Bifida Association, Association for Retarded Citizens-U.S., Muscular Dystrophy Association, United Cerebral Palsy, or Easter Seal Society are other sources to investigate. While many do not fund individual equipment requests, they may provide equipment on loan, as already mentioned.

Insurance companies sometimes cover the cost of equipment ordinarily not covered by the policy, if it is purchased and provided as part of a hospitalization. If your doctors suggest equipment while your child is in the hospital, try to have it delivered, fitted, and checked during the hospital stay. In this type of arrangement, the hospital purchases the equipment and then bills you for it as part of the total cost of the hospitalization.

METHODS TO HELP COMPENSATE FOR VARIOUS DISABILITIES

You probably can think of many daily activities that are easier to do in one position than another. For example, lifting a heavy object is easier if your feet are spread apart than if they are close together. Writing is easier when your arm is supported on a table rather than held in the air. The relationship of body parts to one another and their position in space clearly affects our skill and success at a specific task.

When we start to perform a familiar task, most of us assume a comfortable position without much thought or effort. However, as new skills are learned, many positions may be tried before the ones that make the jobs easier are found. Once effective positions are established, we use them quite naturally. Unlike a person without a disability, a handicapped child may not be able to control his or her body well enough to get into a good position for many activities. As a result, the child's ability to perform many tasks may be diminished. Placing a handicapped child in a proper position and providing appropriate equipment may improve his or her ability to succeed at specific tasks. If, for example, your child cannot hold his or her head and body in balance, equipment can provide the support and proper body alignment to allow the child to do things that would otherwise be impossible. Equipment also can be used to reposition a child in such a way that weak muscles are assisted or stronger ones are allowed to do more of the work.

Some children develop deformities because they cannot change positions easily. Special appliances can help youngsters vary their position periodically and prevent or delay such problems. Use of these devices also may diminish the need for additional procedures such as splinting, casting, traction, or even surgery.

There are other benefits as well. Positioning equipment can allow disabled children to bear weight on their limbs at appropriate ages. Weight-bearing is important for bone structure and formation. As children grow, bones change shape and strengthen in response to the weight they support and the pull of the muscles attached to them.

The best positioning devices provide just enough assistance for a youngster to improve performance, while also encouraging practice in a problem area. For example, a head support should maintain head control loosely, allowing the child to move and adjust his or her head position within a narrow range. The loose fit gives a child the opportunity to improve head control while providing assistance at the same time. A tight-fitting head control device would not allow a child to strengthen the muscles supporting the head. All types of adaptive equipment for positioning and support should be used as directed by your child's pediatrician, orthopaedist, therapist, or other specialist.

GOOD POSITIONING DOES NOT ALWAYS REQUIRE COMMERCIALLY MADE ADAPTIVE EQUIPMENT

While the main focus of this chapter is on adaptive equipment, you should be aware that some of the benefits of positioning discussed here do not require specialized devices. There are numerous ways parents and family members can promote proper alignment and positioning when carrying a child, placing him or her in a chair or on the floor to play, or helping him or her to stand and take steps. Your child's therapist can show you the best ways to work with your child. If your child does not need adaptive equipment but does need ongoing help in achieving proper positions, then you might want to establish a working relationship or partnership with the therapist. That way, you can review your child's positioning needs and keep informed on the best ways to provide assistance.

Some relatively simple positional aids have a wide range of practical applications. Sandbags can be used to support any body part in a correct position. Wedges can help to elevate the head and shoulders. When the child lies on his or her stomach, a wedge or bolster can be used to prop the child on forearms for play. Rolled towels, fuzzy paint rollers, or plastic soda bottles rolled in a towel can be transformed simply into bolsters. An inflatable swim ring can be placed around a child's chest for the same purpose. Therapy rolls of varying sizes also can be purchased commercially.

An adjustable prone board on which a child lies can be used in place of a wedge for propping on hands or forearms, as shown in Figure

Figure 1. Adjustable prone board allows child to be positioned on his or her abdomen.

1. Prone boards can be purchased or improvised from cardboard boxes or boards. Commercially available ones have wings at armpit height to prevent the arms from retracting or drawing back out of a good weight-bearing position.

A side-lyer can provide symmetrical support. The side-lying position promotes the child's use of two hands together in front of his or her body. Side-lyers are available commercially, but a sturdy box with a belt for safety also can be used. A small pillow should be placed under the head and between the legs to ensure symmetry. Be sure to alternate sides, unless your child has a persistent right or left asymmetry.

A hammock can help a child who usually keeps his body stiff and extended get into a curled, relaxed position while lying on his back. A hammock can be made easily from a crib blanket gathered and tied at the ends and hung low across a crib or playpen.

Sitting

For sitting, an infant seat can be padded to provide appropriate support for a small child. Sandbags, towel rolls, or paint rollers placed at the sides can be used to make a snug fit. Placed under the knees, they prevent the child from sliding forward and out of the seat.

Bean-bag chairs are sometimes helpful if your child does not require lots of extra support. For sitting on the floor, swim rings or rubber tubes can be inflated and placed around the child's trunk for support.

You can use one or several of these devices, depending upon how much trunk support is needed.

Corner seats are commercially available, or can be made from a sturdy cardboard box. A corner seat may have high sides to support your child's head and trunk, or low sides to control just the lower trunk. The sides of a corner seat should be kept at shoulder height, if the child has difficulty keeping the arms forward to reach and manipulate toys. Corner seats may be placed on the floor or elevated. Elevated corner seats will allow the child to sit with feet positioned flat on the floor, in order to provide balance. Additional supports may be needed to help keep legs and feet in proper alignment. A harness or belt will prevent your child from falling forward, and a padded dowel between the thighs will prevent him from sliding forward, as shown in Figure 2.

For children who have some head and trunk control, booster seats can be used as children begin to use their legs more actively in support. Initially, a booster seat should be used with a small table, or it can be placed in a cardboard box to keep the child's feet from sliding forward. If the sides of the box are high enough, the child can hold on with his or her hands at a comfortable level.

A wide variety of toddler chairs can be adapted to the needs of your child. Many commercially available seats with a variety of attachments

Figure 2. Corner seat provides trunk support for the child.

can improve a child's ability to sit. These chairs generally offer adjustable backs, side support for the body, adjustable and removable head rests, and other attachments that can properly position both hips and legs. Firm footrests, which can be adjusted for height and angle, as well as straps for keeping the feet in the proper position, are standard accessories. Trays are usually available for most models.

With the advice and guidance of your child's therapist, you also can adapt a sturdy wooden chair to fit your child's needs. A chair with armrests is best. For extra support, a board can be added in the back, extending the chair's height. Standing the entire chair inside a three-sided cardboard box can help keep a child's arms forward. Improvise a harness or seat belt if you need it, and use a tray or table for support in front. Bathtub appliqués, used to prevent slipping in the bath tub, also can be applied to a chair to prevent sliding forward in the seat. Be sure to provide a firm footrest attached to the chair; or a box of appropriate height can be used for the same purpose. Makeshift straps will help steady the feet in good position.

Stools and bed trays can be used as play trays for corner seats. Although commercial models are often available, you can easily make a tray from a sturdy cardboard box by cutting the sides to the child's chest height and carving a semi-circular notch in the top to fit the child's chest. If your child has little trunk control, such a tray should be at chest height. If your child has partial control, you can place the tray at waist height.

Crawling and Standing

Equipment is also available to help children bear weight on all four limbs, when they are unable to balance on their hands and knees alone. Such devices look like small hammocks. They have a sling for the child's trunk, which is attached to a frame by straps or strings. This helps the child prop on both arms and legs without fear of falling. Some frames are mounted on casters, so that children can experiment with creeping on their hands and knees.

Prone standers are used for children who are unable to bear weight on their legs unless fully supported. They are designed to permit standing at an angle, not in a fully upright position, as seen in Figure 3. By standing the child at an angle, the body weight is distributed throughout lower limbs, trunk, and arms, instead of resting only on the feet. Such controlled weight-bearing in prone standers can help promote bone growth and normal development of the hip sockets in young children. Prone standers come with a variety of accessories and adaptations, which allow them to be used in many different ways. Some are designed to lean forward at a table, counter, or other surface. Others are free-standing or fixed to a stable base. There are many varieties of prone standers and a number of accessories. You may want to shop around to find the one that best meets your child's needs.

Standing tables and standing boxes are used for children who can bear their total body weight on their feet but are unable to stand independently. The child is supported loosely by a box with a tray attached

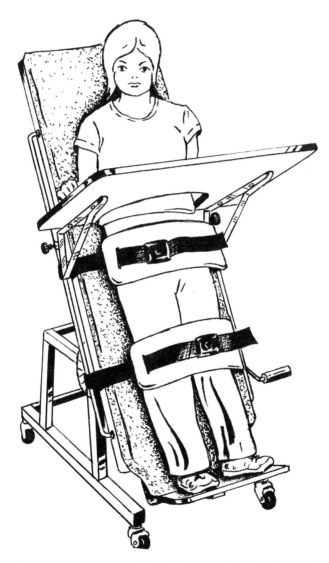

Figure 3.   Adjustable prone stander allows child to be in an upright position and to engage in fine motor activities.

as a play surface. The entire unit is attached to a stable base to prevent tipping over. Standing tables provide an opportunity for the child to practice standing balance without fear of falling.

MEASURING YOUR CHILD FOR ADAPTIVE EQUIPMENT

Most large pieces of equipment are available in a variety of sizes and models, designed to fit your child's size and his or her specific needs. If you plan to use equipment for a long time, you should consider your child's height, weight, and rate of growth. In addition, you should measure your living space, including doorways, halls, and counter heights, to determine the best size and model for your child.

Accurate measurements and careful planning also are essential when you make equipment at home. In addition, your child's therapist may be able to provide plans and helpful hints for construction.

ORTHOPAEDIC APPLIANCES

Orthopaedic appliances make up a special category of adaptive equipment, including prescription items such as traction, casts, splints, braces, shoe corrections, and specialized seating and standing devices. Such appliances are used to improve body position, posture, and symmetry. They also can help maintain good range of motion in the joints as well as reduce, halt, or reverse various deformities. In addition, orthopaedic appliances can help correct and maintain joint mobility, with the ultimate goal of avoiding more invasive surgical procedures.

Orthopaedic appliances frequently are used in conjunction with regular home exercises or direct physical therapy treatments. Children who wear orthopaedic devices for prolonged periods need ample time out of the appliances to experience other positions and experiment with independent movements. No one position is appropriate or beneficial all of the time. Tightness can develop if muscles are maintained in the same position for too long, which in turn can lead to other limitations of movement. However, in some cases the benefits of treatment involving extended use of appliances are considered greater than the risk of new limitations. This is generally true in severe or rapidly progressing problems. In such cases, a therapist or orthopaedic surgeon is faced with a difficult decision of choosing the lesser of the two evils.

Types of Orthopaedic Equipment and Appliances

Traction   Traction is one method used to correct abnormal positioning of the joints. Joints are molded by two separate forces: the position of the bones and the appropriate tension or muscle pull around the joint. Abnormal positioning or muscle function can have a lasting effect with respect to how a joint is shaped and how it moves. Traction also is used after an injury or surgery to maintain correct positioning of bone segments for healing.

Traction usually is introduced in the hospital, where it can be monitored closely. If long-term treatment is necessary, traction easily can be transferred to the home. Equipment can be rented from a medical supply company and monitored by a local public health nurse. Traction equipment generally will include a bed frame, pullies, and weights, as well as cuffs or belts to attach weights at specific angles.

Casts   Casts are used to position and stabilize joints or bones after an injury or operation. Usually, they are made of plaster strips that are soaked and wrapped around a body part. Casts most often are applied for 4 to 6 weeks following muscle surgery and for 6 to 8 weeks following bone surgery or fracture.

Splints   Splints generally are used for a limited period of time to maintain a stable or functional position of the joints. Typically, they are molded to fit snugly. Some splints are available in standard sizes with soft or padded parts that conform to an individual's body shape.

Night splints are used primarily for preventing contractures (limited joint movements), maintaining a good range of motion, and stretching of tight muscles. For example, children with very tight inner thigh muscles might be treated with a splint that stretches the muscles and maintains a desirable range of hip mobility. Without treatment, such children would have difficulty separating their legs adequately for normal posture, movements, and hygiene. Such treatment may have the added benefit of preventing hip dislocations.

Some splints improve the function of specific body parts by providing stability and a good position or by counteracting increased muscle tone. A youngster with spastic cerebral palsy, for example, may use what is called a hip abduction splint in a sitting position to improve independent balance and control. Because the splint keeps the legs separated, it gives the child a broadened base of support for balance and simultaneous control of increased muscle tone.

Splints usually are prescribed by an orthopaedist or physiatrist and are fitted and fashioned by either an occupational therapist, physical therapist, or orthotist. If your child needs a splint, you will be given instructions regarding its use and the indicators of possible problems.

Braces   Braces and splints perform similar functions. Like splints, braces help to maintain passive range of motion and provide proper joint alignment. But braces also are used to increase control of body parts while making specific movements easier. In other words, braces align and support particular joints, so other joints can be used in a more

200 / Procedures, Appliances, and Medical and Surgical Treatments

appropriate way. For example, a body jacket is a brace that provides the trunk with rigid support, and it can be used to counteract an abnormal spinal curvature. When in use, it gives a youngster enough additional control in sitting to permit more success in daily routines and play. Similarly, ankle braces provide enough stability for a child to stand and walk in a more normal fashion.

Static splints (Figure 4) and braces maintain one position in a part of the body without stopping or actively helping movement in another. *Dynamic* splints and braces position certain joints in the best possible way and also actively assist other body parts in performing useful movements. Dynamic devices usually consist of a stable portion, similar to static splints, with attachments to free-moving body parts that produce or make a specific motion easier. These attachments usually incorporate string or elastic bands, which act as substitute muscles. For example, a dynamic splint to improve voluntary grasp release might consist of a static portion to hold the wrist in one position, plus finger slings attached to elastic bands, as seen in Figure 5.

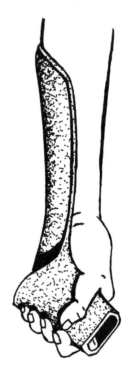

Figure 4.   Static hand splint keeps hand and wrist in one position.

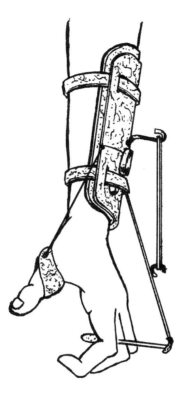

Figure 5. Dynamic hand splint allows finger movement.

Braces, or orthoses as they are sometimes called, usually are named for the joints that they align and support. An *a*nkle-*f*oot *o*rthosis, referred to as an AFO, controls the position of the ankle. A KAFO is a *k*nee-*a*nkle-*f*oot *o*rthosis, and controls both the knee and ankle position relative to one another. A TLSO is a *t*horaco-*l*umbo-*s*acral *o*rthosis, which provides control of the entire spine from chest to pelvis, and an LSO, or *l*umbo-*s*acral *o*rthosis, controls the lower spine. Small, in-the-shoe braces that support the ankle and foot bones during weight-bearing are called UCBs. UCB does not stand for particular body parts, but for the university where the braces were first developed, the *U*niversity of *C*alifornia at *B*erkley. An RGO, or *r*eciprocal *g*ait *o*rthosis, allows a paraplegic child (one whose legs are paralyzed) to move his or her legs one at a time, providing that certain muscles are working.

Ankle-Foot Orthoses (AFO) Ankle-foot orthoses commonly are used to control conditions such as flat arches, tight heelcords, and abnormal rolling and turning of the ankle and heel in a standing position.

The position of the ankle is controlled by the shell of the brace. Ankle-foot orthoses also can control the amount of knee extension by holding the ankle and foot in an approximate 90-degree angle. (See Figures 6 and 7.)

Knee-Ankle-Foot Orthoses (KAFO) A knee-ankle-foot orthosis controls the alignment of the knee and ankle for proper weight-bearing. It also can prevent the knee from going back too far. In addition, knee-ankle-foot orthoses prevent or limit lateral deformities of the knee, such as knock knees (genu valgum) and bowlegs (genu varum). Some knee braces are molded plastic shells, whereas other types are structured from plastic or leather cuffs attached to rigid metal uprights. Metal braces are somewhat heavier than plastic ones, but they provide more stability. When metal uprights are used, they frequently include a locking mechanism at the knee, which allows a locked fully extended knee position for standing and an unlocked bent position for sitting, as noted in Figure 8.

Figure 6.   Example of older type of ankle-foot orthosis, less frequently used today.

Figure 7. Commonly used ankle-foot orthosis controls the position of the ankle. It is made out of plastic material that should fit well in an everyday shoe.

Hips-Knee-Ankle-Foot Orthoses (HKAFO) and Pelvic Bands Some children will require bracing from their hips to their ankles. These braces are usually constructed with cuffs and uprights. They also provide locks that allow full extension or flexing at the hip and knee to accommodate standing and sitting. Waist or pelvic bands are commonly used with bilateral long-legged braces, for both symmetry and control (Figure 9).

Cables Some braces have cables that control the amount of rotation of the leg or foot either inward or outward. Most often, they are used to counteract intoeing. Cables usually are attached to ankle-foot orthoses and to a waist belt. Twisting the cables in the direction opposite to the way the child's foot turns will help to bring the foot into a more neutral alignment.

Parapodiums and Standing Frames Children who require full support of the lower trunk and the legs may be treated with standing frames

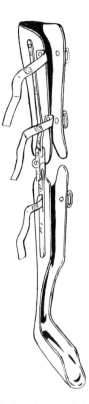

Figure 8. Knee-ankle-foot orthosis with locking device at the knee controls alignment of knee and ankle for proper weight-bearing.

or parapodiums. Standing frames are long-legged braces attached in a rigid position to a broad and stable base. This eliminates the need to balance independently while standing and, therefore, frees the child's hands for all types of activities. Parapodiums are similar to long-legged braces attached to a stable base, but parapodiums have adjustable hip and knee joints for standing and sitting. A parapodium can be worn for a longer period of time, since the child's position can be varied without removing the equipment.

Special Shoes Children with very mild deformities of the foot and ankle often can be treated with simple shoe corrections or with sturdy, specially fashioned footwear. Some children with flat arches or a tendency to walk on the inside of the feet need arch supports or scaphoid pads, commonly called cookies. They are placed inside the shoes and directly lift the arches and improve the position of the ankles. Other shoe corrections include both inner and outer heel and sole wedges.

Outer wedges tip the foot and ankle inward. Inner wedges tip the foot and ankle outward.

If a child has one leg longer than the other, a lift usually is placed under the shorter leg to even the leg lengths. By using a lift, a symmetric position of the hips, trunk, and shoulders can be maintained and the development of major deformities such as scoliosis or sideward curvature of the spine can be prevented.

Thoraco-Lumbar-Sacral Orthoses (TLSO) and Lumbar-Sacral Orthoses (LSO) Thoraco *l*umbar-*s*acral orthoses and *l*umbar-*s*acral orthoses counteract spinal deformities such as scoliosis, excessive kyphosis (a rounded back), and increased lordosis (called swayback). These braces usually are made from a molded plastic shell, which supports the child's spine in a straightened position, as seen in Figure 10. Milwaukee Braces, which also are used to treat scoliosis, actually are thoraco-lumbar-sacral orthoses with rigid metal upright rods that support a neck ring and chin pad to apply slight traction to the spine. A

Figure 9. Hip-knee-ankle-foot orthosis provides bracing from hips to ankles.

Figure 10. Molded plastic shell-type body jacket, which supports child's spine in a straightened position.

physician also may prescribe a fabric corset to control and support the trunk. In addition, collars may be used to enhance head control, visual monitoring, and eye-hand skills through increased support of the neck.

Total Support Systems Children with virtually no muscle control may require specialized total support systems or full body orthoses. These braces enable a child without muscle control to sit and participate in certain daily routines or educational activities. Total support systems must be molded carefully in a precise position and lined with foam to ensure a comfortable fit and to minimize the risk of pressure sores.

Proper Fitting and Prescription of Braces

Although braces are individualized for a proper fit, with frequent use, the equipment may loosen or stretch and require adjustments. Revision also will be needed as your child grows. A brace must fit in order to work properly. Braces usually are measured, fitted, and fashioned by a professional orthotist who works from a prescription written by an orthopaedist or physiatrist. Several fittings may be necessary before the final product is ready for use.

When your child needs a brace, make sure you are taught how to apply it correctly, when and how to use it, and how to check for comfort.

Braces are designed to stabilize and align joints. Whereas this is essential for treatment, it also limits the natural movement of the joint, which is necessary for the development and use of normal balance reactions. Limiting the functional ranges of some joints may cause a child to compensate by developing an abnormal posture or movement pattern in other joints. The likelihood of such secondary problems developing can be lessened by careful fitting, frequent observation, and readjustment if needed. You may expect some problems, yet they should not outweigh the gains achieved by the bracing. Review the pluses and minuses as you see them with your child's orthopaedist, therapist, and orthotist when deciding whether to change the treatment.

PROSTHESES OR ARTIFICIAL BODY PARTS

Children born with certain defects of the body or limbs may need prosthetic devices, or artificial body parts. Malformations of the limbs can include missing parts, shortened segments, or abnormally aligned and formed segments. Some children require a prosthesis because of a trauma or tumor necessitating amputation.

Prostheses for the lower limbs are designed to allow the handicapped child to stand and walk. They may replace a portion of the foot, the whole foot, foot and ankle, lower leg or entire leg, and thigh or hip. Prostheses for the upper limbs are designed to allow the child to perform routine functional activities such as feeding, dressing, writing, playing, reaching, grasping, and manipulating objects. An entire arm or any part of the arm can be fitted with a prosthesis.

All prostheses are helpful in restoring an even distribution of body weight, which improves symmetry in function and helps with balance. They also can improve appearance, which in turn may help a child develop a positive self-image and promote acceptance by peers in social situations. The cosmetic value of a prosthesis should not be underestimated.

Prostheses are highly individualized and are specially made and fitted by a trained prosthetist, according to a doctor's prescription. Artificial limbs usually are constructed to resemble the body parts they replace and to match the corresponding limbs (Figure 11). They may have movable parts and joints, which can be operated by gravitational

Figure 11. Example of a simple lower limb prosthesis.

pull, pulleys and cables, hydraulic systems, or electrical stimulation in which batteries stimulate the child's nerves. The working ends of an upper limb prosthesis may look like a real hand or may be more like a simple tool such as a claw or clamp.

Prostheses are held in place by the fit of the socket or by a special harness or both. Total contact sockets fit the child's stumps snugly. Some have a suction type of fit, which further increases stability. The prosthesis needs to be stable if it is to be reliable for daily use.

Once a good fit is achieved and the child has learned to use the prosthesis, more complex devices can be added. Simple tools that have a single motion such as open and close may give way to more complex devices offering a wider range of motion and positions that will improve control and function.

MOBILITY AIDS

Children who cannot pivot, crawl, creep, or walk, often benefit from equipment that helps them to move about independently and explore their environment. Most frequently, children who need mobility aids have disabilities that affect their central nervous system and musculoskeletal systems. A child with poor muscle tone will have difficulties maintaining a stable position, an essential ingredient in achieving purposeful movement. On the other hand, increased muscle tone often restricts joint motion and prevents a child from moving about freely. A youngster with flaccid or weak muscles may not be able to overcome gravity to move about. Other children may have bony deformities that prevent the usual movement patterns. Children with unsteadiness or poor balance, also called ataxia, may need the help of appropriate devices in order to move about. Another group of children will require mobility aids on a temporary basis—for example, when wearing casts following an injury or surgery.

In general, mobility aids offer support to improve posture as they make moving around easier. Movement can be made easier when support is increased by allowing children to move their extremities with more freedom. Many mobility aids also improve balance and stability by providing a wider base of support for movement, enabling the child to overcome gravity more efficiently.

Types of Mobility Aids

Mobility aids include hammock swings, ramps, wedges, lazy Susans, crawlers, creepers, trolleys, handcarts, wheelchairs, adapted ride-on toys, and other ambulation aids. Most mobility aids are prescription items that are recommended by your child's physician or therapist. They often need to be adjusted to the child's size and disability.

Hammock swings (Figure 12) and *rocker seats* can be used to treat children who have difficulty tolerating movement in space. They are designed to provide slow, controlled motion. Through experience, the child begins to predict the changes in position and learns to tolerate movement in space. These devices can be activated by an adult or can be brought into motion by movements children make on their own.

Ramps and *wedges* can be used to encourage rolling or belly-crawling. Placing a child on the elevated side of the ramp or wedge will permit gravity to assist him or her to slide downward.

A *lazy Susan* allows the child to pivot on his or her stomach with ease. The child is placed on the lazy Susan so the body is supported fully and the hands are free to push against the floor. With the lazy Susan, the

Figure 12.   Variation of a hammock swing allows controlled movements in space.

effects of friction are minimized. Thus, even slight pushes by the child will cause it to turn in a circle.

Scooter boards (Figure 13) can help a child learn to belly-crawl or creep on all fours. These devices eliminate the need for very coordinated movement of the legs, since the body is fully supported by the board.

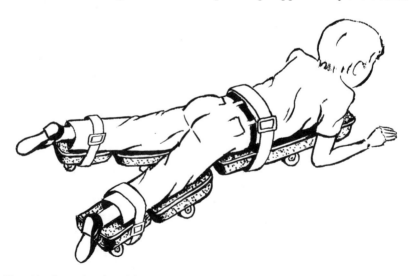

Figure 13.   Scooter board can help a child who is unable to crawl or to creep explore the environment.

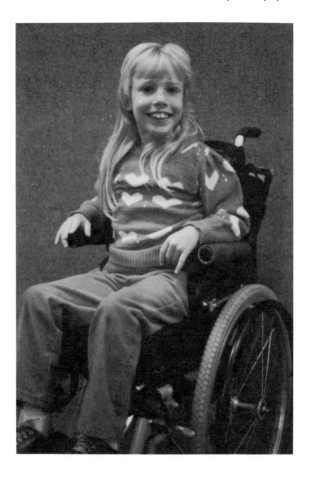

Wheelchairs often are introduced at an early age for children who most likely will not become community ambulators, that is, able to walk most of the time in most places. Some children will use wheelchairs exclusively, whereas others may need them only in specific locations or when long distances must be covered.

Wheelchairs are prescribed by a physician, often with a therapist's assistance. They vary considerably in size, strength, durability, and weight. Some are more adaptable than others and have more accessories. Some permit a greater number of modifications or are easier to fold. Your child's size, strength, and other musculoskeletal factors will need to be taken into consideration when a wheelchair is selected.

Electric wheelchairs are powered by battery packs and can be outfitted with a variety of control systems. For example, wheelchairs have been designed to be operated by hand, foot, mouth, chin, or breath control. They may be adapted to any movement a child can control consistently.

Ride-on toys also can be used to help a child move about in a seated position. Most ride-on toys will need to be adapted to provide more support for the trunk, with a firm, flat seat or high backrest.

AMBULATION AIDS

Ambulation aids are used to help children walk, and include parallel bars, walkers, crutches, canes, and other movable supports. Each device provides a different amount of support. As with other types of equipment, a child should use the aid that provides just the right amount of support. Too much support may interfere with his or her progress.

Parallel bars are used by children who need stable support for their arms in order to move their legs forward. Parallel bars provide a great deal of support. Frequently, they are used as a child begins to learn to walk. As the child gains control of his or her movements, the use of parallel bars is phased out and other aids are introduced.

Walkers are used once a child can balance independently in a standing position for brief periods of time. In using a walker, a child stands alone momentarily as he or she moves the walker forward, either by pushing or lifting and placing it. Walkers come with or without wheels. Walkers with wheels actually may be more difficult to control, as the child has to prevent them from rolling too fast or too far out in front.

Crutches can be used by children who have good control of their trunk and upper extremities and some independent standing for balance. Using crutches, a child can achieve a more typical and efficient walking pattern than with either a walker or parallel bars. This is because the child moves each limb independently in an alternating, reciprocal pattern. Different types of crutches are available to suit individual needs. Some provide axillary support as well as handgrips. This type of crutch needs to be well padded at the top to prevent pressure on the nerves that run through the armpit to muscles of the arm. Other types of crutches provide forearm support and are used by children who have good balance and shoulder control (Figure 14). Platform crutches are used by children who can bear weight on their forearms but not on their hands (Figure 15).

Canes are primarily for balance rather than support. They are available with a single tip or four prongs at the end (the latter called a quad cane), to increase stability. Some children use two canes instead of crutches.

Most children who require continued use of ambulation aids wear some type of brace or corrective footwear. Also, following orthopaedic

Figure 14.   Crutch with forearm support.

surgery, or while a fracture heals, a child temporarily may need to use crutches, canes, or a walker.

Ambulation aids must be adjusted carefully to the child's height and body position, to ensure correct posture and optimal support. Any skeletal problems must be taken into consideration when fitting the equipment. Length should be checked regularly, particularly during periods of rapid growth.

ADAPTIVE EQUIPMENT FOR FINE MOTOR CONTROL

Children who need adaptive equipment for general posture control usually benefit from fine motor adaptations. Fine motor adaptive equipment generally is designed to improve a child's independence in performing specific tasks—for example, feeding, dressing or other activities of daily living. Typically, fine motor equipment provides stability

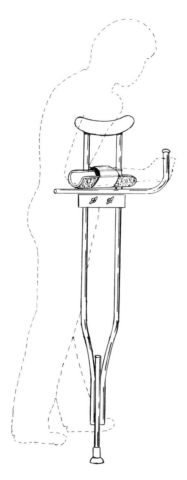

Figure 15. Platform crutch for children who cannot bear weight on their hands.

and positioning for the head, upper trunk, or upper extremities. Usually the arms are supported with the hands in front of the body, so the child can see his or her hands as they are being used. This is important for the development of eye-hand coordination and in all activities involving reaching, grasping, and releasing objects, as well as in motor planning.

Most fine motor appliances aid in learning and enjoyment by increasing opportunities to improve skills using toys, books, tools, and household items. Such equipment also may enable children to become more responsible for their own daily care and grooming.

Equipment to Position Arms and Head

Accessories are available for many seats and standers that can position the head and arms effectively for improved fine motor control. Chair accessories such as head supports, harnesses, lateral trunk supports, and trays help to keep your child's head, upper body, and arms well-supported in a symmetrical posture. Trays keep the arms steady so attention can be focused on using the hands. Elbow blocks can be mounted on armrests or trays to keep the arms forward to bear weight in a proper position and to keep the hands together near midline. Dowels can be mounted on trays to enhance and control the arms and shoulders. When the child grasps a stable object such as a dowel with one hand, the child's shoulders are steadied, and as a result the opposite arm can perform with greater control. Dowels and elbow blocks keep the elbow positioned in front of the shoulder for proper weight-bearing, and dowels keep the forearm in a midposition, which is essential for many manipulative tasks.

Splints and braces are sometimes worn on the arms and hands to improve their position for a variety of activities. They are used to position and stabilize the shoulders, elbows, or forearms in such a way that wrists, hands, fingers, and thumbs can be used with greater control. Some splints and braces keep the elbows straight to facilitate weight-bearing on the hand. Other splints and braces attempt to align the forearm and wrist in a neutral position, which enables the hand to hold a pencil or other utensil. This type of equipment needs to be small and comfortable to allow some movement of the arm.

Straps and weights can be used to hold the forearms steady against a surface for children who cannot control movements and keep their hands on desired objects. With random motions reduced or eliminated, a child is more apt to be successful in reaching, holding, and manipulating items that are placed nearby. Straps and weights can be used by themselves or in conjunction with other positioning devices.

Since all of these devices restrict motion in some areas by fixing the extremity in a particular position, they should be used sparingly—only when needed for a specific activity. Prolonged use of any positioning device may be uncomfortable, cause frustration, and limit the development of other equally important skills.

Modifying Objects for Grasping

At times, you can improve your child's ability to hold and manipulate toys, utensils, tools, clothing, and other things by altering the objects. Simple modifications often can make a big difference. For example, adding handles to toys and household items like pull toys, toothbrushes, combs, and books can enable a child with poor grasp to hold and use the item more efficiently. Another way to adapt materials is to increase the length or width of an object. This makes it easier to hold on to it. Thickening the handle of a spoon or toothbrush by wrapping it with tape or adding rubber can make it large enough to be grasped easily.

Gluing a clothespin to a lightswitch can help a child to operate the switch on his or her own. Large tabs can be attached to pages in a book to make it easier to turn pages.

Adding texture to an object or surface can make grasping easier and improve the stability of objects during manipulation. Try putting tub appliqués on smooth surfaces for stability. Sandpaper or double-backed tape can be added to blocks, utensils, and other objects for texture. Use your imagination to create ways to make objects safer and easier to handle. For writing, select implements that need minimal pressure and accuracy in orienting the tip, such as Magic Markers® and jumbo crayons. Even removing the paper from crayons can make writing easier, as less precision will be needed in orienting the crayons to the paper.

ADAPTING SWITCHES FOR SEVERELY DISABLED PEOPLE

Electrical and battery-operated household items and toys such as lights and radios can be adapted for severely physically disabled persons by wiring a simple switch into the electrical circuit. Some switches are sensitive to the slightest pressure on a large surface. Others are sensitive to either the light or shadow cast upon a surface. Still others such as mercury switches are sensitive to the slightest movement of almost any body part. Certain switches can be operated by sucking or blowing and need very little control of the muscles of the head, neck, and the four extremities. Some children with adequate head control, but poor control of their body and extremities, can be fitted with head sticks and pointers to turn pages, operate simple controls, or point to symbols on a communication board.

EQUIPMENT TO IMPROVE THE LINE OF SIGHT

Many children have difficulty positioning their head and eyes in such a way that they can see their hands as they manipulate objects. Methods to help a child visually attend to a fine motor activity can be devised easily. Strategically placed mirrors, for example, will enable children who have difficulty positioning their head to see their hands at work. Children who have limited range of motion of the arms and head benefit the most from mirrors.

Easels, lap boards, and felt boards can be adjusted to the proper height and angle for easy viewing or manipulation of materials. Book rests also can be adjusted to position pictures and books at the right level. Some materials can be suspended to achieve a good position, using household items like dowels, hooks, coat hangers, and strings.

The height of chairs and tables or other work surfaces can be adjusted to keep hands and objects in the line of sight. Extenders for table legs often are available, as are adjustable seats and trays for many seating systems.

CLOTHING MODIFICATIONS

Clothing fasteners can be modified for ease of operation by making simple changes such as adding loops or large handles to zippers or replacing zippers and buttons with Velcro® closures. Using large buttons and snaps in place of the small ones usually found on children's clothing is also helpful. Selecting clothing with large or loosely elasticized openings rather than snaps or buttons can make dressing easier. For older children, the tips of laces on shoes or clothing can be enlarged to facilitate handling, and, if possible, large eyelets can be substituted for small ones. Many companies now offer stylish clothing specially adapted for disabled persons.

MEALTIMES

Specialized seats to support a child's head and body in the right position are useful at mealtimes. These items usually are covered with a stain-resistant, water-repellent material for easy cleaning. Feeding seats are designed to keep the child's head in midline with the chin, tucked slightly to encourage proper movements of lips, tongue, and jaw. Most standard high chairs provide inadequate support for the child with poor postural control.

Changing the angle and orientation of the utensils can improve efficiency. Spoons and forks are available with bent handles for children who have trouble turning and rotating their wrist to put them into their mouth. Silverware with a swivel handle is available for children who have difficulty keeping the utensil level while bringing food to their mouth (Figure 16). Many different types of bottles and nipples are available to make bottle-feeding easier for babies who have a weak suck or grasp. When purchasing your mealtime equipment, keep in mind that the weight of the utensil can facilitate or inhibit its use.

Figure 16. Example of an adapted spoon. The bent, easy-to-grasp handle makes self-feeding easier for children with fine motor problems.

BATHING

Bath seats secure a child safely while in the tub and free your hands for bathing. They are particularly helpful if your child requires total body support due to weakness or low muscle tone, or because the child moves about too much or too forcefully. Bath seats generally resemble chaise lounges and often are made from lightweight plastic piping. The seats themselves are of a washable mesh or similar material for easy drainage and drying. The legs usually are equipped with suction cups to secure the seat in the tub. Foam cushions are also available for bathing young infants in the sink. After the bath, they can be squeezed out to dry. In addition, the cushions can be used for support on the changing table.

TRANSFER AND TRANSPORTATION DEVICES

Lifts are mechanical devices that can transfer a physically handicapped child from one spot to another—for example, from a bed to a wheelchair or from a wheelchair to a tub. Platform lifts are used to transfer a child while in a wheelchair to and from specially equipped vans. Some public transportation vehicles also are equipped with platform lifts. Simple boardlike devices also can be used to provide a surface on which the child can slide.

Children who require total support in almost all situations will need adapted strollers or wheelchairs, safe and supportive car seats, and proper seating in the home. Travel chairs can serve all three purposes. They adjust to several different heights and angles of recline and have multiposition rear wheels that fully retract under the seat, permitting use as a carseat. In the car, a travel chair can be secured with a standard seat belt. Travel chairs can be equipped with trays for home uses such as meals or play and can be pushed outdoors like any stroller. These chairs are relatively easy to adjust and maneuver. They have a full range of accessories and usually can be adjusted to fit as the child grows.

With minor adaptations, standard car seats can be used for many disabled children. Some are available with hard shells to fully enclose and protect the child from a jolting forward motion. A therapist may be able to help you select the best and safest model for your child and adapt it as necessary. Remember that children and infants never should be transported in an adult's lap or unrestrained in any seat. Many states have laws prohibiting traveling with unrestrained children in the car.

TOILET TRAINING AIDS

A regular potty seat can be used with many children with handicaps when they are ready to be toilet trained. A few manufacturers offer adaptive potty seats with high backs, side supports, and desk-like front supports. For some children, a standard potty seat positioned at a small table may work just as well. Remember that tables and desks are strictly for support, and should not be used to provide entertainment that distracts the child from the business at hand. Adaptors for the standard toilet seat generally do not provide adequate trunk or foot support for children with physical disabilities.

HOME MODIFICATIONS

Since activities of daily living are intimately related to home management, the physical layout of your home can be planned to ease care of your child. Ramps can be added. Counter tops, sinks, tables, and beds can be constructed or adapted to convenient heights. Doorways and hallways of adequate width are critical for children who rely on wheelchairs. Grab bars can be installed in the bathroom. Nonskid appliqués can be placed in a tub or shower for extra support and safety. Plans can be made to store vital equipment and special supplies in convenient locations for quick and easy access. Some children may require hospital beds to be managed at home, particularly those children who sleep in a particular position.

Other environmental changes can be made to maximize a child's mobility. Making these changes will be an ongoing process as your child grows and expands his or her skills. The key to modifications as well as to any adaptive equipment is to help children while at the same time encouraging their independence and furthering their development.

ACKNOWLEDGMENT

Contributions have been made to this chapter by Barbara Bush, R.P.T.

Chapter 24

Medications May Be Necessary for Your Child

Many children with developmental disabilities take medications as part of their treatment. For example, children with seizure disorders take medicines to control the seizures, and youngsters with severe attention problems may take medicine to improve their concentration. Many different medications are available to treat these and other problems. Each has advantages and disadvantages, and each has unique effects on the body.

This chapter discusses some of the medications commonly prescribed for children with developmental disabilities. Medicines are identified by either their trade name or common name, with the generic name given in parenthesis. We describe how and when these medications are to be taken, how they work, and their side effects and toxic effects. Moreover, we discuss how to recognize and monitor these side effects, and how certain medicines interact with other medications. Before information on individual medications is provided, some general considerations on side effects and toxic effects are discussed.

SIDE EFFECTS

Side effects are undesirable but not unexpected reactions to a proper or therapeutic dose of a medicine. Some side effects occur often, whereas others are rare. Not all people will experience side effects, even when they are taking the same medication in the same amount. Certain side effects, such as an upset stomach or a skin rash, are noticeable and can cause discomfort. Others may not be so obvious and may be detected only by a laboratory test or a doctor's examination. For example, some medicines may affect the child's blood count or liver function. Your doctor or pharmacist can inform you of the common side effects of particular medications. Before starting any medication, be sure to find out what the signs are of adverse reactions and toxicity. Also, if tests are needed to monitor the medication blood levels, make certain you know how often the tests must be done (see also Chapter 22 on "Tests and Procedures").

Sometimes side effects cannot be avoided. They may have to be tolerated in order for the medicine to work. In general, the benefits of taking the medication should outweigh any discomfort or undesirable effects it causes. An example of a valuable medicine that causes side effects is the seizure medication, Dilantin. It helps prevent seizures, but it may cause the gums to grow, which is called gingival hyperplasia.

If your child develops side effects after starting a medication, call your doctor and discuss your observations with him or her. Your doctor needs to know about anything unusual that occurs while your child is taking a medication. Keep in mind though, that your child's complaints may not be a side effect at all, but, instead, part of the illness or just a coincidence.

TOXIC EFFECTS

Toxic effects often develop when a person is taking too much medication. This is always a serious concern and must be dealt with immediately. Therefore, if a child has any unusual symptoms or is very uncomfortable, inform your physician immediately so the youngster can be checked. If a toxic effect is present, the doctor will adjust the dose or change the medication. Keep in mind that two people taking the same medication and dosage may react differently; one may become toxic whereas the other may not.

Whenever a medication is prescribed, it is of utmost importance that the directions provided on the label be followed carefully. The directions tell how much and how often the medicine is to be taken. A good rule to follow is to consult your child's physician if you have any questions or concerns about a medication.

SEIZURE MEDICATIONS

There are many different types of seizure disorders. Some seizures are treated more effectively than others with specific medications. Your doctor will tell you which medication is best to use for a certain type of seizure.

Before medicine is prescribed, your child's physician or a pediatric neurologist must determine what type of seizure is occurring. Therefore, the doctor may ask for a detailed description of the seizures and then order a brainwave test.

Many children need more than one medication to control the seizures effectively. For some children seizure medications are only required for 1 or 2 years, whereas others will need to take medications for their entire lives. In the beginning of treatment, it is usually difficult to predict how long a medication will be needed. Your physician will give you information about the type, severity, and prognosis of your child's seizure disorder.

Ordinarily, seizure medications work by quieting the brain and stopping the spread of seizure activity from one part of the brain to another. In some instances, this quieting effect can help the brain to "heal" itself. In other situations, however, the damage to the brain is so severe that complete "healing" is impossible.

In order for any seizure medication to be effective, there has to be enough of it in your child's body. If too little medicine is in the body, then the quieting effect will not be strong enough to prevent a seizure. If there is too much medicine, brain activity can be slowed down to such a degree that lethargy, drowsiness, or sleepiness may result. The doctor aims to prescribe just the right amount of medicine to prevent seizures, but not so much as to cause undesirable symptoms. This correct amount is called the therapeutic level. Once the therapeutic level has been established, the only way to maintain it is to take the medicine regularly as it is prescribed. If a child forgets to take the seizure medication, the level of the medication in the body may fall below its effective range, which in turn may lead to the reappearance of seizures. Your doctor will monitor the therapeutic level of the medication with a blood test, usually done two to four times annually.

Levels of most seizure medications usually do not change abruptly, but change gradually over time. For instance, a therapeutic level usually is not reached immediately; several days of taking the proper dosage may be required. Therefore, a child who is having seizures may not notice the benefits of the medication right away. Conversely, when medicine is discontinued, it may take several days or more before the child's system is totally free of the medication. If seizures continue to occur when a therapeutic range of a seizure medication has been reached, then the doctor may either change or add one or more seizure medications in an attempt to control seizure activity.

If your child has been seizure-free for several years, the doctor may want to discontinue the medication. Children usually are weaned off a medication by reducing the dose gradually over the course of several days to weeks. An abrupt stoppage of certain seizure medications might trigger a seizure within several days of the final dose. It is important that any changes in your child's medication be made under the supervision and guidance of your physician.

The pages following describe some of the more common medications used to treat seizures.

Dilantin (Diphenylhydantoin)

Dilantin is a very effective seizure medication used for the treatment of several different kinds of seizures, but particularly those that have a limb-jerking and stiffening (tonic-clonic) component. Dilantin has been used successfully for grand mal seizures, in which all four limbs are involved, as well as for focal seizures, in which jerky movements are localized to one or two limbs. Dilantin also can be used to treat psychomotor seizures, which sometimes are accompanied by unusual motor behaviors such as lip smacking or eye blinking.

Dilantin can be given in liquid, tablet, or capsule form. It usually is taken two or three times a day, but in older children it may need to be taken only once a day.

Common side effects are swollen gums, increased hair growth, and anemia. Less common side effects include dizziness, insomnia, emotional disturbances, headache, nausea, vomiting, constipation, skin rash, enlarged lymph glands, liver damage, bone softening, unsteadiness, and coarsening of facial features. Toxic effects include lethargy, sleepiness, slurred speech, poor balance, double vision, blood in the urine, and a severe rash. See your doctor immediately if toxicity is suspected.

Your child's blood count and liver function should be monitored by a physician at least two to three times per year. If these tests are abnormal, then Dilantin should be discontinued and another seizure medication used instead.

Dilantin often is given together with other seizure medications. This may affect its level in your child's body. Thus, close monitoring with blood tests is essential. Dilantin also should be taken with caution whenever medications to prevent blood clotting, or anticoagulants, are being taken at the same time.

Phenobarbital

Phenobarbital is another very effective seizure medication used for the treatment of grand mal seizures. It also is the primary drug used to treat recurrent or complicated febrile seizures. At home it can be given by mouth in liquid form, tablets, or capsules. In the hospital, it often is given intravenously (IV) or intramuscularly (IM).

Common side effects of phenobarbital are lethargy, irritability, and hyperactivity. Less common side effects include dizziness, insomnia, disturbances in thinking, lowering of heart rate and breathing, nausea, vomiting, constipation, skin rash, anemia, and bone softening. Toxic effects are pronounced lethargy, sleepiness, poor balance, and a severe rash.

Phenobarbital often is taken together with other anticonvulsant medications. This may affect its level in your child's body as well as the level of the other medications. Therefore, close monitoring is required. Phenobarbital also has a tendency to decrease the effectiveness of anticoagulants, steroids, and birth control pills.

Mebaral (Mephobarbital)

Mebaral is very similar to phenobarbital, and in fact, is converted to phenobarbital by the body. Consequently, its use, side effects, and toxicity are the same as those of phenobarbital. It is sometimes used instead of phenobarbital because it tends to have fewer emotional and behavioral side effects such as irritability and hyperactivity. It is available in tablet form only.

Mysoline (Primidone)

Mysoline also resembles phenobarbital in its action and is used to control similar types of seizures, including grand mal, focal, and psychomotor seizures. It is dispensed in tablet and liquid form. The initial dose is usually small and subsequently is increased over the course of a week.

Common side effects are irritability, hyperactivity, balance problems, and vertigo (the sensation that the room is spinning). The balance problems and vertigo usually disappear with continued usage. Less common side effects are nausea, vomiting, loss of appetite, fatigue, emotional disturbances, double vision, drowsiness, and skin rash. The toxic effects and drug interactions are similar to those of phenobarbital.

Tegretol (Carbamazepine)

Tegretol often is used for the treatment of psychomotor seizures, that is, seizures that are accompanied by unusual behaviors. This type of seizure sometimes is referred to as partial-complex or temporal lobe seizure. Tegretol also is given to children with grand mal and focal seizures. It comes in tablet form only and is given two to four times a day. The dose is usually small at first and then is increased gradually in an attempt to avoid side effects.

Common side effects are dizziness, drowsiness, unsteadiness, nausea, and vomiting. Less common side effects include reduced blood cell production in the bone marrow and liver toxicity. Even though these side effects are rare, they are potentially very serious and need to be watched for. Thus, your child's physician will want to monitor your child's blood count and liver function closely. These studies should be obtained two to three times a year. Other less common side effects include emotional and visual disturbances, ringing in the ears, pain in the limbs, retention of urine, and cardiovascular disturbances. Toxic effects are severe dizziness, unsteadiness, drowsiness, vomiting, restlessness, and tremors.

Depakene (Valproic Acid)

Depakene is a newer form of anticonvulsant medication that seems to work well in controlling so-called minor motor seizures. These are seizures that are manifested by short spells, occasional jerking or twitching, or drop attacks, in which the patient suddenly falls to the ground. Depakene also has been found to be effective in reducing the frequency of seizure activity in severely brain-damaged children, whose brainwave studies show evidence of diffuse and widespread abnormalities. Depakene comes in liquid and capsule form, and usually it is given two to three times daily.

Common side effects of Depakene are nausea, vomiting, and indigestion. Less common side effects are liver and bone marrow toxicity, similar to effects seen with Tegretol. These are potentially serious side effects and require close monitoring of blood count and liver function by your child's physician. Other less common side effects include unsteadiness, dizziness, headache, tremor, weakness, emotional upset, skin rash, and tremors. Toxic effects are lethargy and sedation.

Concerning drug interaction, Depakene can increase the blood level of phenobarbital and decrease the blood level of Dilantin. These effects have to be monitored closely by your child's physician. If necessary, appropriate adjustments to the various medications should be made so therapeutic levels can be reached.

Clonopin (Clonazepam)

Like Depakene, this medication often is used for minor motor seizures and drop attacks. It also can reduce the frequency of seizure activity in severely brain injured children. Clonopin comes in tablet form and is given two to three times a day. The initial dose usually is small and then is increased gradually. Tolerance to the medication may develop over time; therefore, a periodic upward adjustment of the medication may be necessary.

Common side effects include drowsiness, unsteadiness, irritability, and hyperactivity. Less common side effects are confusion, depression, forgetfulness, abnormal eye movements, slurred speech, increased salivation, loss of appetite, and liver disorders.

Zarontin (Ethosuximide)

This medication is the drug of choice for the treatment of typical petit mal seizures. Petit mal seizures are minor seizures characterized by brief lapses of consciousness, or "absences," that are sometimes associated with the abnormal eyelid movements or lip-smacking (see also Chapter

16 on "Seizure Disorders"). The brainwave test shows a characteristic pattern that distinguishes petit mal seizures from other minor motor, absencelike seizures. Zarontin comes in capsule and liquid form. It usually is given one to two times a day. The initial dose of Zarontin typically is low. Then, it is increased slowly in order to avoid side effects.

Common side effects are stomach upset, loss of appetite, nausea, vomiting, cramps, and diarrhea. Less common side effects include liver and kidney disorders. Children on this medication should have periodic blood counts, liver function studies, and urine checks. Other less common side effects include drowsiness, lethargy, headache, irritability, unsteadiness, and sleep disturbances. In rare instances, a disease called systemic lupus erythematosus develops following treatment with Zarontin.

Adrenocorticotropic Hormone

Adrenocorticotropic hormone or ACTH, a drug frequently used for endocrine and rheumatic disorders, has been used successfully with a specific type of seizure disorder known as infantile spasms, infantile myoclonic seizures, or hypsarrhythmia. ACTH is not available as an oral medication and needs to be injected into muscle tissue. This can be done when the child is hospitalized, or sometimes a visiting nurse may go to the parent's home to inject the medication.

Side effects of ACTH include elevated blood pressure, water retention, swelling of the face, susceptibility to infections, thinning of bones, and muscle weakness.

PSYCHOSTIMULANT MEDICATIONS

Hyperactive youngsters who have attentional problems typically have difficulty focusing on activities and tend to flit from one thing to another. Poor concentration and distractibility also are signs of hyperactivity.

Psychostimulant medications are used to reduce hyperactive behavior and attentional problems by helping the child concentrate. For a long time, doctors were baffled by the fact that stimulant medications seemed to slow down hyperactive children rather than perking them up or stimulating them further. Many called this a paradoxical effect. Today we know that there is no paradoxical effect. These medications work in hyperactive children by stimulating their brains so that they can attend better to the necessary details of an activity. Once the children's distractibility is reduced, they do not jump from task to task, and their overall amount of activity is lessened.

Psychostimulant medications differ from anticonvulsant medications in that a therapeutic level is reached relatively quickly, and the medications begin to work usually within the first hour after they have been taken. However, the effects of psychostimulants do not last long, usually 4 to 8 hours at the most. The medicine essentially is cleared from the body overnight, and by the next morning a new dose is needed if the beneficial effects are to be achieved.

A number of studies have documented the benefits of these medications in children with attentional problems and hyperactivity, but these medications do not work for all hyperactive children. The reasons for this are unclear, but they probably relate to the fact that there are many different causes of hyperactivity and the psychostimulant medications are effective only for a few. It is difficult to predict who will and who will not respond positively to psychostimulant medications. For this reason, the medications ordinarily are started on a trial basis. Initially, children are given a low dose. If no improvement is noted in the first few days, the dosage may be increased. If there still is no effect after several increases or after a similar medication has been tried, then the psychostimulant medications should be stopped and an alternative form of therapy should be sought. The therapeutic trial period should not take longer than 3 months.

If the medication does work, it can be helpful to both children and their families. However, it should not be the only form of treatment for hyperactivity. It should be thought of as one part of the total treatment plan. The medication alone rarely solves all behavior problems. Other helpful therapeutic interventions include family therapy, individual psychotherapy, adjustment of a child's educational setting, and a behavior modification program.

Psychostimulant medications usually are given only on school days, since this is when children need to pay attention the most. It often is recommended that these medications be withheld on weekends and holidays. However, if parents find that managing a child's behavior without medication is too difficult on weekends, it makes sense to give the medicine even on nonschool days. Generally, this helps to foster better parent-child relations.

The three medications used most often to treat hyperactivity and attentional problems are described next.

Ritalin (Methylphenidate Hydrochloride)

Ritalin is the most frequently used psychostimulant medication. It is available in tablet form and usually is given in the morning before school and at noon. The effect of Ritalin usually wears off by the time the child arrives home from school. Sometimes a third dose is given in midafternoon so that the effect can continue beyond regular school hours.

Ritalin is also available in a sustained release form, given only once in the morning. This can be particularly beneficial for children who do not like to take their medicine at school. Many youngsters are sensitive about their problems and do not want to draw attention to them by taking medication.

Common side effects are loss of appetite and difficulty falling asleep. These side effects usually are transient and pass within a couple of weeks. Less common side effects are nervousness, nausea, dizziness, headache, talkativeness, moodiness, palpitations, stomach aches, and a possible slowing of the child's growth rate.

There are no real toxic effects, since Ritalin does not accumulate over time. Overdosage, however, can occur, as with any other medications, either by accident or on purpose. Symptoms of acute overdosage result primarily from overstimulation of the brain and include vomiting, agitation, tremors, twitching, rapid heartbeat, and palpitations.

If Ritalin is taken with anticonvulsants or antidepressant medications, the dosages of those medications may have to be decreased, since Ritalin may interfere with the process of their elimination from the body.

Dexedrine (Dextroamphetamine Sulfate)

Dexedrine is available in both tablet and liquid form. The medication usually is given in the morning and at midday. A third dose may be given in the afternoon if necessary. Dexedrine also comes in a long-acting capsule (spansule), and like the sustained-release form of Ritalin, only needs to be given once in the morning. Although both Ritalin and

Dexedrine have similar effects, for unknown reasons some children respond better to Ritalin, whereas others respond better to Dexedrine. Therefore, if one of the psychostimulants is ineffective, it may be worthwhile to try a different one.

The side effects and overdose symptoms of Dexedrine and Ritalin are basically the same, as are their drug interactions.

Cylert (Pemoline)

Cylert, like Dexedrine and Ritalin, has similar effects on the body. Cylert usually is started at a low dose and built up gradually, so that the desired effect may not be noticed for several weeks. It is dispensed in tablet form. The duration of the effect of Cylert is longer than that of Ritalin and Dexedrine; therefore, it is given only once a day, usually in the morning. Again, for some unknown reason, a child who does not show any beneficial response to Ritalin or Dexedrine may respond well to Cylert.

Side effects and overdose symptoms of Cylert are the same as for Ritalin and Dexedrine. Blood tests measuring liver function should be obtained periodically on children receiving long-term therapy with Cylert.

ANTISPASTIC MEDICATIONS

Children who are physically handicapped because of brain damage or cerebral palsy frequently have problems with spasticity. Spasticity is the tightening of muscles that occurs when the nerve cells in the part of the brain that ordinarily controls the muscles are damaged.

In cerebral palsy, the damaged nerves stimulate the muscles continually and do not allow them to relax. Thus, the muscles of affected limbs continue to contract, and are getting tighter (see also Chapter 15 on "Cerebral Palsy").

Three medications are used primarily to reduce spasticity: Valium, Lioresal, and Dantrium. Since each of these medications works in slightly different ways, patients with a particular problem may find one of these drugs more effective than the others. To date, few comparisons have been made of the three medications to determine which works best under what circumstances.

Valium (Diazepam)

Valium, best known as a tranquilizer, is the medication used most often by physicians to treat symptoms of spasticity. It is available in tablet form and as an injectable liquid. Valium is started at a low dose and is built up to the point where the maximum antispastic effect is achieved with minimal tranquilizing effects.

Common side effects of Valium are drowsiness, fatigue, problems with balance, weakness, and dizziness. Less common side effects include confusion, constipation, depression, headache, bladder problems, speech disturbance, tremors, vision problems, and skin rashes. On rare occasions, insomnia, anxiety, hostility, and hallucinations are observed. Generally, these are seen only after long-term use of Valium. Toxic reactions include sleepiness, confusion, and unresponsiveness.

Valium may depress the function of the brain, and should be taken with caution when anticonvulsants, antidepressants, and antipsychotic medications are given at the same time.

Lioresal (Baclofen)

Lioresal is used most often with paraplegic and quadriplegic patients who have suffered damage to the spinal cord by multiple sclerosis or trauma. Its use in children with cerebral palsy has not been well studied. Theoretically, it may be helpful in children who have spasticity associated with spina bifida.

Lioresal comes in tablet form. It usually is given three times a day. One generally begins with a low dose and builds up to the point where there is a maximum relief of spasticity.

Common side effects are occasional drowsiness, dizziness, weakness, and fatigue. Less common side effects are confusion, headache, insomnia, low blood pressure, nausea, constipation, and bladder problems. Rarely, hallucinations and speech and vision problems are noted. Toxic effects include vomiting, weakness, lethargy, nonresponsiveness, and seizures.

Dantrium (Dantrolene Sodium)

Dantrium works directly on the muscle, causing it to contract less, even in the face of continued stimulation from a damaged nerve. Theoretically, Dantrium appears to be the ideal treatment for spastic cerebral palsy. However, a few studies indicate that Dantrium is not any more effective than Valium in reducing spasticity.

Dantrium is available in tablet form. Like the other antispastic medications, the initial dosage is low and is increased gradually over time until an effect is seen. If the maximum dosage is reached and no positive effects are observed, the medication should be discontinued.

Common side effects are drowsiness, dizziness, weakness, fatigue, and diarrhea. Less common side effects are liver damage, stomach problems, speech disorders, urinary problems, abnormal hair growth, and acne. Rarely, cardiac problems and seizures are observed.

PSYCHOTROPIC MEDICATIONS

Many children with developmental disabilities also have emotional difficulties. Some children's emotional problems are so severe that they interfere with their school performance, peer relationships, and normal bodily functions. Children's emotional problems often are related to difficulties in their home, school, or other environments. In such situations, eliminating the underlying cause of the child's problems may relieve the emotional disturbance. However, this is not always possible; sometimes the psychiatric disturbance is so severe that medical intervention is required.

Medications commonly used to help individuals with emotional or psychiatric problems are called psychotropic medications. Two main categories of psychotropic medications are discussed here: antipsychotic and antidepressant medications.

Antipsychotic Medications

Antipsychotic medications are used in children and adolescents who show symptoms of severe psychiatric disturbance such as bizarre thinking patterns, delusions, hallucinations, severe confusion, aggressive behavior, agitation, and restlessness. How antipsychotic medications work to improve these symptoms is not well understood. They often have a sedative effect, which tends to calm down a severely agitated child. Recent evidence suggests that some symptoms of psychiatric disturbances are due to chemical imbalances within the brain. The antipsychotic medications alter the chemistry of the brain and thus improve behavior and thinking.

Like anticonvulsant medications, these medicines provide a beneficial effect when taken on a regular basis, so that adequate levels are maintained in the body. It may take a few weeks before a positive effect is seen. Specific therapeutic blood levels have not been designated for many of these medications. An adequate dosage generally is determined by the patient's behavior rather than by defined blood levels.

Numerous antipsychotic medications are available. Some of the more common ones are *Thorazine* (chlorpromazine hydrochloride), *Stelazine* (trifluoperazine hydrochloride), *Mellaril* (thioridazine hydrochloride), and *Navane* (thiothixene hydrochloride). All of them work in a similar way and have similar side effects.

Side effects include lethargy; sleepiness; sluggishness; weakness; dry mouth; blurred vision; and unusual muscular contractions (dystonia), which can lead to head-tilting, facial grimacing, unusual tongue movements, and difficulty speaking. There may also be tremulousness, rigidity, and restlessness. Another side effect of long-term use of these medications is tardive dyskinesia, a condition characterized by repetitive ticlike movements of the face, tongue, lips, and sometimes the limbs. It is more commonly seen in adults than in children. There is no known effective treatment for tardive dyskinesia.

Less common side effects are rapid heartbeat, electrocardiogram changes, a fall in blood pressure, minor liver problems, changes in blood count, breast enlargement, nasal congestion, constipation, difficulty urinating, increased sweating, and salivation. Seizures, exacerbation of psychiatric symptoms, allergic reactions, and fever are rare side effects.

These medications depress the function of the central nervous system and should be taken with caution when other medications that act similarly, such as anticonvulsant, antispastic, and antidepressant medications, are used.

Haldol (Haloperidol) Haldol is a commonly used antipsychotic medication with potent sedative effects. It also is prescribed frequently for children with Gilles de la Tourette's syndrome, a disorder in which uncontrollable tics of the face and extremities and bizarre vocalizations are present. The exact way Haldol works is still unclear. But like so many similar medications, Haldol may correct chemical imbalances in the brain and thus help to reduce the abnormal behaviors.

Haldol is available in tablet and liquid form. A trial with the medication consists of starting at the lowest possible dose once or twice a day and gradually increasing it until a positive response is noted or the side effects limit any further increase. The ideal dose is one that provides maximum therapeutic effect with minimum side effects. Since this medication is one of the antipsychotics, the side effects, toxic effects, and drug interactions are similar to those of the other antipsychotic medications described here.

Cogentin (Benztropine Mesylate) Cogentin deserves special mention since some of the movement side effects of the antipsychotic medications—such as tremors, rigidity, and dystonia—can be alleviated by using Cogentin. Although Cogentin may diminish some of the adverse reactions, it may cause dryness of the mouth, blurred vision, constipation, and difficulty urinating. Also, tardive dyskinesia may be more likely to occur when Cogentin is combined with antipsychotic medications. For these reasons, Cogentin should be used cautiously when treating patients already taking antipsychotic medications. Sometimes, physicians may elect to decrease the dose of antipsychotic medication in an attempt to prevent movement side effects before adding Cogentin to the drug regimen.

Antidepressant Medications

Antidepressant medications are used in children and adolescents who manifest symptoms of severe sadness, hopelessness, and worthlessness. Sometimes poor school performance, difficult peer and family relationships, aggressive behaviors, lack of interest, withdrawal, hostility, early waking, loss of appetite, weight loss, and general slowness also are observed in depressed children.

How the antidepressant medications work is not fully understood. There is some evidence that, like the antipsychotic drugs, they correct chemical imbalances in the brain and thus improve mood, sleeping, eating, and other physiological functions.

Antidepressant medications are somewhat similar to anticonvulsant and antipsychotic medications in that a certain therapeutic level has to be reached before the medications become effective. It sometimes takes 2 to 4 weeks before any improvement is noted. These medications have to be taken on a regular basis in order to maintain an effective drug level in the body. Blood levels of these medications can be tested from time to time and dosage adjustments made when necessary.

A number of antidepressant medications share common side effects such as constipation, dryness of the mouth, blurred vision, difficulty urinating, sleepiness, weakness, lethargy, stomach upset, and low blood pressure, which is sometimes associated with dizziness. Toxic effects may include restlessness, agitation, delirium, convulsions, and cardiac problems.

Lithium Lithium has been used successfully in treating patients with manic-depression, an illness characterized by marked mood swings between depression and mood elevation. How Lithium works is unclear. Again, there is some evidence that the chemical environment of the brain is altered by this medication.

Unfortunately, Lithium can be very toxic. Therefore, its levels should be followed very closely to make sure that the medication stays within the therapeutic range. If no behavioral improvement is noted by the patient even when the medication is in the therapeutic range, it should be stopped to prevent toxic effects. Lithium is available in tablet and capsule form for oral use and generally is given three to four times daily.

Common side effects are tremors, frequent urination (particularly at night), thirst, nausea, fatigue, lethargy, and stomach upset. Less common side effects are heart and thyroid abnormalities and dizziness. Early signs of toxicity are diarrhea, vomiting, drowsiness, weakness, and loss of coordination. Later signs are giddiness, balance problems, blurred vision, a ringing in the ears, and increased urine output. Serious toxic signs include seizures, confusion, stupor, heart problems, and low blood pressure. Lithium and antipsychotic medications should not be taken together.

Tofranil (Imipramine Hydrochloride) Tofranil is one of the more commonly used antidepressant medications. It also is used to treat wetting, or enuresis. Tofranil may be prescribed after other causes of enuresis have been ruled out. This medication is available in tablet form. It usually is started at a relatively low dose and then increased weekly until either improvement is noted or the maximum dosage is reached. If no improvement is seen, the medication should be stopped. Even with improvement, treatment of enuresis with Tofranil should last only a few months. Then the medication should be withdrawn gradually. If a child again starts to wet, a second trial of Tofranil can be instituted.

Common side effects of Tofranil are constipation, dryness of the mouth, blurred vision, sleep disturbances, weakness, lethargy, stomach upset, low blood pressure, nervousness, and agitation. Less common side effects include heart abnormalities, anxiety, disorientation, numbness, tingling or burning sensations of the extremities, balance and coordination problems, skin rash, breast enlargement, and altered liver function. Rare side effects are seizures, blood changes, and hair loss. Toxic effects include marked drowsiness leading to unresponsiveness, balance problems, restlessness, nervousness, movement disorders, seizures, rapid or irregular heartbeat, and low blood pressure.

Decongestants should not be taken together with Tofranil, and medications like Ritalin should be taken with caution when prescribed at the same time. Tofranil increases the effect of other medications that depress brain function such as Phenobarbital and Valium. It should not be given to an adolescent if alcohol or drug abuse is suspected.

Chloralhydrate Chloralhydrate is one of the medications prescribed for sleeping problems in children. Many developmentally disabled children have sleeping problems. Although numerous products are sold over-the-counter to help people get to sleep, many are not suitable for children. Chloralhydrate can help break an abnormal sleeping pattern and allow a more normal pattern to take its place.

Chloralhydrate comes in capsule or liquid form. It usually is given half an hour before bedtime. This medication should not be used for more than a few weeks at a time. It can be discontinued for a week or so and then used again. It is not meant for long-term use.

Chloralhydrate also is used frequently as a sedative prior to such tests as an electroencephalogram, CT scan, or special hearing tests.

Side effects of chloralhydrate include stomach upset, disorientation, incoherence, skin rash, and blood changes. Rarely, excitement, dizziness, and dependence are observed. Toxic effects are severe sleepiness leading to unresponsiveness, low blood pressure, depressed breathing, and severe stomach irritation. Chloralhydrate should be used cautiously with medications that prevent blood clotting or anticoagulants.

THYROID MEDICATIONS

A number of thyroid medications are on the market for treating hypothyroidism. Congenital hypothyroidism, a disease detected in infancy that can cause brain damage, results from the body's inability to produce essential thyroid hormone. Early treatment can prevent brain damage. Synthroid and Levothroid (levothyroxine) are two forms of thyroid hormone used most often to treat hypothyroidism. These medications perform as well as thyroid hormone produced naturally in the body. Generally, the child with hypothyroidism takes one tablet a day. Levels of thyroid hormone in the blood are monitored to ensure that the child is getting the appropriate dose.

There are no side effects to these medications, but it is possible to have overactive thyroid function or hyperthyroidism if the dosage is too high. Some common signs of hyperthyroidism are poor growth, diarrhea, rapid heart rate, increased body temperature, sweating, headache, increased appetite, fatigue, overactivity, and poor sleeping.

MEDICATIONS FOR BOWEL PROBLEMS

Several groups of medications can be used to help physically handicapped youngsters who have bowel problems. Each group has its own mode of action.

Stool Softeners

Stool softeners may be prescribed for children who have chronic problems with constipation, fecal soiling, or impaction of the bowel. They work by either drawing water into the stool or retaining water. Water keeps the stool soft and thus helps to prevent constipation. A common stool softener is *Colace* (docusate sodium), which is available over-the-counter in tablet, capsule, powder, or liquid form.

Mineral Oil

Mineral oil lubricates stool, keeping it soft so that it can be moved easily through the intestines and thus be eliminated easily. Mineral oil generally is taken at bedtime. It has an unpleasant taste, but when mixed with milk, juice, yogurt, or other foods, it is less apparent. If mineral oil is to be used on a long-term basis, it is recommended that a multivitamin also be taken daily, as mineral oil has a tendency to block the absorption of fat-soluble vitamins. Mineral oil should not be taken by severely handicapped children, who might have a tendency to vomit and aspirate. If aspirated, mineral oil can cause a severe form of pneumonia.

Bulk Laxatives

Bulk laxatives generally have three actions. First, they act like stool softeners, drawing water into the bowel to keep the stool soft. Second, they frequently add bulk to the stool, which stimulates elimination. Third, they usually contain an ingredient that also stimulates the intestine to move the stool through quickly. Some common laxatives include *Peri-Colace, Metamucil, Senokot,* and *Doxidan.* Side effects may include intestinal cramps or diarrhea. If used for extended periods, some laxatives may be habit-forming.

Stimulants

Dulcolax (bisacodyl) is one of the more common laxatives used for constipation. It directly stimulates the large intestine and thus enhances stool elimination. It is not as gentle as most of the just-mentioned medications, and may cause cramps in a child who is constipated.

Dulcolax is available both in tablet and suppository form. Tablets can take up to 8 hours to work and are frequently taken at bedtime. Suppositories usually have an effect within an hour after administration. Dulcolax may be habit-forming, but may also be the only alternative for regular bowel function in some patients.

Glycerin suppositories are used for younger children or when only mild bowel stimulation is required.

Enemas

Enemas are used when a child is severely constipated. A liquid solution is administered rectally, which then induces elimination and serves to clean out the bowel. *Fleet enemas* are the most commonly used enemas. Besides the regular waterlike enemas, there are also mineral oil and soapsuds enemas. Elimination is usually induced within 2 to 5 minutes after administration. Enemas often are used when impaction is diagnosed. Cramps are the main side effects.

MEDICATIONS FOR URINARY TRACT PROBLEMS

Urinary tract infections and a condition called spastic bladder are common problems in children with certain developmental disabilities such as spina bifida. There are several categories of medication used to treat these problems: antibiotics, acidifying agents, and anticholinergic medications. Antibiotics combined with agents that make urine slightly acidic are used to prevent and fight infection. Anticholinergic medications will help relax a tight or spastic bladder so that it will fill more efficiently and not cause constant dribbling of the urine. Once the bladder is filled, clean, intermittent catheterization can be used to empty the bladder (see Chapter 22 on "Tests and Procedures" for discussion of catheterization).

Antibiotics

Antibiotics are used to treat and prevent infections caused by bacteria. Children who are prone to infections, or who are at risk for kidney damage due to frequent infections, are given antibiotics.

Numerous antibiotics and sulfa drugs are available today. Some of the more commonly used medications for urinary tract infections include *Ampicillin, Amoxicillin, Gantrisin, Keflex, Bactrim,* and *Septra.* These medications come in tablet and liquid form and can be taken either on a short-term basis to treat an infection or on a long-term basis to prevent an infection.

The most common side effects include stomach upset with possible diarrhea, nausea, or vomiting. Bactrim, Septra, and Gantrisin may also cause serious blood problems, although this is rare. All these medications are safe when taken over a short period to fight an infection. If Bactrim, Septra, or Gantrisin is used for long-term treatment, then periodic blood counts should be obtained.

Acidifying Agents

Acidifying agents make the urine more acidic. Since most bacteria do not grow and thrive in an acidic environment, making the urine acidic then helps to prevent infection. The most common acidifying agents used are *vitamin C* and *cranberry juice.* Large doses of vitamin C can be taken each day (5 g) without apparent ill effects.

Anticholinergic Medications

Choline is a chemical found in many parts of the body. One of the actions of choline is to cause the bladder to contract. In some bladders with impaired or absent nerve function (neurogenic bladder), the bladder contractions can be excessive and thus prevent the bladder from filling properly, causing continual urinary dribbling. Anticholinergic medications block the effect of choline and allow the bladder to relax and fill. The most common anticholinergic medications used for this purpose are *Ditropan, Probanthine,* and *Donnatal.* These medications come in tablet and liquid form.

The most common side effects are a dryness of the mouth, blurred vision, decreased sweating, increased heart rate, constipation, nausea, vomiting, drowsiness, weakness, dizziness, difficulty falling asleep, and allergic reaction. Toxic effects include restlessness, excitement, psychotic behavior, low blood pressure, decreased breathing effort, and loss of consciousness.

CONCLUSION

Medications used appropriately can be of great help to people who are in severe distress. They are, in fact, life-saving in many situations. But despite the benefits, many medications have potentially dangerous side effects, which must be considered.

Medications must be kept out of the reach of children, as well as others who are at risk for ingesting them and for whom they are not intended. If children take any medicines that have not been prescribed for them, the nearest Poison Control Center should be telephoned immediately. It is also wise to have *ipecac syrup* on hand (available from the pharmacy), should the Poison Control Center advise inducing vomiting. vomiting. (Vomiting *should not* be induced with all poisonings.)

Whenever a medicine is prescribed, the physician's instructions must be followed closely to achieve a therapeutic effect and to avoid toxic effects. If suspicious symptoms are ever noticed, they should be discussed promptly with your child's physician. It is your responsibility as a parent to monitor all medication effects, whether good or bad. Also, as potentially beneficial as medications can be, they will not work if they are not taken. As a parent, you must ensure that your child is given the chance to benefit from the medicines that he or she takes.

ACKNOWLEDGMENTS

Contributions have been made to this chapter by Daniel T. Marwil, M.D., and Siegfried M. Pueschel, M.D., Ph.D., M.P.H.

◀ Chapter 25 ▶

Some Children May Have to Undergo Surgery

A child with special needs requires regular medical care just like any other child. However, in addition to routine pediatric checkups, your child may need the services of one or more medical specialists. It also is possible that your child may need to have an operation and thus require the services of a surgeon.

This chapter describes a number of surgical interventions that may be needed by youngsters with developmental disabilities. Of course, just as there are many kinds of developmental disabilities, there are also numerous associated medical and surgical problems that can arise. The medical and surgical needs of each child are unique, and, therefore, the goals and type of treatment will vary from child to child. This chapter focuses primarily on describing surgical interventions themselves. The characteristics and prognoses of the conditions necessitating surgery have been discussed in previous chapters.

Surgery, itself, has become highly specialized. Many individual surgeons are concentrating on the treatment of particular organ systems. For example, cardiac surgeons operate on the heart, orthopaedic surgeons operate on muscles, tendons, and bones, and urologists operate on kidneys, ureters, and bladder.

GENERAL CONSIDERATIONS

Whenever surgery is planned, some general issues should be considered. Decisions must be made, for example, about the operative procedure to be followed, as well as the best time to do it. In nonemergency situations, factors such as the child's stage of growth and development, the possible effects of immobilization and decreased stimulation during hospitalization, and the impact of interrupting educational programs and ongoing therapy need to be taken into account. Families also should consider how their child reacts to unusual situations, new people, and changes in school. Many youngsters regress behaviorally during prolonged hospitalization. Recognition and anticipation of potential behavior problems may help manage and even avoid behavior problems.

It is important to discuss with your child any anticipated surgery shortly before the operation is to take place. Explain in detail, perhaps together with the surgeon, the steps involved in admission to the hospital, preparation for surgery, and having the operation, without causing undue anxiety and fear. Be honest about possible discomfort of blood tests, the pain that may be felt after the operation, and the length of the recovery. Your child also should be told the reason for the surgery, in terms he or she can understand. Even if children do not understand all the reasons, they usually grasp how the surgery is expected to benefit them. Sometimes hospitals invite children to visit and become familiar with the routines of a hospital stay, preparation for surgery, what an operating room and a recovery room look like, and what nurses do to make the hospital stay more pleasant. Books that show pictures of operating theaters and describe what is going on during an operation are also available. These preparatory efforts can alleviate much of a child's anxiety and concern.

Surgery is undertaken only when it is judged that its potential benefits outweigh its risks. Before an operation, patients should be in the best health possible. Other medical problems should be treated prior to surgery. Good nutrition before surgery also is important, as nutrition plays a vital role in wound healing and resistance to infections.

ANESTHESIA

Anesthesia is a part of almost all surgical procedures. Without anesthesia, surgery would be virtually impossible, because it is through the administration of anesthetic medications that the patient's awareness of pain is altered or eliminated.

Local Anesthesia

Most people are familiar with local anesthetics such as *Novocain* or *Xylocaine*. These medications block the pain by making the nerves numb in the area where the medication is injected. For example, if your child has a cut that needs stitching or a tooth that needs drilling, then prior to the procedure the medication is injected into the respective location.

Another form of local anesthesia is called a nerve block. In this case the anesthetic is injected into a specific nerve. When a nerve block is used, the entire area supplied by that nerve temporarily loses its sensation. Depending on the type and amount of anesthesia used, the effects will wear off between 15 and 60 minutes later.

Spinal anesthesia can be thought of as a more extensive form of nerve block. When spinal anesthesia is given, a needle is used to guide a small tube between the bones of the spine into the spinal canal, which contains the spinal cord. An anesthetic then can be injected through the tube into the space around the spinal cord. This will numb all the areas of the body supplied by nerves branching off from this level of the spinal cord and below. Also, the muscles supplied by these nerves will be paralyzed temporarily.

General Anesthesia

General anesthesia is the most frequently used type of anesthesia during major surgery. Some general anesthetics can be injected into the bloodstream, and some are gases that need to be inhaled. When inhalation anesthesia is used, the patient is unconscious during surgery. In addition, the patient's muscles may be paralyzed temporarily, including the muscles needed for breathing. When general anesthesia is used, a tube is placed through the nose or mouth into the windpipe or trachea, permitting the anesthetic and oxygen to be given to the child during an operation.

As with any medication, general anesthesia can have side effects. In rare instances, certain anesthetics have caused liver damage. Also, a condition called malignant hyperthermia, in which the body's temperature rises to dangerously high levels of 105°F to 107°F, has been reported in some patients with specific neuromuscular diseases. However, your doctor and the anesthesiologist (medical doctor who administers anesthesia) will be aware of these potential side effects and will try to avoid them to the best of their abilities.

Following general anesthesia, small segments of the lungs may collapse in some patients. This condition is known as atelectasis. Also, the lungs' mechanisms for clearing secretions may be less efficient temporarily. This is the reason a patient's respiratory system is considered so carefully when an operation is being planned and why coughing and deep breathing are encouraged after surgery.

NEUROSURGICAL INTERVENTIONS

Surgical Treatment of Hydrocephalus

Cerebrospinal fluid surrounds the brain and spinal cord and circulates through cavities inside the brain known as ventricles. This fluid acts as a cushion between the brain and the bones of the skull (See Figures 1 and 2). Sometimes the normal flow of cerebrospinal fluid is blocked or is

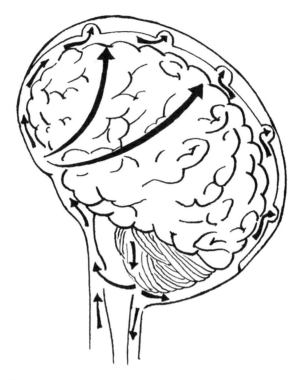

Figure 1.   Arrows indicate flow of cerebrospinal fluid around the brain.

produced in excess. When this happens, the cerebrospinal fluid builds up in the ventricles of the brain, causing them to enlarge and squeeze the brain against the skull, which can cause hydrocephalus and brain damage. In a baby whose skull bones have not yet fused together, the increased pressure inside the skull can cause bulging of the soft spot on top of the head and may lead to rapid enlargement of the head. In an older child whose skull bones have fused together, increased pressure inside the skull produces symptoms such as headache, nausea, vomiting, drowsiness, and even coma.

Hydrocephalus can be corrected surgically. To relieve the pressure inside the skull and reestablish the normal flow of cerebrospinal fluid, a neurosurgeon places a plastic tube called a shunt inside the brain. One end of the shunt is inserted into the enlarged ventricle with its excess fluid, and the other is threaded under the skin along the neck and chest into the abdomen, where the surplus cerebrospinal fluid is drained. This type of shunt is called a ventriculoperitoneal, or VP, shunt (Figure 3).

Another type of shunt, known as a ventriculojugular shunt, has one end inserted into the ventricle of the brain and the other emptying

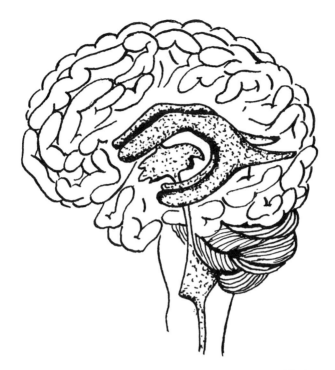

Figure 2.   Ventricles or cavities inside the brain in which the cerebrospinal fluid is produced.

into the jugular vein, a large vein in the neck. Shunts may require replacement from time to time as the child grows. Sometimes they may become infected or blocked and then need to be removed.

The shunt operation is done on an inpatient basis under general anesthesia. Children usually remain in the hospital for 5 to 10 days following the procedure. Before the youngster is discharged, parents should be taught the signs and symptoms of a malfunctioning shunt (see also Chapter 26, on "Hospitalization and Aftercare").

Surgical Repair of Spina Bifida

In spina bifida, or meningomyelocele, the development of the spinal cord, its coverings called the meninges, and the bones of the spine or vertebrae are defective. A sac formed by the meninges, with its disorganized nerve tissue and cerebrospinal fluid, is exposed on the surface of the back. One of the first steps in the treatment of meningomyelocele is closure of the back defect by a neurosurgeon. After the skin around the sac is thoroughly cleansed, the sac and its content are removed and the skin edges are stitched together.

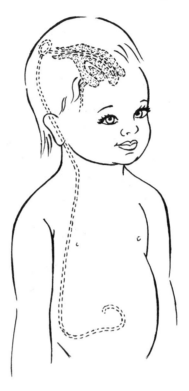

Figure 3. Ventriculoperitoneal shunt used in treatment of hydrocephalus. Shunt drains excess cerebrospinal fluid from the ventricles on the brain into the abdomen.

SURGICAL PROCEDURES OF THE GASTROINTESTINAL TRACT

The gastrointestinal, or GI, tract is a long tube consisting primarily of the food pipe or esophagus, stomach, and small and large intestines. Food enters at one end and is broken down chemically as it passes through the intestines. Water and nutrients are absorbed into the blood stream, and residual waste is eliminated as bowel movement through the rectum.

During early embryonic development of the gastrointestinal tract, mishaps may occur resulting in birth defects. These birth defects, which can occur alone or together with certain developmental disabilities, require surgical intervention in early life. Birth defects of the gastrointestinal tract can take several forms. Three of these are discussed here: stenosis—a narrowing of a tube; fistula—an abnormal connection between two parts; and atresia—a failure of a part of the system to develop. Hernias, a fourth disorder of the gastrointestinal tract, sometimes requiring surgery, are also discussed.

Surgery of Stenosis

Pyloric stenosis is the term used to describe a narrowing at the lower end of the stomach, or pylorus. It is treated by cutting muscle fibers of the wall of the pylorus to relieve the narrowing at that point.

Narrowing of the duodenum, or the part of the bowel that is close to the stomach, is called *duodenal stenosis*. In this case, surgery involves removing the stenosis and reuniting the two ends of the intestine.

In another condition called *Hirschsprung disease,* there is a narrowing of a segment of the large bowel, caused by a lack of nerve endings. This often results in persistent constipation. Special X rays, such as a barium enema, will show this condition. Again, surgery is necessary; the narrow segment is cut out and the two normal ends of the large bowel are surgically united.

These operations are performed under general anesthesia and require a hospital stay of 1 to 2 weeks. Recovery takes approximately 1 to 4 weeks.

Surgery of Fistulas

Fistulas occur most often between the esophagus and the trachea (the latter is also known as the windpipe). This condition is called *tracheoesophageal fistula.* The surgeon repairs the problem by removing the abnormal connection between the esophagus and trachea. Repair of tracheoesophageal fistulas is important to prevent food from entering the lungs, which can cause recurrent pneumonia.

Surgery of Atresias

A blind pouch of the esophagus, known as *esophageal atresia,* may accompany a tracheoesophageal fistula. When an atresia interrupts the continuity of the esophagus, the surgeon will attempt to connect the separated ends by sewing them together to form what is called an anastomosis. If a connection is impossible, a part of the intestine is used as an extension between the two ends of the esophagus.

An atresia of the duodenal segment of the bowel is another common birth defect, particularly in children with Down syndrome. Like a duodenal stenosis, a *duodenal atresia* must be repaired surgically. The operation consists of cutting out the blocked segment of bowel and rejoining the two ends of the intestine.

An atresia in which the anal opening at the end of the large bowel fails to form is called an *anal atresia* or *imperforate anus.* This condition may be accompanied by fistulas of other sections of the lower intestine to structures such as the urethra or vagina. In addition, kidney malformations, congenital heart disease, esophageal atresia, tracheoesophageal fistula, and bone deformities of the pelvis, spine, and the arms are observed together with anal atresia.

Normally, the lower end of the large intestine, the rectum, passes through a funnel-shaped sling of muscles in the pelvis. If the blind end of the rectum, the imperforate anus, lies below these muscles, correction can be done in the first few days of life by creating an opening for the rectum in the usual position. If the end of the rectum lies above these muscles, then correction may require two or more operations. During the initial operation, which is usually done in the first few days of life, a colostomy is performed by which the colon or large bowel is attached to an opening, or stoma, on the skin of the abdomen. Through this opening stool passes to the outside and is collected in a plastic bag that is attached to the stoma. Later, when the baby is about 12 to 15 months of age, a second operation is performed to pull the rectum through the muscular sling and to create an opening for the rectum at the anal area. When recovery from this second procedure is complete, the opening of the colostomy, the stoma, is closed and the ends of the large bowel, which were separated at the time the colostomy was performed, are reconnected. There are variations of this surgical procedure, which depend on the individual circumstances as well as the surgeon's preference.

Surgery of Hernias

The term *hernia* means a protrusion of an organ through a weakened area of a muscle. There are different types of hernias; for example, a *hiatal hernia* occurs when part of the stomach or bowel pushes through the diaphragm muscle; an *inguinal hernia* results when part of the intestines pushes through muscles in the groin; and an *umbilical hernia* is a weakness in the navel area where the umbilical cord was attached.

Hernias can become life-threatening if the protruding portion of the organ, most often a part of the intestine, gets stuck (incarcerated) outside the opening, causing an interruption of the blood supply. This condition, called strangulation, requires immediate attention and in many cases, emergency surgery. As a preventative measure, hernias often are repaired surgically before they become incarcerated.

Surgical repair of a hernia involves pushing the protruding part of the organ back through the opening in the muscle and closing the opening with stitches. Most umbilical hernias never cause problems and do not need surgical attention, since they disappear with time.

A more serious condition, in which abdominal organs such as liver and intestine may protrude through the front of the abdominal wall, is called an *omphalocele*. A related condition, *gastroschisis,* is a hole in the abdominal wall that occurs at a point other than the navel or umbilicus.

In the case of a large omphalocoele or gastroschisis, returning the organs back into the abdominal cavity usually is a gradual process involving several operations. At first, if the opening is very large, a synthetic covering may be used to enclose the organs. Then, after the organs are contained within the abdominal cavity, the skin from both sides is sewn together.

SURGICAL PROCEDURES TO CORRECT FEEDING PROBLEMS

Treatment of Severe Feeding Disorders

Some children have severe impairments of the muscles and nerves needed to coordinate chewing and swallowing. Problems in chewing and swallowing can lead to inadequate nutrition, choking, and aspiration of food particles into the lungs, resulting in recurrent respiratory infections. For youngsters for whom feeding by mouth is impossible, an operation called a gastrostomy can be performed. This procedure enables food to enter the stomach directly. The surgeon creates an opening in the abdominal and stomach walls and places a gastrostomy tube through the opening into the stomach. Liquid or pureed food then can be given through the tube (see also Chapter 22 on "Tests and Procedures").

In a condition called gastroesophageal reflux, the stomach contents may flow back into the esophagus. Sometimes the material spills over into the trachea, causing aspiration into the lungs and, subsequently, pneumonia. Gastroesophageal reflux occurs because of a weakness in the muscle that encircles the lower end of the esophagus, known as the esophageal sphincter. This muscle normally keeps food in the stomach from backing up into the esophagus. Severe gastroesophageal reflux may require correction by surgery. The procedure is known as *fundoplication*. In this operation the upper part of the stomach is wrapped around the lower end of the esophagus and sewn in place.

SURGERY OF CONGENITAL HEART DEFECTS

Not all of the congenital heart defects described in Chapter 13's discussion of birth defects require surgery; a few will correct themselves. For example, patent ductus arteriosus and small ventricular septal defects often close spontaneously. Also, the heart is able to compensate for some structural defects such as small atrial septal defects, small ventricular septal defects, and minor degrees of narrowing of pulmonic and aortic stenosis.

With severe congenital heart defects such as tetralogy of Fallot (combines four cardiac defects), endocardial cushion defect, large atrial and ventricular septal defects, severe pulmonic and aortic stenosis, or coarctation of the aorta, the heart's means of compensating are only partially or temporarily effective. Over time, further structural changes in the heart and pulmonary blood vessels may occur, including enlargement of the heart's chambers, thickening of the heart's walls, and narrowing of the pulmonary arteries. Subsequently, as the efficiency of the circulation diminishes, the strain upon the whole body becomes obvious, and symptoms such as poor growth, shortness of breath, exercise intolerance, and frequent infections may develop. Heart surgery is undertaken to prevent this downhill course.

Cardiac catheterization is a surgical procedure usually done before a heart defect is repaired to assess the extent of the problem. This procedure allows the cardiologist to visualize the inside structures of the heart as it pumps. A detailed description of cardiac catheterization is provided in Chapter 22, on "Tests and Procedures."

With the development of the heart-lung machine and the advent of open-heart surgery, great strides in the treatment of congenital heart disease have become possible. During open-heart surgery, blood is diverted from the heart to a machine where it is oxygenated and then returned to the child. This allows the surgeon to operate on structures inside the heart while the machine pumps the blood. Sometimes, preliminary surgery is indicated, such as *pulmonary banding* if total correction of a severe cardiac defect is not feasible at an early age.

The type of surgery needed to correct congenital heart disease will vary according to the kind and degree of the cardiac defect present in the child. In infants with patent ductus arteriosus, surgical treatment consists of eliminating the increased flow of blood to the lungs by tying off the ductus arteriosus vessel that failed to close after birth. Likewise, in some infants where the foramen ovale did not close spontaneously, surgical closure may be necessary.

If the problem is an opening between two chambers of the heart— for example, a ventricular septal defect—then the hole is closed by either sewing it shut directly or patching it, depending on the size of the hole.

Valves that are either too tight, as in pulmonic stenosis and aortic stenosis, or too loose, as in mitral insufficiency, may need to be corrected by surgery. Excessive tightness of a valve can sometimes be relieved by cutting the band of fibrous tissue surrounding the valve, a procedure known as *commissurotomy.* Sometimes, the defective valve will have to be replaced with an artificial one. Similarly, a loose valve can be reconstructed surgically in an operation called *valvuloplasty,* or if necessary, replaced. In coarctation of the aorta, the narrow portion of the blood vessel is removed and the normal sections sewn together.

If the problem is decreased blood flow to the lungs, as in tetralogy of Fallot, then the aim of the surgery is to deliver the oxygen-poor blood to the lungs for oxygenation. A variety of procedures have been devised to accomplish this, including connecting a branch of the aorta to a branch of the pulmonary artery or creating a connection (an anastomosis) between the aorta and the pulmonary artery. Today, total correction of tetralogy of Fallot can be accomplished. This involves enlargement of the connection between the right ventricle and pulmonary artery and closure of the ventricular septal defect.

SURGICAL CORRECTION OF
PROBLEMS OF THE MUSCULOSKELETAL SYSTEM

Damage to the neuromuscular system including the muscles, nerves, and bones, or problems in the areas of brain and spinal cord that control muscle function, can cause muscle dysfunction and deformities of bones and joints (for a discussion of various neuromuscular disabilities, see Chapter 18 of "Diseases of Muscles and Bones"). Severe deformities and disabilities sometimes can be corrected or improved with surgery. Procedures that are used to treat *contractures* (shortening of muscles and tendons) caused by spasticity, hip dislocation, club foot, muscle weakness, and paralysis are described next.

Surgery of Contractures

Children with spastic cerebral palsy have overactive reflexes and tight muscles. Because of the spasticity, the child's arms and legs may be pulled into abnormal positions, which often limit normal movements. To prevent permanent shortening of muscles and tendons (contractures), physical therapy is used in an attempt to relax and stretch muscles. Often such therapy cannot completely prevent a contracture from developing; in these cases, surgical intervention may then be necessary.

Contractures can be treated surgically by procedures to release and lengthen muscles and tendons, called *myotomy* and *tenotomy*, respectively. The procedure involves cutting either the shortened muscle or tendon to allow the affected joint to be manipulated into a central position. After the operation, a cast is applied to the affected limb to keep the joint in proper position, while the cut ends of the muscle or tendon heal. When the cast is removed, physical therapy becomes important to prevent the recurrence of contractures. In some cases, myotomy or tenotomy can be done on an outpatient basis, as in heelcord lengthening. The casts usually remain on the affected limbs for about 4 to 6 weeks. The time of recovery depends on the child's underlying neuromuscular problem and the type of surgical procedure performed. In complex situations, inpatient care is advised.

Surgical Intervention in Hip Dislocation

The unbalanced forces that spastic muscles exert on a joint also can cause dislocation of the bones at the joint. A common example is dislocation of the hip, which develops if the muscles that flex the thigh and those that pull it toward the midline are spastic. These forces tend to pop the head of the bone of the upper leg, the femur, out of its socket (Figure 4). In addition to muscle and tendon releases, it may be necessary to perform an *osteotomy* as well, to correct the dislocation. During an osteotomy, the femur is cut transversely, and after rotation the pieces are realigned so that the two ends of the femur fit together. Sometimes, a wedge of bone from another site is used to help position the cut ends of bone at the desired angle. The bone segments are then fixed in the corrected position with metal screws or wires.

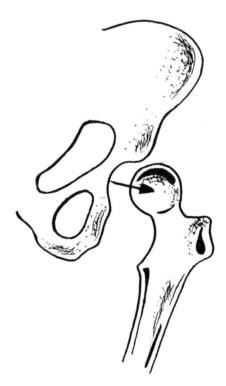

Figure 4.   Dislocated hip. Upper part of femur or leg bone has slipped out of the hip socket, shown by the arrow.

Congenital hip dislocation occurs in some children either as an isolated defect or in association with other defects such as spina bifida. Early treatment of a congenitally dislocated hip is aimed at repositioning the head of the femur in the joint socket, called the acetabulum, and keeping it there in good position (Figure 5). Frequently this can be accomplished by casting or traction alone. In an older child the surgeon may have to "build" an acetabulum through osteotomies and bone grafts.

Surgical Procedures of Clubfoot Deformity

Another common congenital defect of the bones is a *clubfoot,* or *equinovarus deformity.* Before surgery is performed, correction may be attempted with a serial casting procedure. If casting alone is unsuccessful, then treatment may require a combination of tendon releases, muscle transfers, osteotomies, and casting.

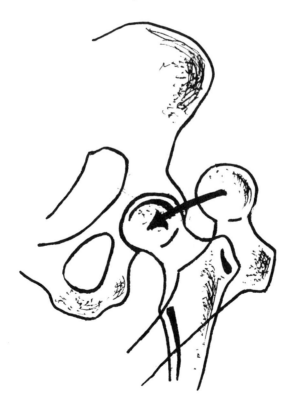

Figure 5.   Arrow shows repositioning of the dislocated leg bone in its proper place in the hip socket.

Surgical Procedures for Muscle Weakness and Paralysis

Any disability that interrupts or prevents the electrical impulses that travel down the nerves to a muscle can cause muscle weakness or paralysis. The degree of muscle weakness or of paralysis of a muscle or group of muscles depends on the number and kinds of nerve fibers affected. Muscles that do not receive nerve impulses, do not grow well and become small or atrophied. Sometimes, movement can be restored or strengthened by a muscle transfer operation. During this procedure an appropriate, normal muscle that is near the weak or paralyzed muscle is separated from the bone to which it normally is attached. This free end then is transferred to the bony attachment of the affected muscle. When the transferred muscle contracts, it then produces movement at the new joint, in effect, replacing the weak or paralyzed muscle. Whether a muscle transfer is practical in a child depends on the kind of deformity present, the particular joint and limb involved, and the status of the muscles available for transfer.

Surgical Procedures for Joint Problems

When a joint is unstable—for example the ankle in a paralyzed foot— sometimes a joint fusion, or *arthrodesis,* is performed. This operation is done both to correct the existing deformity and to prevent a potential progressive deformity. In this procedure, pieces of the bones that come together at the affected joint are removed and the joint is aligned in the desired position. This joint is then stabilized by casting. As healing progresses, the cut surfaces of the bones that are in contact with each other grow together, thus fusing the joint in the corrected position.

Surgical Correction of Spinal Deformities

The spine is composed of many small bones called vertebrae. The vertebrae are lined up one on top of another, creating a bony column in which the spinal cord rests. Moving from the head down, the spine is divided into four regions: cervical—refers to the neck area; thoracic— refers to the chest; lumbar—refers to the lower back; sacral—refers to the pelvic area.

When viewed from the side, a normal spine is not straight like a broomstick, but, rather, is slightly S-shaped, with a mild curve forward of the cervical and lumbar regions (mild lordosis), and a slight curve backward of the thoracic and sacral spine (mild kyphosis).

There are three general types of spinal deformities: too much forward bend, or marked *lordosis;* too much backward curve, or marked *kyphosis;* and an abnormal sideways curve, called *scoliosis* (Figure 6). The spinal abnormalities may be congenital as a result of structural abnormalities in the bones, or, more often, they may develop after birth as a

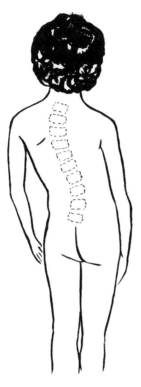

Figure 6. Spine with scoliosis.

complication of neuromuscular disorders such as cerebral palsy, spina bifida, or muscular dystrophy. In many children with scoliosis, the cause of scoliosis is not known; it is then called idiopathic scoliosis.

Patients with a very mild degree of scoliosis most often do not require surgical treatment. However, these children will need regular follow-up to check whether the curvature is increasing over time. Sometimes electrical stimulation of the back muscles is used in mild scoliosis. Moderate degrees of scoliosis can be treated with bracing. Several different kinds of braces have been devised for this purpose. Today lightweight plastic material is used for most braces. Severe scoliosis and gradually increasing scoliosis despite bracing may require surgery. The usual procedure is a *spinal fusion*. The goal of a spinal fusion is to straighten the curve as much as possible and to prevent the vertebrae from shifting further. In order to accomplish this, metal rods called Harrington rods are wired along the spine to maintain proper alignment, accompanied by bone grafts. After surgery the child must wear a plastic body jacket for about 6 to 8 months.

SURGERY OF THE URINARY TRACT

Damage to the nerves that supply the muscles of the bladder, as in spina bifida, will impair normal urination. If the bladder cannot be emptied, the urine that accumulates may become infected with bacteria, and urine reflux, or backing up of urine into the ureters and kidneys, may occur.

Children with spina bifida or a paralyzed bladder can usually prevent these complications by regularly emptying the bladder. This can be done by either pressing on the bladder—which is referred to as Credé's maneuver—or a tube called a catheter can be inserted through the urethra into the bladder at regular intervals (see also Chapter 26 on "Hospitalization and Aftercare").

If these nonsurgical procedures are not successful in preventing reflux of urine into the ureters and damage to the kidneys, then surgery may be necessary. The goal of surgery is to provide unobstructed drainage of urine from the kidneys without the possibility of reflux. Sometimes, this is accomplished by connecting the ureters directly to a stoma, a surgically created opening on the surface of the abdomen. A plastic bag is worn over the stoma to collect the urine. If the ureters are too short or have been damaged, then an ileal loop may be performed. In this operation, a piece of small intestine is used to form a connection or conduit between the ureters and the stoma. (See also Chapter 13, Figures 2 and 3).

In some individuals who lack urinary sphincter control, artificial sphincters may be used, whereby a balloon-type mechanism is surgically implanted around the urethra.

SURGERY TO CORRECT HEARING DISORDERS

The structures of the ear that are primarily responsible for transmitting sound waves are the eardrum, or tympanic membrane, and the small bones in the middle ear, called the ossicles. The inner ear, or cochlea, then transforms the sound waves into nerve impulses that are sent along the auditory nerve to the brain. In order for sound waves to be transmitted, the ear canal must be clear, the eardrum must be able to move freely, and the ossicles must work well and transmit the vibration to the inner ear. An ear canal full of wax, an immobile eardrum, ear infection, fluid in the middle ear, abnormalities of the ossicles, or any combination of these can impair hearing. For additional information on hearing problems, see Chapter 8, on "Sensory Disorders."

Two operative procedures can alleviate a hearing impairment.

1. In severe cases of otitis media (inflammation of the middle ear) where there is an increasing accumulation of pus, a small cut can be made in the eardrum to relieve the pressure and to drain the pus. This procedure is called a *myringotomy.*
2. In chronic serous otitis media with fluid accumulation in the middle ear, a small plastic tube called a ventilation or tympanostomy tube often is placed through the eardrum into the middle ear to enable drainage of the fluid.

SURGERY OF THE EYE

Visual impairment may be an isolated disability or part of a complex of disabilities. Cataracts, glaucoma, and strabismus are among the more common conditions that impair vision, and often are treated surgically.

Cataract Surgery

The lens is the part of the eye that focuses a visual image on the back of the eye known as the retina. A lens that has lost its normal transparency and has become cloudy is said to have a cataract. Some dense cataracts can be identified easily, whereas others can be detected only when the eye is viewed through special instruments such as an ophthalmoscope or slit lamp.

Cataracts as an isolated problem may be inherited or caused by trauma. Cataracts are also associated with a wide variety of disorders including: congenital infections, such as rubella syndrome, inborn errors of metabolism such as galactosemia, hypoparathyroidism, diabetes mellitus, chromosome disorders such as Down syndrome, and other hereditary disorders including myotonic dystrophy.

Surgery is undertaken whenever the cataract significantly interferes with vision. Cataract surgery is done either by extraction of the abnormal lens or by using special, delicate instruments that pulverize the cataractuous lens and simultanously suck up and remove the debris. Following removal of the cataract, the child is fitted with either contact lenses or glasses to correct his or her vision.

Surgical Treatment of Glaucoma

Glaucoma is a condition in which there is increased pressure inside the eye. This elevated pressure can damage the retina and the optic nerve and cause permanent changes in the cornea.

The goal of surgical treatment in glaucoma is to control the pressure inside the eye. This is accomplished by draining the increased fluid in a procedure called a *goniotomy*. If this is unsuccessful, a filtering procedure known as a *trabeculectomy* is performed.

Surgical Correction of Strabismus

Strabismus is an abnormal alignment of the eyes. It includes esotropia (cross-eyedness) in which the eyes turn inward, and *exotropia* (wall-eyedness) in which the eyes turn outward. Some cases are due to underlying defects such as cataracts, tumors, nearsightedness (myopia) or farsightedness (hyperopia). Also, an imbalance in the muscles that move the eyes can cause strabismus. Eye muscle surgery can correct the alignment problem. Amblyopia, or lazy eye, which often accompanies strabismus, usually is treated by patching the normal eye. This promotes the use of the weaker eye until vision in the two eyes is equalized.

RECONSTRUCTIVE SURGERY

The goal of plastic or reconstructive surgery is to restore the normal structure and function of parts of the body that either developed abnormally or have been damaged by disease or trauma. Repair of a cleft lip or cleft palate is an example of a common type of reconstructive surgery.

The plastic surgeon works with soft tissues and muscles as well as with nerves and bones. Grafting of skin, muscle, and bone as well as the use of synthetic prostheses are often part of the reconstructive process. One area in which there has been major progress in recent years is in the surgical treatment of defects of the face and skull, as seen in Crouzon disease and Apert syndrome. The exact type of procedure performed is dictated by the extent of the structural defect present.

ACKNOWLEDGMENTS

Contributions have been made to this chapter by Katherine C. Castree, M.D., and Siegfried M. Pueschel, M.D., Ph.D., M.P.H.

◀ **Chapter 26** ▶

Hospitalization and Aftercare

Being admitted to the hospital often is a frightening experience for children and their parents. With the proper information and preparation, however, a hospital stay can be made much less upsetting for you and your child.

For many developmentally disabled children, frequent trips to the hospital are common. If your child has to be admitted to a hospital, be sure you understand why it is recommended and what is to be gained from the hospitalization. If you are not familiar with certain technical terms, ask that they be explained. Also, ask your child's doctor about the risks involved in any treatment or procedure planned. After all, in order to make decisions regarding your child's best care, you need adequate information about both the benefits and risks of any procedure and therapy.

Some procedures may be absolutely necessary, perhaps life-saving, leaving you little choice. Even for these procedures, you should be informed about the risks and possible adverse side effects.

Anticipated hospitalizations or surgery should be discussed with your child's pediatrician for at least two reasons: First, the doctor should know what the specialists are recommending. Second, the pediatrician may be able to offer a second opinion, if it is warranted. In addition, the pediatrician also may be helpful in recommending other specialists if they are needed for diagnosis, care, and treatment of your child.

PREPARING YOUR CHILD FOR THE HOSPITAL ADMISSION

If your child is old enough to understand that he or she will be admitted to the hospital, tell him or her in simple words shortly beforehand what is going to happen, why he or she is to be hospitalized, and what the outcome will be. Be honest. If you know that there will be some discomfort or something is going to be painful, tell him about it and offer your support and reassurance. Explain how long the pain might last, if you know, or ask the doctor to do this if he has a good rapport with your child.

Some hospitals have programs designed to help children get used to the hospital setting. These programs sometimes include tours of the

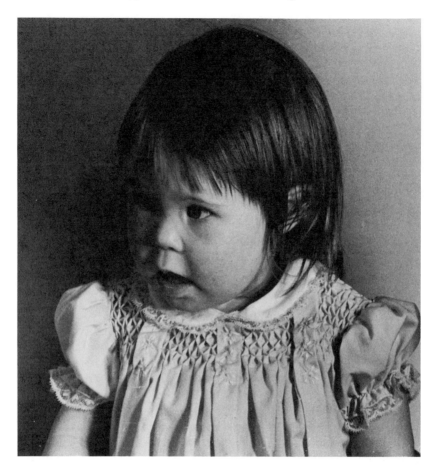

pediatric section of the hospital, discussion of treatment procedures, introduction to play activities, films, and other information that will prepare children for a hospital stay. You may want to check with your hospital before your child is admitted, to see if such a program exists.

You also may find that books for children describing a hospital stay are helpful. Having your child talk to another child who was hospitalized or had a procedure that your child is scheduled to undergo is another way of preparing your child. Such preparation generally helps to reduce fears and apprehensions.

YOUR ROLE IN CARING FOR YOUR CHILD IN THE HOSPITAL

Once your child is admitted to a hospital ward, it is a good idea to get to know the people who will be caring for your child. Introduce yourself to the people who are involved in your child's care. Get to know the staff persons' names and inquire about their respective roles. The more interest you show in what is happening, the more likely it will be that the staff will respect the suggestions and requests you may have. If you can help with your child's care and if it does not interfere with the professional duties of the staff, do so, as it will make your child more comfortable. Many hospitals have unlimited visiting hours for parents and permit overnight stays.

Sometimes parents become frustrated and angry when the hospital staff treat their child differently than the parents do at home. Do not be afraid to tell the hospital staff the ways to approach your child or to explain his or her likes and dislikes. As a rule, the hospital staff would like to make a youngster's stay as pleasant as possible. For example, if a certain position is more comfortable for your child or has been suggested to prevent pressure sores, be sure to show the staff this. You can make helpful reminders by putting a sign in colorful letters over your child's headboard such as "Please sit me up to watch TV."

DISCHARGE PLANNING

If it has not been suggested by the hospital staff, ask to meet before discharge with those persons who have been caring for your child in the hospital. This is particularly important if special equipment, medications, or nursing care is required at home. Such discharge planning should take place far enough in advance to allow time for special arrangements to be made.

If special equipment is needed, a social worker or nurse may be able to help you arrange for its rental or purchase. These professionals also may have valuable information on how to obtain funding for expensive equipment.

HOME CARE FOR YOUR CHILD

Learning What Is Necessary for Home Care

Once a child has been discharged, parents are expected to carry out the basic care procedures at home. For example, a youngster might need ongoing treatments, changes of dressings, or care of a cast. Whatever procedures are needed, they should be taught to you by the nursing staff before your child leaves the hospital. You probably will be asked to be with your child while a nurse demonstrates the procedure. Often, nurses ask parents to practice the procedure while they watch you.

It may be helpful to make a daily plan for your child's care at home that is similar to the one that has been carried out in the hospital. By mapping out a daily schedule, you will be sure not to miss giving medicine, changing a dressing, or doing any other necessary procedures. Be sure to include some fun activities between treatments. This is a good way to pass the time, and generally will help to improve your child's spirits.

Recuperation

The recuperation period, or the time it takes the individual to resume everyday activities, depends on the nature and severity of the disability, the type of surgery done, or the medical problem that led to the hospitalization. The doctor can give you an idea of how long this may be.

While the child's body adjusts to the changes brought on by an illness or an operation and while healing is taking place, frequent periods of rest will be required. This does not mean your child has to sleep during these periods; he or she can play quietly, read, watch television, listen to records, or do other quiet activities.

If your child is confined to bed and activities are severely limited, dietary changes may be necessary to prevent constipation. Also, after certain types of surgery, special diets may be required. Be sure to check with the hospital and with your doctor for any special dietary instructions.

The doctor also can give you some idea of how long your child's activities should be restricted. Following the period of restriction, routine activities should be increased gradually until the child is able to resume his or her usual level of functioning without fatigue. During recuperation from surgery, particularly following orthopaedic surgery, some youngsters will need physical therapy or special exercises.

At times, it is important for your child's progress toward recovery to be monitored by someone with training in health care. If this is needed, a visiting nurse can be involved in home care following hospitalization. Around-the-clock nursing care may be necessary for some children with complex problems requiring numerous procedures. A nurse can assist you with changing dressings, equipment, care of a cast, positioning, and other health-related concerns that may come up. Nurses also can be a valuable tie between you and other health care specialists.

Take Care of Yourself

For severe medical problems that require constant monitoring, there are programs and facilities that can help with your child's care. Some states have pediatric nursing care centers or special programs that provide respite, babysitting, or home care for severely ill children (see also Chapter 31 on "Resource Development").

Many parents with severely ill children may feel guilty about wanting a break from their responsibilities occasionally. In fact, taking a break from the strain of caring for a chronically ill youngster is not only a good idea but is often essential for stressed parents. Spending 24 hours a day, seven days a week attending to the needs of a sick child can quickly use up all of your energy and patience. If such demands on your physical and mental resources continue unabated for a long time, it might even be harmful to your own health. Therefore, taking advantage of any available services can benefit parents and children alike. You may want to check with your local health department, hospital, visiting nurse, pediatrician, health clinic, or social service department for information about respite care and other services for families.

HEALTH AIDS, EQUIPMENT, AND TREATMENT USED DURING POSTHOSPITAL CARE

Many children leave the hospital with prescriptions for special equipment and treatment. Some types of equipment are simple to manage and require little care on the part of the parent or caregiver. Others, however, require some training in order to operate and to keep them in proper working order. For example, you will need to become familiar with specific care procedures if your child is discharged with a plaster cast, tracheostomy, or other appliance.

Casts

If your child goes home with a cast, you will need to make sure that the cast is kept clean and dry. If your child is not toilet trained and the cast is near the diaper area, the edges can be protected by plastic such as Saran Wrap. The edges of the cast should be bound off or covered with adhesive tape to prevent them from causing sores to the skin. The hospital nurse or visiting nurse can show you how to do this.

Other things to watch for are stains that appear on the cast indicating possible bleeding beneath the cast. If you see this, you should call your child's doctor right away. It is a good idea to circle the area using a wax pencil or Magic Marker® and write the date and time on the edge of the circle. Then you will be able to tell if there is any further bleeding.

If you note any odor, especially if foul smelling, coming from beneath the cast, this should be reported to your child's doctor. It could indicate that an infection has developed.

If the case is on an arm or leg, the circulation or blood flow to the area should be checked several times a day, in particular during the first few days after the cast has been applied. Ordinarily, the toes or fingers should be warm to the touch, pink in color, and should not appear swollen. The circulation can be checked by using a process called blanching, which means pressing the tip of a toe or finger between the thumb and the index finger. This causes the toe or finger to turn white. When you release the pressure, you should see an immediate return of pinkness to the toe or finger, indicating that the circulation is good. If the toes or fingers appear bluish-purple in color, are cold to the touch, seem painful, or if they do not blanch, then you should report this to the doctor immediately. It may mean that the cast has become too tight and is interfering with circulation.

Shunt Care for Hydrocephalus

A shunt is a plastic tube that is used to drain excess fluid from the brain in conditions such as hydrocephalus or subdural effusion. During shunt implantation, one end of the tube is placed in one of the ventricles of the brain where the fluid is made or in the subdural space in case of subdural effusion. The other end is inserted into the abdominal cavity where the excess fluid can be absorbed. The rest of the tube lies just under the skin and can usually be seen and felt behind the ear, running down the side of the neck to the chest and abdomen. For more details, see Chapter 25 on surgery.

If your child has a shunt, ask the neurosurgeon how to check for shunt failure, what you need to know about general shunt care, and the signs and symptoms that would indicate that the shunt is not working. Such symptoms include drowsiness, listlessness, irritability, a high-pitched cry, vomiting, seizures, and in the case of very young babies, a bulging soft spot or fontanel on the top of the head. If you think that the shunt is not working and you observe these symptoms, call the physician who put the shunt in place in the hospital or take your child to the nearest hospital emergency room.

Tracheostomy

A tracheostomy is a surgical opening at the front of the throat into the windpipe, or trachea, to make breathing easier. A tracheostomy is usually done when someone is having a severe breathing problem caused by a blocked airway. A tube is placed into the opening of the windpipe, to which a respirator can be attached. It also provides an opening through which oxygen can be administered and mucous suctioned from the main passageways of the lung. Suctioning may be required on a regular basis to keep the airway open. If your child is to have a tracheostomy and particularly if your child is going home with a tracheostomy in place, you will need to be instructed in how to suction your child and how to take care of the tracheostomy.

Because tracheostomy tubes do not allow the child to talk, it becomes important to devise some way to know when the child is trying to communicate with you. Some parents become accustomed to the differences in the child's breathing pattern and can tell if the child is crying or is in need of attention. Sometimes breathing monitors or cardiac monitors are used at home, especially during the night, to be sure the tracheostomy does not become plugged.

You should be aware of the signs and symptoms of respiratory distress or severe difficulty in breathing. They include restlessness; duskiness or a bluish tint to the skin, especially around the mouth, lips, and tongue; gasping for air; rapid breathing; and limpness. Know what to do and who to call if these signs are observed: First, find out quickly whether the airway is obstructed by mucous or whether the tracheostomy is dislodged. If you have been well instructed, you most likely will be able to remove the obstruction by suctioning or by putting the tracheostomy in its proper position. If you cannot relieve the obstruction, then immediately call a local rescue squad or your child's doctor, or take your child to a close-by emergency room, whichever will be the most expedient way to get help for your child. Most important, be prepared for such emergencies.

Respirator

There are many different types of respirators. If your child is placed in a respirator, a respiratory therapist, nurse, or doctor can explain how it works, how to use it, and how to monitor its functioning.

A respirator may assist your child's breathing. The respirator is a machine that can push air, often mixed with oxygen, into the lungs when the lungs or other part of the respiratory system are not functioning properly. The respirator is attached to either a tracheostomy tube or an endotracheal tube. An endotracheal tube is a plastic tube that is placed through the mouth and down the throat into the windpipe, to make a clear passageway for air to enter the lungs. Respirators also are often used during surgery.

When the respirator is no longer needed, you may hear the medical staff talking about weaning your child off the machine. Weaning, in this case, means gradually decreasing a child's dependency on the respirator by giving the child alternate periods of time to breathe on his or her own. Weaning is a normal part of being taken off the respirator.

Oxygen Administration

If your child needs oxygen, it can be administered in one of several ways: by a mask, a nasal cannula, or through a tracheostomy tube. Oxygen masks are usually worn over the nose and mouth. A nasal cannula is a piece of narrow plastic tubing with two short extensions that fit into the nostrils. The different methods of administering oxygen usually include the use of a fine water mist, which keeps the nasal and respiratory passages moist.

The oxygen used in hospitals ordinarily is delivered through an outlet in the wall of the child's room. If oxygen is needed at home, it usually is provided in steel flasks, tanks, or compressors, which can be serviced and maintained by a medical supply company.

Oxygen administered in the home typically is used in combination with a humidifier, oxygen concentrator, or compressor. Be sure to understand how the oxygen supply works, what the auxiliary machines are used for, and who to call if the equipment fails to work properly. Someone from the company that provided the equipment should be able to answer all your questions.

Some children need certain medications mixed in a mist or aerosol solution that is inhaled into the lung. Often these are administered through an oxygen system like the ones just described.

Suctioning

Children with respiratory problems often need to be suctioned to rid the respiratory tract of the excess mucous that is accumulating. During suctioning, one end of a small tube is placed in the respiratory tract and the other end is attached to a suction machine that uses negative pressure, like a vacuum, to suck the mucous and secretions out of the child's nose, throat, tracheostomy, trachea, and lung passages. The technique for suctioning, if your child should need it, should be taught to you by a respiratory therapist or nurse.

Cardiopulmonary Resuscitation

If your child has severe respiratory or cardiac problems, knowing cardiopulmonary resuscitation, or CPR, can be very important. It may help save your child's life in a medical emergency. Courses in cardiopulmonary resuscitation are offered through most chapters of the American Heart Association and the American Red Cross.

Feeding Tubes

There are several ways to feed a child who cannot take food by mouth. Each involves using different types of tubes.

Nasogastric Tube   If a child does not suck well or cannot eat normally, a tube may have to be passed through the nose down the back of the throat into the food pipe or esophagus and then into the stomach. Food, in the form of a formula or other special pureed nourishment, is given through the nasogastric tube. A feeding bag or pouch is attached to the end of the nasogastric tube and then its content is drained into the stomach by gravity. When you insert the tube, it is important to make sure it is in the stomach. Tube insertion should be taught by the hospital staff. They also will instruct you about how often and what to feed your child before leaving the hospital.

For some children, nasogastric tube feedings are used only as a supplement. These children continue to receive some part of their daily nourishment by mouth. Typically nasogastric tube feeding is limited to a short period of time. If feeding problems are chronic or severe, other means of feeding may be used.

Gastrostomy Tube   A gastrostomy is a surgical opening into the stomach, made through the wall of the abdomen. A gastrostomy tube is then placed into this opening. This tube has a balloon cup at its end which is inflated after it is inserted into the stomach. This helps to hold the tube in place inside the stomach.

Special formulas, pureed foods, and other liquids can be given through the gastrostomy tube. The feedings usually flow by gravity, but in some instances may be given by means of a special pump. The type of foods, and how and when they are to be administered should be determined by the attending physician and nutritionist. You may be instructed to add different foods to your child's diet on your own, but it is always a good idea to check with your doctor before making any changes.

When the tube is not in use, a small clamp may be attached to it in order to keep it closed. This clamp usually is pinned to the child's underwear or diapers so that its weight does not pull on the tube.

Central Line   A central line is a means of intravenous feeding and another way of providing nutrition. It is used when there are problems with the intestines and absorption of nutrients. An intravenous catheter is placed surgically into a large blood vessel such as a vein in the neck.

A special intravenous solution called hyperalimentation is administered for a number of hours during the day or night. There are procedures for cleansing the area where the tube enters the skin. Be sure to get instructions from the nurse or doctor before your child is discharged with a central line. Also, arrangements for obtaining special solutions should be made before the child goes home.

Oral Stimulation   For children fed by nasogastric tube, gastrostomy tube, or central line, oral stimulation and good mouth care are very important. Otherwise, these children may come to dislike having things placed in their mouths. If possible, they should be given some food by mouth, even if it is a very small amount. This will help them to accept different tastes and textures later, as well as to keep the sucking, chewing, and swallowing mechanisms working. If your child cannot have any food by mouth, an occupational therapist or speech therapist can advise you about exercises and oral stimulation activities. This is particularly important if your child is expected to feed orally at some time in the near future.

When a child is not fed by mouth, the mucous membranes or linings of the mouth as well as the tongue and lips can become very dry. Good mouth care, gentle brushing of the teeth, and running your finger. covered with a soft wet cloth, over the child's gums and the insides of the cheeks can prevent problems. These techniques help moisten the membranes of the mouth and clean away debris. Lemon and glycerine swabs also can be used to clean the gums and mouth. Vaseline or similar lubricants should be applied to the lips to keep them from becoming cracked and dry.

Bladder and Bowel Aids

Children with spinal cord injuries or spina bifida or who have sustained damage to the urinary bladder or other parts of the urinary tract may need assistance in passing urine. There are two major ways urinary elimination can be assisted: by catheterization or through an ileal loop or conduit (see also Chapter 25 on surgery). Some children will need a colostomy if specific congenital anamolies, tumors, or other gastrointestinal disorders do not allow natural elimination of stool.

Urinary Catheters For children who have poor or no bladder control, intermittent catheterization may be necessary to prevent urinary tract infections and other complications of the kidneys. In addition, catheterization may help reduce the likelihood of children wetting their clothes, and the accompanying embarrassment. A urinary catheter is a thin plastic tube that can be inserted into the urinary bladder to drain urine. Intermittent catheterization is carried out by the parent or other caregiver for the very young, but it is taught to older children so they can do the procedure themselves. It involves passing the catheter through the small opening that leads to the urinary bladder. Intermittent catheterization reduces the chance of infection by preventing urine from remaining in the bladder too long or flowing back into the tubes or ureters that lead to the kidneys.

Ileal Loop or Conduit With the advent of intermittent catheterization, the need for an ileal loop has decreased markedly and is rarely done today. This surgical procedure involves creating a stoma, or opening at the abdomen, through which urine is collected in a drainage bag worn over the stoma. The drainage bag attaches to an adhesive-backed wafer that sticks to the area around the stoma. The wafers are changed as necessary, and the bag is emptied periodically throughout the day (see detailed discussion in Chapter 25 on surgery).

Colostomy   A colostomy is a surgical procedure in which a stoma is created (see Chapter 25 on surgery). A small segment of bowel is surgically brought through an opening of the abdominal wall (stoma), which carries the stool or bowel movement to the exterior of the body. A drainage bag, worn over the stoma, is used to collect the stool. This bag is emptied and cleaned at regular intervals. Good skin care around the stoma is very important, since stool and secretions that are normally in the intestinal tract can be irritating to the skin. Specific care of the colostomy as well as information on nutrition can be obtained from the surgeon or nursing staff who have cared for your child in the hospital.

ACKNOWLEDGMENTS

Contributions have been made to this chapter by Carol A. Musso, B.S., R.N., and Barbara D. Remor, B.S., R.N.

◀ **PART V** ▶

Assessments, Education, and Resource Development

◀ Chapter 27 ▶

Assessing Developmental Disabilities

Psychological Tests and Procedures

Earlier chapters in this book have discussed the many ways developmental disabilities can be detected. This chapter describes the more complex process of assessment. The discussion focuses on evaluation of developmental and intellectual abilities and the psychological tests and procedures used in the process. The following test categories are examined:

Screening tests
Mental and intelligence tests
Developmental tests
Infant tests
Adaptive behavior scales
Achievement tests
Behavioral procedures
Personality tests and procedures
Neuropsychological approaches

Tests in a number of these categories are summarized in Table 1.

Before describing the different types of instruments, a general overview of assessment is provided. It is important to be aware of what various psychological tests and procedures can and cannot tell you. Each type of test is designed to provide a particular kind of information, and each has limitations. Knowing the limitations can help you interpret the results more accurately.

ASSESSING DEVELOPMENTAL PROBLEMS

Assessment, or evaluation, refers to a careful, systematic examination of a child's skills and deficits in order to determine current levels of functioning and future expectations. Basically, an assessment involves

Table 1. Summary of commonly used tests

Test and publisher	Ages	Comments
Screening Tests		
Denver Developmental Screening Test Lodoca Project and Publishing Foundation Denver, 1973	6 weeks to 6 years	Screening test. Identifies possible developmental disabilities in four areas: language, gross motor, fine motor, and personal/social development.
Intelligence Tests		
Stanford-Binet Intelligence Scale Riverside Publishing Co. Chicago, 1986	2 years to 18 years	Norm-referenced intelligence test. Revised in 1986 to provide scores in four subtest areas: verbal reasoning, abstract/visual reasoning, quantitative reasoning, and short-term memory. A full-test composite score also is provided.
Wechsler Preschool and Primary Scale of Intelligence (WPPSI) The Psychological Corp. New York, 1967	4 years to 6½ years	Norm-referenced general intelligence test. Provides a verbal IQ, performance IQ, and full-scale IQ scores. Gives a profile of strengths and weaknesses.
Wechsler Intelligence Scale for Children–Revised (WISC–R) The Psychological Corp. New York, 1974	6 years to 16 years/11 months	Norm-referenced general intelligence test. Provides scores for each subtest, a full-scale IQ score, performance IQ score, and verbal IQ score. Also provides a profile of strengths and weaknesses.
Wechsler Adult Intelligence Scale–Revised (WAIS–R) The Psychological Corp. New York, 1981	16 years and beyond	Norm-referenced general intelligence test for adults. Like WISC–R, it provides a verbal IQ, performance IQ, full-scale IQ, and a profile of strengths and weaknesses.
McCarthy Scales of Children's Abilities The Psychological Corp. New York, 1972	2½ years to 8 years	Norm-referenced test. Provides scores in five areas—verbal, perceptual performance, quantitative, memory, and motor—and offers a general cognitive index for total test performance.
Kaufman Assessment Battery for Children (KABC) American Guidance Services Circle Pines, MN, 1983	2½ years to 12½ years	Norm-referenced intelligence test. Designed to assess learning potential and preferred learning style. Scaled scores for mental processing subtests and composite scores are provided.

Table 1. *(continued)*

Test and publisher	Ages	Comments
Infant Tests		
Bayley Scales of Infant Development The Psychological Corp. New York, 1969	1 month to 2½ years	Norm-referenced test. Provides a mental developmental index, psychomotor developmental index, and infant behavior rating.
Alpern-Boll Developmental Profile Psychological Development Publications Indianapolis, IN, 1972	6 months to 12 years	Developmental scale. Uses interview format to assess abilities in five areas of functioning.
Brazelton Neonatal Behavioral Assessment Scale J.P. Lippincott Co. Philadelphia, 1972	Newborn	Tests newborns' behavioral and neurological status, including responses to environmental events, organization, and behavioral state or level of arousal.
Ordinal Scales of Intellectual Development University of Illinois Press Champaign, IL, 1975	1 month to 2 years	Developmental scale based on Piagetian theory. Contains six ordinal scales measuring level of achievement of the baby on various cognitive abilities.
Adaptive Behavior Scales		
Vineland Adaptive Behavior Scales American Guidance Services Circle Pines, MN, 1984	Birth to 30 years	Adaptive behavior scale. Measures communication, daily living, socialization, and motor skills. Provides standard scores and age-equivalents.
AAMD Adaptive Behavior Scale American Association on Mental Deficiency Washington, DC, 1975	3 years to adult	Contains rating scale for behavioral domains and a scale for maladaptive behavior. Test has been standardized on mentally retarded children.
Achievement Tests		
Peabody Individual Achievement Test (PIAT) American Guidance Service Circle Pines, MN, 1970	Kindergarten to grade 12	Individual achievement test. Assesses skills in mathematics, reading comprehension, spelling and general information. Grade equivalent and age equivalent scores for each subtest and a composite score are available.
Wide Range Achievement Test (WRAT) Jastrak Associates Wilmington, DE, 1978	Kindergarten to adulthood	Individual achievement test originally published in 1936. Contains three subtests: reading, spelling, and arithmetic. Grade equivalent percentile ranks and standard scores available for each subtest. No composite score provided. Test was renormed recently.

(continued)

Table 1. (continued)

Test and publisher	Ages	Comments
Metropolitan Achievement Tests The Psychological Corp. New York, 1978	Kindergarten to grade 12	Achievement test originally published in 1930; revised most recently in 1978. Includes survey batteries for skill assessments and three instructional batteries for diagnostic purposes. Provides fall and spring norms for each grade level.
Iowa Tests of Basic Skills Primary Battery 1979 Multilevel Battery 1978 Riverside Publishing Co. Chicago, 1979	Kindergarten to grade 9	Achievement test battery. Assesses performance in reading, mathematics, spelling, language usage, and work study skills.
Neuropsychological Test Batteries		
Halstead-Reitan Neuro- psychological Test Battery for Children V. H. Winston & Sons Washington, DC, 1974	9 years to 14 years	Comprehensive battery of cognitive, motor, and perceptual tests from which an index of neurological impairment is calculated. Includes 11 tests and can take 6 or more hours to administer.
Luria-Nebraska Neuro- psychological Test Battery— Children's Version Western Psychological Services Los Angeles, 1981	Children	Standardized test battery containing 11 subscales including gross and fine motor, tactile and visual functions, rhythm, speech, memory, reading, writing, arithmetic and intellectual processes. Test takes approximately 2½ hours to administer.

gathering information through observing behavior, interviewing children and families, and testing. What actually takes place during a specific assessment depends on what information the parent and evaluator want to know. In other words, the purpose of the assessment determines the types of tests and procedures used. There are numerous reasons for having evaluations. One parent may want to know how a child is developing in general compared to others his or her age. Another may be concerned about a specific performance area such as speech or motor coordination. Evaluations can be tailored to answer both general and specific concerns of families.

Formal testing can thus answer a variety of questions, each having a different purpose. The list following summarizes a number of assessment purposes, including diagnosis, prediction, selection, intervention, and program evaluation.

Diagnosis: to determine whether an individual has a problem and, if so, what kind.

Prediction: to make a scientific guess about what is likely to happen in the future for some individual or group of individuals.

Selection: to choose individuals for inclusion in a group. In developmental disabilities, tests may be used to determine who may benefit from special services, or who may be ready to change from one program to another.

Intervention: to obtain information about how a specific individual functions and to use this information to plan appropriate education or treatment programs.

Program Evaluation: to determine how well an educational or treatment program is succeeding in achieving its goals.

When testing children for possible developmental disabilities, professionals usually are concerned about diagnosis, prediction, and intervention. They want to determine if a youngster has a developmental problem, the extent of the disability, and the best type of intervention for the identified problem.

During an evaluation, professionals have to judge whether an individual child's performance on a test deviates from the normal or typical performance of children of the same chronological age. This type of comparison of a specific child to average children forms the basis of many useful assessment scales. Such scales, sometimes referred to as norm-referenced or normative tests, are designed so results can be summarized easily and expressed as numerical scores. An intelligence test, which provides an IQ score, is an example of a norm-referenced test. Many IQ tests also are standardized; that is, the procedures for administering and scoring the test are clearly specified and are performed the same way every time the test is given. When an individual's test score is significantly below the norm and parents and evaluators feel the child's performance during testing accurately represented his or her skills, then the evaluator is likely to conclude that there is a developmental problem. Minor deviations from the norm are more difficult to interpret. In some individuals, the test score will reflect a mild disability, whereas in others, it may indicate that the child was not performing up to par during the evaluation. When the findings are ambiguous, periodic retesting may be needed to get a better picture of the child's rate of development and learning.

Comparing an individual child's test score to the average is just one way to evaluate ability. Professionals also observe the child's behavior during testing and inquire about self-care skills and other adaptive abilities. Noting how a child approaches a task, interacts with the examiner, focuses on test items, and attends to events in the environment are some of the observations evaluators make during testing. Such information, along with test scores, gives a truer picture of the youngster's capability. For children with handicapping conditions, the impact of the handicap on opportunities to learn, the effect of adaptive equipment, and the youngster's attempts to compensate for the handicap all must be considered during the assessment. For example, a youngster with severe cerebral palsy who has difficulty controlling facial muscles may not be able to speak intelligibly. Yet, the child may have developed age-appropriate skills in understanding language and in communicating in other ways. The evaluator is faced with the task of assessing the child's language abilities, whether they involve sign language, total communication, use of communication boards, or other alternative systems. Regardless of the impairment, examiners of developmentally disabled children have to assess areas of strength, deficits, and methods of compensation. The more accurate the assessment, the better tailored to the individual can be the necessary educational and treatment programs.

Many psychological tests and procedures can be used effectively to assess the skills of handicapped children. Some developmental disorders, however, are so severe or affect one area of functioning to such an extent that it becomes impossible to use certain standardized tests. In such instances, special tests designed for impaired children or modifications to existing instruments will be necessary. In general, the greater the impairment of one or more senses—seeing, hearing, feeling—and the greater the disruption of the child's response systems—speaking, gesturing, and moving—the harder it will be to discover the child's skills and competencies.

Evaluators of developmentally disabled children must consider the impact of the impairment on the child's ability to show what he or she knows. They also must consider what interpretations and generalizations can be made from results obtained from modified tests and procedures. And they need to be comfortable working with children with handicaps, to help them feel at ease and to encourage them to attempt tasks that may be difficult.

To summarize, professionals assessing children with developmental disabilities administer tests and procedures to answer questions about children such as: Is the sequence or rate of development normal or unusually retarded? Is a particular area of development affected, or is the effect observed in all areas? Can a specific disorder be recognized, and if so, are effective treatments available? Are there ways to compensate for the functional effects of a handicap? In addition, many professionals view assessment as an ongoing process in which progress toward developmental goals can be monitored through periodic assessments or recurring evaluations.

TEST VALIDITY AND RELIABILITY

Psychological tests and procedures vary in length, format, and purpose. Some are administered individually, while others are given to groups of people. Some are paper and pencil tests, others are oral, and still others involve object manipulations. Some seem like tests taken in school; others seem more like play or games.

Different tests are designed to measure various aspects of development. How well a test succeeds in measuring what it is expected to measure is called the *validity* of the test. When selecting assessment instruments, professionals consider a test's validity. For results to be meaningful, the test first has to be valid. As an example of how validity can affect findings, imagine a test of mathematical skills that only asks a child to count sets of objects. Although the test involves numbers, the child does not have to demonstrate any computational skills. Thus, the results would not be a valid measure of mathematical ability for a school-age child.

Another important consideration is test *reliability*. Reliability refers to the consistency of a test's results. A test administered twice to the same individual should yield the same or very similar results. If the findings are very discrepant, then the test would not be considered reliable. The more reliable a test, the more confidence the evaluator can have in the value of the results. Of course, individual characteristics of the child, the testing situation, and other circumstances still must be considered when interpreting the findings.

In developing tests and proedures, professionals begin with a particular theory or belief of how children grow and develop. These theories and beliefs influence what types of test items will be included, the purpose of the test, how the test is constructed and, how the results will be interpreted. It is helpful for parents and others who are the recipients of a child's test results to understand something about the test itself, how it was developed, its theoretical basis, and what it purports to measure.

TYPES OF TESTS

The majority of tests and procedures used in assessment can be classified as either *norm-referenced* or *criterion-referenced* tests. These terms describe how the tests were developed and whether the findings are compared to the average performances of others or to some standard criteria. Other types of tests, sometimes referred to as *process-oriented* procedures, look at the specific strategies children use in solving problems or in responding to events in their environment.

Norm-referenced Tests

As previously stated, norm-referenced tests compare an individual's test score to the average score of a group. Norm-referenced tests can be developed for any subject matter or area of functioning. Both intelligence tests and achievement tests, discussed later in the chapter, are norm-referenced tests. The norms are the average scores or standards against which an individual score is evaluated. They typically are found in tables in the test manual and show the expected scores for children at various ages. These comparison scores, often referred to as age norms, are established through painstaking research, usually with hundreds of children at each age level.

Instead of age-norms, certain tests utilize grade level norms as the standard of comparison. Thus, scores are reported as the level of functioning expected of youngsters in a particular grade. For example, a score of 4.1 on a mathematics achievement test with grade level norms indicates that the child's mathematic skills are equivalent to those expected of a youngster in the first month of the fourth grade.

Norms can be established for any group of interest, such as children with a common developmental disability or medical diagnosis or even a common cultural background. It is important to know if the comparison group on which the test is based differs from the child being tested in important ways. If significant differences exist, the test may not be appropriate for the child, and if administered, the results could be incorrect or misleading. For example, if a child tested on a norm-referenced intelligence test is found to have a lower than expected score, at first glance you might conclude that the youngster lacks certain expected thinking abilities. But, if the child tested is severely hearing impaired and the normative group consisted only of hearing youngsters, the appropriateness of the test and results suddenly is called into question. The hearing impaired child would be at a disadvantage, particularly if the test contained many oral questions and answers. The test would not be evaluating this youngster's thinking skills at all, but rather the responses to questions that were heard. In the same way, if the normative group included only native English-speaking children but the child being tested speaks a foreign language, then the results would be inaccurate. At times, it may be useful to know how a child who differs from the norm performs on particular test items when compared with the general population, but one must be very careful about such comparisons, so that certain problems are not misdiagnosed.

Criterion-Referenced Tests

Criterion-referenced tests compare a child's performance to a specific standard or criterion. The criterion outlines what the child is expected to do and how he or she is expected to perform it. Whereas the results of a norm-referenced arithmetic test might tell you how a child's performance compares to that of other children in the fifth grade, a criterion-referenced arithmetic test would show exactly what arithmetic skills the child possesses. Each kind of test is useful for different purposes.

Criterion-referenced measures concentrate on finding out what a particular child has accomplished. The test presents the child with an ordered sequence of test items. Each item is considered to represent an essential component of the area being tested. In arithmetic, items might include counting, demonstrating one-to-one correspondence, adding single-digit numbers, adding double-digit numbers, subtraction, and other similar items. If a youngster successfully completes all questions up to adding double-digit numbers, the evaluator will know that the youngster has learned the necessary prerequisite skills but requires instruction in addition of more than one digit.

This approach can be very helpful to professionals planning educational or remedial programs for specific children. Criterion-referenced tests assume, however, that the essential skills needed have been defined, analyzed, and sequenced properly for the subject being tested. More success in defining tasks in motor development, self-care skills, and academic achievement has been achieved than has been the case for social or emotional development and thinking abilities.

Process-Oriented Measures

Certain tests are designed to assess the methods children use to solve problems or to complete tasks. Such tests often are referred to as process-oriented measures, as they focus on the process or strategy the child employs. An example of a strategy used by very young children working on puzzles is trial-and-error. They typically select pieces at random and try to fit them into openings on the puzzle board. Older children who have had experience with puzzles develop more efficient strategies such as looking for openings with particular shapes or finding pieces with characteristic edges, colors, or pictures.

A number of psychological tests and procedures use a process-oriented approach. Some of these are based on the work of the well-known Swiss psychologist Jean Piaget, who studied thinking strategies of young children. From his observations, he developed a theory on the development of intellectual abilities. The Ordinal Scales of Intellectual Development is an example of a process-oriented test based on Piaget's theory.

Instead of process-oriented measures, some psychologists use the term *qualitative-developmental assessment* to refer to the evaluation of a youngster's thinking strategies. This term indicates that it is the quality of thinking not the quantity of knowledge that is of interest, and it suggests that the quality of thinking changes as children develop and mature.

The sections following describe the basic categories of tests and procedures. The tests described generally are constructed as norm-referenced, criterion-referenced, or process-oriented measures. As space does not allow a description of all of the published psychological tests, only a few are highlighted here. For further reading, additional references are provided in the bibliography at the end of this book.

Screening Tests

The purpose of a screening test is to quickly distinguish individuals who are at risk for having or developing a particular problem from those who

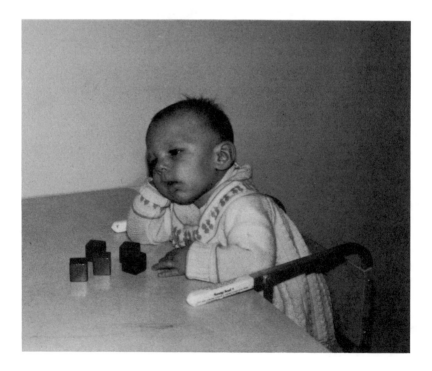

are not. The job of developmental screening tests for children is to identify those youngsters who might have a developmental disability.

Screening tests often are a first step in the evaluation process. Many school systems, physicians, health centers, and visiting nurse associations routinely administer screening tests to locate those children who might be in need of special services.

One of the most frequently used screening tests is the Denver Developmental Screening Test. It assesses four areas of development in children from birth to 6 years of age and can be administered in 15 to 20 minutes. Areas screened include the child's fine motor abilities, personal and social development, language development, and gross motor abilities. When a child fails items that 90 percent of children of the same chronological age successfully complete, the results are considered questionable or abnormal depending on the total number of items failed. When a child passes all or most items, the results are called normal. Children with questionable or abnormal findings will need to be followed closely, with rescreening after a few weeks or perhaps a full comprehensive evaluation.

Compared to screening, a comprehensive assessment is a more detailed, more complete process that provides both descriptive and diagnostic information. An assessment should include a discussion of the factors that help, hinder, or influence a child's performance, as well as recommendations for remedial or rehabilitative programs for the child.

Mental and Intelligence Tests

Mental and intelligence tests traditionally have been among the most frequently used psychological tests. Yet, the concept and validity of intelligence testing remains controversial. Professionals disagree on definitions of intelligence, on what constitutes an appropriate measure of intelligence, and how so-called intelligence tests differ from tests of school achievement. Despite the controversy, many people believe that intelligence tests have validity as assessments of the combination of abilities that enable a person to deal competently with situations according to the society's values. In short, intelligence tests attempt to measure an individual's thinking and problem-solving skills.

Mental or intelligence tests are intended to measure cognitive abilities. *Cognition* is a general term for thinking and includes: sensing; perceiving; recognizing; remembering; differentiating one thing from another; developing concepts; understanding pictures, words, and numbers; judging; solving problems; and reasoning. Tests that assess cognitive skills are concerned with thinking and how a person takes in, thinks about, and uses information. Intelligence tests also frequently tap specific knowledge or facts. Items typically included in intelligence tests may ask a person to define a word, compare two pictures, sort objects into groups, make a drawing, complete a puzzle, solve a problem, answer questions, or perform other kinds of mental activities. Most intelligence tests rate a child's responses on the different test items and compare this performance rating, or score, to the average score of children of the same chronological age. The Stanford-Binet Intelligence Scale, Wechsler Intelligence Scale for Children–Revised (WISC–R), and the McCarthy Scales of Children's Abilities are well-known examples of this kind of test. A new intelligence test, the Kaufman Assessment Battery for Children (KABC), was published in 1983. It is a useful, easy-to-administer test that gives information on a child's learning style.

Test results usually are expressed as a number, but the number alone is meaningless unless something is known about the range of possible scores and the average score for the age group. For example, if you were told a child obtained a score of 49 on a test, it would not be clear if this was a passing or failing mark or perhaps an excellent score. If you were told the maximum score possible was 50, you would know the child did very well. If 100 was the top score, then this youngster did poorly. If the youngster was 5 years old and the average score for a 5-year-old was 50, you would conclude that this child achieved what would be expected for his age.

Mental Age   Some intelligence test results are given as a mental age score, or MA. Mental age provides an age equivalent for the child's test score. To illustrate, suppose that a particular test has the following norms: the average score for 5-year-olds is 50; for 6-year-olds, 55; and for 7-year-olds, 60. Then suppose a 7-year-old child was tested and obtained a score of 55; one would say that this youngster was functioning at a mental age of 6 years old on this test.

The terms *test age, functional age,* and *developmental age* mean much the same thing as *mental age.* You may see these terms used in psychological reports as well as in other developmental evaluations. They all convey the relationship between a specific child's performance and the age at which that level of ability is considered typical.

Although the concept of mental age is useful and relatively easy to understand, it has some limitations that should be kept in mind when interpreting test results.

First, a specific score means very different things when earned by youngsters of different chronological ages. A 2-year-old who achieves a mental age of 5 years has much greater potential than a 10-year-old earning the same score.

Second, by itself mental age does not reveal anything about an individual's strengths and weaknesses. Knowing that an 8-year-old child earned a mental age of 6 years does not tell you whether the youngster does well in language tasks or has trouble in arithmetic, or perhaps has exceptional skills in object manipulations and verbal abilities. For the results to be more meaningful, you should know the mental age score expected for the child tested and something about the child's pattern of achievement on test items.

Intelligence Quotient An intelligence quotient, or IQ, is a test result expressed as a number that conveys how a child did on the test and how the performance compares to what was expected for the youngster's age.

Many tests use IQ scores. Among the most frequently used are the Stanford-Binet Intelligence Scale and the Wechsler Intelligence Scales, including the Wechsler Preschool and Primary Scale of Intelligence (WPPSI), the Wechsler Intelligence Scale for Children–Revised (WISC–R), and the Wechsler Adult Intelligence Scale–Revised (WAIS–R). The McCarthy Scales of Children's Abilities uses a General Cognitive Index, or GCI, that is basically the same as an IQ score. The Bayley Scales of Infant Development offers both a Mental Development Index (MDI) and a Psychomotor Development Index (PDI), which are similar in nature to the IQ. IQ tests have been designed statistically so that the average score, also called the mean, expected at each age is 100 and the standard deviation is 15 or 16 points.

The standard deviation is a standard against which specific scores can be evaluated. It describes how much better or worse an individual score is when compared to the expected score for the population. In statistics, each standard deviation above or below the average represents a percentage of the population. For example, scores falling within one standard deviation above and one standard deviation below the average or mean will always represent 68 percent of the population of interest. Scores within two standard deviations of the mean account for about 95 percent of the population. Figure 1 shows the standard deviations and corresponding population percentages for a test with a mean of 100 and a standard deviation of 15.

Intelligence tests and IQ scores have been shown to be related to other abilities of the child, particularly academic achievement. Examining the patterns of correct and incorrect answers on the test can provide information about the youngster's abilities and can help clarify problem areas. IQ tests also can be used in measuring change over time.

Intelligence tests and IQ measures also can be misunderstood and misused. Intelligence tests measure a number of skills but do not provide a complete study of abilities or characteristics. They do not tell us, for example, whether the child is creative and imaginative, musical, talented in painting or drawing, or has leadership abilities. How the child works during the test can reveal something about eagerness to

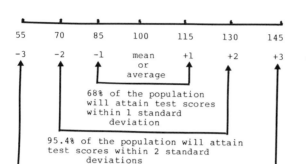

Figure 1.   Standard deviations and corresponding population percentage for a test with a mean of 100 and a standard deviation of 15.

achieve, interest, and concentration, but the IQ score does not tell us how motivated the child is in other situations or how hard that child will work to get something accomplished. Nor does the IQ score measure the value of a person. Whether one is kind or cruel, loving or selfish, for example, is not a matter of IQ at all. In addition, many factors may affect a child's performance on the day the test is taken and, consequently, the IQ score. Fatigue, nervousness, and illnesses all can influence a youngster's performance.

Keep in mind, too, that some intelligence tests are known to give higher or lower IQ scores than others. Thus, there can be variations in a child's IQ simply due to the test used. IQ scores also may change over time for the reasons that some tests measure different skills at different ages, children themselves change, and children may perform differently in one place than another.

It is best to regard IQ scores simply as one of many measures of a child's abilities that can be useful in planning needed educational or treatment services.

Developmental Tests

Developmental tests arrange test items into steps or periods in the order in which the child is expected to learn or acquire the skills the items represent. These tests assume that development occurs in an orderly or predictable way, that persons do not necessarily mature at the same rate, and that the level or stage of maturity can be measured by performance on certain tasks or activities.

Developmental tests usually are norm-referenced, criterion-referenced or process-oriented, and may be used to assess cognitive, language, social, motor, or self-care skills.

Some developmental tests may require the child to answer questions and perform activities in a number of different skill areas. Others may use an interview or checklist format where the examiner obtains information about the child's skills from the parent or other person who knows the child well. Test results may be reported as a developmental quotient or DQ, but findings often are described in terms of developmental age or level. A number of developmental tests are planned with educational or training activities to help the child make developmental progress once the child's developmental status has been measured.

Frequently, developmental tests are administered several times during a period of treatment or special programming to monitor a child's progress. As children change, the kinds of learning opportunities or support services they need also can be expected to change. Assessments may need to be repeated periodically to assess changes in the child's level of functioning and to be sure that the best possible match between the child's needs and opportunities is being maintained.

Infant Tests

Assessment of infants has become increasingly important as people become more and more concerned about identifying as early as possible children who have or may have developmental disabilities.

Like other tests, many infant tests are norm-referenced or criterion-referenced measures. The Bayley Scales of Infant Development, a norm-referenced test, is one of the most widely used infant devices. It is used with children up to 30 months of age and gives a Mental Developmental Index or MDI, a Psychomotor Developmental Index or PDI, and an Infant Behavior Rating or IBR. The Mental Development Index is much like an IQ measure and has many of the characteristics, uses, and limitations mentioned earlier.

An example of a process-oriented infant test is the Infant Psychological Development Scale, developed by Uzgiris and Hunt and based on the work of Jean Piaget. This well-known measure provides valuable information about thinking abilities considered important for all babies. The Brazelton Neonatal Assessment Scale is another type of infant test developed specifically to assess the behavioral status of newborns. It considers a newborn's responses to a variety of stimuli along with the baby's "state" or level of arousal.

The development of tests and procedures for newborns and very young babies has come about for a number of reasons. One is the group of discoveries by professionals showing what many sensitive parents have felt all along—that newborns and young babies are much more competent and capable of purposeful behavior than was believed previously. Another reason is the increased interest in identification and treatment of developmental problems as early as possible. Through research, professionals have learned that signs of developmental disabilities can be detected in preschool years and even in infancy. One does not have to rely solely on a baby's motor performance or the onset of language to find out what the baby knows. Other measures such as changes in heart rate and in sucking patterns, observations of visual attention, and evaluation of an infant's abilities to attend to, recognize, understand, and remember visual and auditory stimuli, all provide valuable information about infant capabilities.

Infant tests in general use have been most successful in predicting later performance when the baby's current performance is much below what is generally expected for his or her age. Very little success has been achieved in predicting future performance with infants, particularly ones under 1 year of age, who are developing normally. Generally, the older the child and the shorter the time between testings, the more likely that one test performance will predict the next. One reason for this seems to be that many of the items on infant tests examine motor skills, whereas tests for older children concentrate much more heavily on language and thinking skills. Although movement is important for its own sake, there is not always a direct relationship between movement and the kind of thinking that is occurring in young infants and older children.

Babies and very young children can be delightful to work with, but they are not easy to evaluate. They often need to be fed or changed, they tire easily or fall asleep, and they may become distressed when handled by an unfamiliar person. And infant tests can be difficult to conduct. The examiner cannot ask questions or simply give the baby directions to follow. Considerable training and practice is needed to carry out the testing procedures correctly and to gain the baby's cooperation. When testing infants, knowledge of normal infant development is essential, as is an awareness of developmental problems and of how they can influence the results of assessments. As with all types of assessment, if a disability is detected, it is important for the professional to be able to translate the assessment findings into programs to help the baby progress developmentally and to be able to interpret the results and recommendations clearly to the parents and other interested professionals.

Adaptive Behavior Scales

In order to gain a better understanding of how people get along in the world, we need to know about what is called their adaptive behavior. *Adaptive behavior* refers to skills in social interactions, emotional adjustment, and self-care.

In all areas of self-help skills, there is a developmental sequence of increasing independence. Most individuals learn to take care of their own needs to be fed, clothed, sheltered, and kept clean.

Social skills also are achieved in a developmental sequence. These involve tasks such as learning to respond to and interact with people, to play with games and toys, to participate in social activities, and to work at increasingly complex jobs. The ability to exchange information, ideas, and feelings with other people plays an important part in developing social competence.

Rating scales typically are used to assess adaptive skills. The most frequently used instruments are the Vineland Adaptive Behavior Scales and the American Association on Mental Deficiency Adaptive Behavior Scales. A psychologist goes through the rating scale with an informant, usually a parent, who knows the individual being evaluated very well. The parent answers questions about the child's skills, such as "Can he feed himself neatly with a spoon and fork?" "Can he play cooperatively at the kindergarten level?" or "Can he wash his hands unassisted?" Some scales provide an overall rating, which is reported in terms of age scores. Others indicate how well an individual performs in a number of areas of functioning, compared to a normative group.

Information about adaptive behavior is crucial when a diagnosis of mental retardation is being considered. There must be significant impairment or delay in both adaptive behavior and cognitive ability before a person can be diagnosed as mentally retarded. The information derived from adaptive behavior scales is useful in educational programs. Teachers can see when a student needs extra instruction to learn a skill and to achieve greater independence.

Achievement Tests

Achievement tests are used to measure what a child has learned. Often this means the subject matter that has been learned in school—for example, reading, spelling, and arithmetic. Like mental tests, achievement or educational tests may be administered individually or to groups of children. They must be both reliable and valid, and must produce results that will give meaningful information about each child's skills. Commonly used individual achievement tests include the Peabody Individual Achievement Test (PIAT) and the Wide Range Achievement Test (WRAT). The Metropolitan Achievement Tests and Iowa Tests of Basic Skills are examples of widely used achievement batteries that often are administered in groups. Many achievement and educational tests report scores in terms of grade level norms.

In order to find out which tasks a child needs to master, many different kinds of skills may be tested. When the child's specific areas of weakness are defined, appropriate remedial programs can be planned.

The goal of remedial instruction is to improve a youngster's abilities in the deficit area. If the problem is one that cannot be corrected or improved, then it is important to help the child learn alternate ways to accomplish what needs to be done.

Educational tests are usually administered by educators, including classroom teachers, resource teachers, special educators on a diagnostic team, or by psychologists. Remediation, or the development of alternate methods to correct a problem, usually is done by teachers who have special training in helping children who have learning difficulties. These teachers use the information from both mental and educational tests to plan an individual remediation program for each child.

Sometimes pretests and posttests are used to help evaluate a child's progress. Pretests are given before a specific intervention program is begun, whereas posttests are administered after the intervention to assess its effectiveness.

Behavioral Procedures

Behavioral assessment is a method of collecting and analyzing information about a child's responses to specific situations. The major goal of behavioral assessment is to measure reliably what the child does under certain circumstances or environmental conditions. The term *behavior* is used in the broadest sense and can refer to any activity of the child that is of interest. It could be anything a child says or does. *Environment* refers to those conditions that exist when the behavior occurs.

To understand the relation between behavior and the environment, behavioral psychologists first must collect the necessary information, often referred to as the ABCs of behavior. *A* is for *antecedent*, or events that happen before the behavior occurs. *B* stands for the particular *behavior* of interest, or what is observed. *C* is for the *consequence*, or what happens immediately after the child displays the behavior.

Psychologists conduct behavioral assessments to clarify a behavioral problem—that is, discover when it occurs, how often, and under what circumstances—and to devise strategies for changing or modifying the problem behavior.

Behavioral assessment typically involves direct observation. Observations are best completed in the settings where the problem behavior occurs. If direct observation is impossible for the professional, parents or others can supply the necessary information.

The measurements used in behavioral assessments usually consist of *frequency* measures, which count how often a particular behavior occurs within a given period of time in a particular setting or environment; and *duration* measures, which record how long the particular behavior lasts. These measurements may be taken continuously, counting all the behaviors during a certain period of time; or by time sampling, counting the behaviors in a representative period of time (e.g., the first 15 minutes of each hour throughout the day, every 10 minutes during the morning, 5 minutes of each period of seatwork assigned). This information is summarized, so changes in how often the behavior occurs or how long it lasts can be noted easily while a behavioral program is being carried out. Typically, these data are shown on a graph. This type of analysis provides the psychologist with the necessary information to develop a treatment strategy to bring about a change in the target behavior.

Behavioral assessment is a very useful technique for planning ways to help an individual change. And it can be used to measure how much change has occurred. One potential drawback to behavioral assessment is that a complete, thorough analysis of behavior can be very time-consuming. However, if the assessment leads to an effective intervention for a serious behavior problem, the time is well spent.

Personality Tests and Procedures

Each individual reacts to the environment with a particular set of characteristics and behaviors that are unique. Personality is the term often used to refer to those patterns of behavior. People typically describe aspects of someone's personality with adjectives like *friendly, aggressive, shy, hostile, energetic, fearful,* and *outgoing,* to name a few.

Assessment of personality may be useful for a variety of reasons, such as vocational counseling or planning for treatment of emotional disorders. There are three basic methods of assessing personality:

1. *Observational techniques* involve systematically watching an individual in a natural setting, such as at home or in school. The information gathered may be organized in several ways—for example, by rating various characteristics and behaviors.

2. *Personality inventories* are questionnaires completed by the individual being assessed. For instance, a person might be asked to mark "True" or "False" in response to questions such as "I am often ill-at-ease in a large group of people," or "Being a success at anything I do is very important to me." Results of inventories can be interpreted to give a description of an individual's personality.

3. *Projective techniques* involve the presentation of stimuli such as ambiguous pictures, incomplete sentences, or inkblots. The individual is asked to respond to the stimuli—for example, to tell a story about a scene depicted in a picture, to finish the sentence, or to describe what the inkblot looks like. Projective techniques tap the individual's imagination and encourage the use of personal experi-

ences, feelings, attitudes, and desires. The interpretation of information from projective techniques is difficult and should be done by well-trained professionals.

Neuropsychological Approaches

Neuropsychological testing is an orderly way of using psychological tests and observations to study relationships between the brain and behavior, that is, how the function of the brain affects our abilities, strengths, and weaknesses. Neuropsychological assessments may be used to detect specific problems in the brain, where the problems are located, and what the impact of the problem is on a person. A variety of standard neuropsychological test batteries are in use.

Areas generally assessed by neuropsychological test batteries include the sensory-perceptual systems such as vision, touch, or hearing; cognitive or thinking activities such as memory and comprehension; motor coordination; and left-right dominance patterns in use of hands, feet, and eyes. Other areas often investigated are problem solving, reasoning, concept formation, language, and emotional responses.

The tests may be interpreted in several ways: by comparing the individual's performance with others in the same group, by an analysis of the pattern of scores obtained on the various tests in the battery, or by detection of an abnormal sign indicating grossly unusual functioning.

Two neuropsychological test batteries frequently used are the Halstead-Reitan and Luria-Nebraska test batteries. Neuropsychological testing is often quite lengthy and may be more expensive than other types of psychological testing. It is usually reserved for very special cases where information cannot be gathered in any other way, and it is most often used along with information from physicians and other professionals.

THE PSYCHOLOGICAL REPORT

After a psychological assessment, a report of the findings should be written. The following information should be included in a psychological report and should be stated clearly and concisely.

1. The purpose of the assessment; why the child was seen.
2. How the information was obtained, including the tests used and observations conducted.
3. The results of the tests, interpretation of the findings, and conclusions of the assessment.

In addition to the above, specific recommendations about education or treatment and about how developmental progress for that child can be encouraged should be included if the purpose of the assessment was to plan for a child who has developmental difficulties.

The psychological report should not be a simple recounting of test scores; it should also be accompanied by an interpretation. Interpretation of tests depends in large measure on the examiner's understanding of human behavior, skill in relating to the child, and knowledge of assessment techniques. The examiner must be able to describe the outcome in ways that can be understood by parents and others who will work with the child, and thus be useful to parents and professionals as they plan strategies to help the child.

Those who receive a report of psychological assessment, whether parents or other professionals, should feel free to ask for explanations if they are uncertain about why the assessment was needed; which tests or procedures were used; why these choices were made; what the results mean; or how the assessment can be used in planning for the child. The more clearly the results are explained, the more likely the assessment findings will be used to benefit the child.

ACKNOWLEDGMENTS

Contributions have been made to this chapter by Ellen I. Rollins, Ed.D., Leslie E. Weidenman, Ph.D., and James A. Mulick, Ph.D.

◀   Chapter 28   ▶

Helping Children Learn

Children with developmental disabilities, particularly those with mental retardation, often learn more slowly than other youngsters. Acquiring new skills and ideas may take handicapped children more time and practice and require more opportunities. But developmentally disabled children do learn and, like all of us, they learn from their experiences. For youngsters who are at a disadvantage because of a physical or mental disability, help from parents and professionals can foster learning.

This chapter outlines ways to help developmentally disabled children learn. Both the types of programs available to help very young disabled children and the principles by which children learn are covered.

EARLY INTERVENTION PROGRAMS
FOR DISABLED INFANTS AND TODDLERS

Interventions for developmentally disabled people are aimed at enhancing development and preventing or lessening problems that may result from a developmental disorder. *Early intervention* is a general term describing programs for very young disabled children and their families. Throughout the country, what constitutes an early intervention program, or EIP, and the age range of children served varies. But in most states, early intervention applies to youngsters in the birth-to-3-year-old age range. At age 3, most of these children then are eligible for special education programs in the local school system. New federal legislation, Public Law 99-457, which was passed in 1986, requires that all states provide preschool special education for children in need by 1990. The same law also offers all states an incentive to develop early intervention programs for infants and toddlers by 1991.

How Early to Start?

Since the mid-1950s, ideas about when to begin helping children with handicapping conditions have moved rapidly down the age scale from school-age to preschool to infancy.

In the 1960s, much interest and attention were focused on the impact on children of discrimination and poverty. From this beginning, a special concern emerged about the effects of deprivation, poor nutrition, and unusual early experiences on the development of very young children. During this time, work with preschoolers in programs such as Head Start was emphasized. Important medical advances were also made in the early diagnosis of genetic disorders and birth defects and in their care and management. Parents who wanted help for their children with developmental disorders formed parent groups and became very active in arranging the needed services. The combination of increased knowledge about and activities for children with many kinds of developmental disorders brought this population very much into the public awareness. As a result, programs were developed and professionals began to study the ways disabled infants and toddlers and their families could be helped.

Interest in early intervention has continued to grow. Today, professionals are working to discover ways to detect disabilities as early as possible and to provide the best treatment for the problems identified. This means starting to work with disabled infants at birth or soon thereafter, or as early as the developmental disability is detected. In addition to working directly with disabled infants and toddlers, programs have expanded their focus to include the entire family. Many early intervention programs now offer parent training, counseling, and support groups for families.

Recent research on the learning capacities of infants provides a sound reason for early intervention. Scientists studying very young children have found that infants are much more active learners than was previously believed. The sheer extent of the competencies of newborn and young infants that now are recognized and the amount of learning that occurs indicates that infancy is indeed an appropriate time to begin intervention. For example, scientists have learned that infants as young as 48 hours of age can make fine discriminations in what they hear. Newborns distinguished between noise and vocal-instrumental music. In a study with 1-month-olds, infants were shown to recognize differences in sounds such as "da," "ba," or "a."

Such findings have caused researchers to reevaluate their ideas about normal development, the effects of various skills on each other, the consequences of impaired function, and the possibility of influencing development in beneficial ways.

Researchers also have been evaluating intervention programs to see if particular programs really are helpful. There is now little doubt that intervention can have a powerful and beneficial effect. We seem to be past the initial question: Does intervention work? Researchers now have started to ask more precise questions, such as: What are the characteristics of effective programs? How do different developmental disorders, different ages at entry, length of involvement, and level of participation affect a program's outcome? What are the consequences of particular program design, curricula, and staffing patterns?

There is much to learn about successful ways of encouraging a young child's development. No child is too young to participate in a good early intervention program. Many children are indeed helped, and numerous parents find such programs helpful for themselves as well.

EIPs: A General Description

Early intervention programs vary widely. Differences can be found in all aspects of a program such as the structure, format, focus, services offered, eligibility, and frequency of contact with children and families. Some programs are designed for particular groups—for example, children with Down syndrome or youngsters with autism or severe behavior disorders. Some programs are center-based, to which parents bring their children for individual therapy or group programming. Others are primarily home-based, in which early intervention workers provide services for children at home and show parents how to carry out treatment programs. The required level of parental participation is another variable in early intervention programs. In some programs, parents must attend all sessions with their children. In others, professionals work directly with the youngsters, and parents are encouraged to participate, but are not required to do so.

To meet the variety of needs of families in today's complex society, many programs are offering an array of services in several different formats. With this increased flexibility, programs are better able to individualize service plans to accommodate families. Early intervention programs are becoming increasingly aware of the importance of tailoring programs for specific families and children, for the chances of active participation and success are enhanced when the program fits into the family's daily schedule and life-style.

Early intervention programs generally have representatives from a variety of disciplines on staff to conduct evaluations, outline the needs of the child and family, and develop an appropriate treatment or service plan. Typically, psychologists, social workers, educators, speech therapists, occupational therapists, physical therapists, and nurses are part of early intervention teams. Many programs work closely with hospitals, clinics, or school systems and also share personnel.

Unlike traditional school programs with structured classrooms, early intervention programs, particularly home-based programs, attempt to help families help their infants and toddlers within the context of everyday activities. Many effective teaching programs can be carried out during diaper changes, baths, meals, and play activities. In many instances, guidance and coaching can help parents make their time spent with their child even more productive and more likely to encourage development.

What to Look for in an Early Intervention Program

When choosing an intervention program, one of the most important considerations is whether a match exists between the program services offered and the needs of the child and family. The program should be able to provide the essential services the child requires. Of course, other factors are important too. For example, basic safety and health conditions of the program should meet regulations and parent approval. A clearly specified plan of treatment should be developed for the child, based on needs identified during assessment. Progress on program goals should be monitored regularly and reevaluations performed routinely.

There should be sufficient staff from various disciplines to meet the basic program requirements. Staff members should show interest and pleasure in working with very young children. It also is important for parents to feel comfortable discussing their child's treatment with the program staff. Staff should understand how teaching affects the immediate performance and the ongoing development of the child. They should know the levels at which the child is functioning, understand the relationship of one aspect of the child's behavior to another, be able to design a program specifically for that child's skills, interests, and learning styles, and be able to carry out the program effectively. This requires that program staff be keenly sensitive to the individuality in children, based on a sound understanding of human development, adequate knowledge of the kinds of problems or disorders that can occur, and a thorough knowledge of the materials, methods, and sequences of learning.

Where Are Programs Available?

The majority of states offer some form of early intervention program, although some do not begin until age 2 or 2½. Many programs are administered by a state's Department of Education, Department of Health, Department of Human Services, or other state agency responsible for the care of persons with mental retardation and developmental disabilities. To find out what your state offers, try contacting the state agency for handicapped persons, the Department of Education, or local chapters of national organizations such as the Association for Retarded Citizens-U.S., United Cerebral Palsy, or Easter Seal Society. If your community has a college or university that offers courses or conducts research in developmental disabilities, or if there is a hospital nearby that has a clinic or program for developmental disorders, you might inquire there as well. In addition, the Council for Exceptional Children in Reston, VA, keeps records about educational services that are available for young children with developmental disorders, and will provide information on request.

BASIC TEACHING STRATEGIES

Children's first and most important teachers are their parents; home, in a sense, is their first classroom. Long before children actually go to school, they learn an enormous amount with their parents' help. Basic skills such as walking, dressing, feeding, talking, and playing with toys are just a sample of what children learn in their first few years. Many parents are unaware of exactly how they accomplished so much teaching in such a short time. For parents of handicapped children, understanding how children learn and how to be an effective teacher can be very important, as effective teaching can promote development. This section of the chapter reviews basic teaching strategies.

For any learning to occur, a child first has to pay attention. Paying attention involves focusing one or more of the senses on what is to be learned. Looking, listening, touching, tasting, and smelling are all examples of paying attention. Very young children attend to new and interesting things more readily than familiar, unchanging ones, although using familiar objects in novel ways can quickly capture and hold an infant's attention.

In general, children attend more readily to things they like—things that are fun, taste good, satisfy, or provide comfort—instead of boring, unpleasant, or difficult things. Attention also is affected by one's expectations. As infants' experience broadens, they learn to anticipate changes from the cues in the environment. The cues that predict pleasurable changes generally attract attention well, but children also will attend to cues that predict unpleasant events so they can avoid them if at all possible. Parents can use cues to direct a child's attention to specific activities and learning opportunities. Examples of cues commonly used by parents and teachers are instructions and gestures.

Once children are paying attention, teaching and learning can occur. The most basic principle of learning is that the consequences of our actions affect learning and behavior. This is not a difficult concept, and understanding it gives parents and teachers the most practical learning tool we know. This principle has two basic parts. The first focuses on the effects of positive consequences and is called positive reinforcement. It states: When a child does something that is followed immediately by a consequence the child enjoys or values, the child is more likely to perform the action again. The second concerns the effects of negative consequences or punishment. It states: When the immediate consequence of a child's actions is unpleasant or not valued, then the child is less likely to repeat the action. In short, positive reinforcement increases the likelihood that the behavior it follows will occur again. Punishment is the opposite. It decreases the chances that the behavior it follows will be repeated.

Different children enjoy different things, so considerable care must be taken to ensure that a particular child values a specific consequence in the anticipated way. Even parents who feel certain about their child's likes and dislikes have been surprised. An easy way for parents to test their hunches about their children's likes and dislikes is simply to observe what they do. By noticing what their children choose to play with, eat, drink, and watch on television as well as who they elect to play with, parents can be reasonably certain about what their children find reinforcing and what they dislike. For most children, attention from parents, playing with a favorite toy, special foods, praise, and love are effective positive reinforcers. Children's preferences change as they grow and develop new interests, so effective positive reinforcers and punishers also will change. Remember, you always can tell whether a consequence is a reinforcer or a punisher by observing its effect on the child's behavior.

In general, consequences have to be immediate to be effective. They also have to be provided consistently. This is particularly important when trying to teach a new skill. Children typically need lots of practice, encouragement, and positive reinforcement to learn and refine a new skill. However, once a skill has been acquired, the amount of positive reinforcement needed may decrease, as many skills become satisfying on their own. For example, once a child has mastered spoon feeding, the reward of eating usually is enough to motivate the child to feed himself. Parents no longer need to provide positive consequences every time the child brings the spoon to his mouth. Children generally do not have to be praised to keep eating favorite foods.

Another important aspect of learning relates to the fact that learning takes time. Most tasks are made up of a sequence of steps, each of which must be learned in just the right way and in the right order. Often, useful tasks can take a child many days or weeks to learn. Additional time then is needed for the child to refine the skills. Parents should be patient and expect their teaching efforts to be rewarded by their child's learning on a gradual but steady basis.

Because learning takes time and occurs in small steps, it may be hard to see the steady changes that are occurring. One way to be sure that progress is being made is to keep records. This may involve noting which steps in a complex skill have been mastered, the amount of time needed to complete a task, or the number of times an action has occurred.

To summarize, these basic learning principles operate all of the time and affect children and adults alike. They influence learning whether or not specific teaching is going on. Remember, children learn from all of their experiences. Therefore, a world that contains many opportunities for exploration, play, and stimulation is an important way to ensure that learning can occur. Similarly, all of the things that parents do with children can be instructive and convey love, security, as well as the challenge of new mastery.

DISCIPLINE AND MANAGING BEHAVIOR PROBLEMS

All children initially learn the limits of acceptable behavior from the adults who care for them. Their sense of what is right and wrong develops over the years as a result of the consequences of their behavior, the direct effects of their actions, the reactions of others, and their observations of people around them.

Through discipline, parents begin teaching appropriate social behavior. Later, brothers and sisters, classmates, friends, teachers, and the extended family continue the process by providing feedback in the form of approval or disapproval for a child's actions. This is an important teaching tool. Like other consequences of behavior, the feedback functions as either positive reinforcement or punishment.

Children are keen observers of what others do. Frequently, new behaviors are learned by trying out ways of acting that seem to work for others. Children tend to imitate the actions of important people in their lives, usually people in control, including parents, siblings, popular classmates, and teachers. This is one of the reasons why it is so important to set good examples for children.

Behavior problems do occur. Handicapped children are no different from other children in this respect. All children lack the judgment to understand the effects that their behavior might have on others, and thus require the corrective feedback that parents and others can provide. Many of us treat chronically handicapped children as if they were exempt from discipline. This may be because people feel sorry for children with disabilities or view these youngsters as sick and helpless and, therefore, not subject to the normal rules or standards of behavior. However, unlike a temporary illness that may be associated with understandable lapses in conduct, a developmental disability in many cases represents a lifelong condition to which the child must learn to adapt. Like all of us, children with handicaps will be judged by society according to widely shared values. To the extent possible, disabled youngsters should learn to act and react as any child would under similar circumstances. When handicapped children behave in ways similar to other children, they are accepted more readily into social and recreational activities that can lead to lasting relationships and enhance personal growth.

Developmental disabilities complicate the task of judging whether or not a child is behaving appropriately. In some cases, developmental delays are not associated with impaired physical development, and affected children often physically look like others their age. People tend to expect children who look normal to behave appropriately, regardless of their ability. In other instances, marked physical handicaps are present, but without delays in intellectual development. Such youngsters often are treated as if they were intellectually impaired. First impressions can be misleading.

Behavior problems can be extremely stressful for everyone concerned. Many parents of handicapped children often are not sure how to view some of their children's behaviors. They often ask, Is this something I should be concerned about? or Is this behavior normal? Parents' concerns about how others will perceive them when their children misbehave are common and are quite natural, and in no way unique to parents of handicapped children.

The truth is that behavior problems are normal. Managing behavior problems is easier if they are considered one at a time and viewed as teaching opportunities. Most behavior problems fall into the category of normal problems of childhood—for example, following family rules, using toys and household materials properly, avoiding dangerous and unhealthy substances, and performing everyday tasks. Another set of problems may be related to a child's developmental disability. These include emotional difficulties that result from the disability itself or from the way the child is treated by others.

It can be helpful to think of behavior problems as teaching problems in which there may be behavioral deficits, excesses, or a combination of the two. A behavioral deficit indicates that the child lacks a skill necessary for a particular situation, and thus, behaves inappropriately. An example of this would be a child who eats with his hands because he never has been taught to use utensils. A behavioral excess indicates that a child is doing something too often or too intensely to be tolerated. An example might be the child who cries excessively or has tantrums in order to get his way. A problem resulting from both deficits and excesses is described in the following example. A child becomes disruptive in the classroom when difficult work is presented for which the child lacks the prerequisite skills. Disruptions involve frequent outbursts and antics at which other children in the classroom laugh. The disruptive acts that are the result of a deficit are being reinforced by the attention of the other children.

Managing problem behavior, then, becomes a matter of setting the stage for effective teaching. The problem behavior must be well defined, so that it can be handled consistently by all involved. It is usually a good idea to count or measure problem behavior for some time before trying to change it. This allows one to tell whether or not the consequence selected is working. If the behavior problem happens less often or lasts for shorter and shorter periods of time after the intervention is started, then the strategy for decreasing the unwanted behavior has been successful.

Selecting the specific strategy is a little more tricky. Behavioral specialists and psychologists often work with families on developing intervention strategies for problem behaviors. Behavior problems that are the result of skill deficits are best handled by teaching the required skills. Sometimes the child does possess the necessary skills, but does not exhibit them consistently. This may mean that performing the skill is not followed by satisfying consequences; that is, the behavior is not positively reinforced. Behavioral deficits of this kind can be turned around by ensuring that the good behavior always is rewarded. Attention from parents including praise, hugs, and other expressions of appreciation and love are among the most universal positive reinforcers. Behavior that is followed by this kind of attention usually is strengthened rapidly. Parents always should consider using their attention and praise to increase desirable behavior before other material reinforcers.

Unfortunately, misbehavior often is followed by parental attention. We have a tendency to ignore or take for granted good behavior and to intervene when problems develop. But, because parental attention is such a strong reinforcer, even the attention associated with anger that is lavished on problem behavior can actually strengthen it. When no longer followed by attention, many annoying problem behaviors, such as tantrums and some mild forms of aggression, are eventually abandoned by children.

This is why many parents are encouraged to ignore problem behavior. However, this is easier said than done. Many misbehaviors or behavioral excesses cannot be ignored without the risk of harm to the child or others. Further, even if parental attention had been strengthening the problem behavior accidentally, there also may have been other sources of positive reinforcement for the child's actions. For example, aggressive behavior may result in material gain or temporary resolution of a conflict. A misbehavior may actually feel good to the child when it is performed. Other sources of reinforcement for misbehavior are other people. Attention from friends and neighbors following the misbehavior can negate the effects of ignoring by parents. Finally, even if the original form of problem behavior decreases, there is no guarantee that the child will behave appropriately thereafter. There is still the question of whether the child has the ability to behave appropriately.

Instead of simply trying to eliminate the problem behavior, it is better to determine what you would like to see the child doing in its place. Then, you can go about making the occurrence of desired behavior more likely by teaching it, seeing that it is rewarded, and doing everything possible to make the misbehavior less likely to occur in the future.

Often, increasing desirable behavior serves to displace undesirable behavior, simply because the child cannot do both things at once. Another way to make misbehavior less likely is to change the environment in a way that makes it harder to do anything undesirable. When a room is child-proofed and breakable objects are placed out of reach of small children, an environmental change has been made. We are less likely to think of a child who actively explores an environment that has been child-proofed as hyperactive or destructive. Such precautions can give us an opportunity to introduce the child to potential problems in a controlled fashion over a longer period of time.

When ignoring, displacing, or avoiding excess behavior are incomplete solutions, methods are available to decrease the strength of a misbehavior directly. Self-stimulatory behavior or repetitive self-injurious acts, although relatively unusual, do occur in developmentally disabled youngsters and tend to be highly resistant to change. Punishment can have fairly rapid effects on such misbehavior. If punishment is immediate, consistently implemented, and truly something that the child dislikes, it will reduce the occurrence of the misbehavior.

There are several drawbacks to using punishment, whatever its form (e.g., spankings, reprimands, extra chores). Most of us dislike using punishment so much that we delay administering it until long after the misbehavior has occurred. A comment like "Wait until your father comes home!" is one example of delayed punishment. Another drawback is that we are not always consistent with punishment. For example, we may say, "You'll be in trouble the next time!" Frequently we give into whatever it was that motivated the child's misbehavior in the first place. Another practical consideration is that what is selected as punishment may not be so undesirable from the child's point of view. These are all things that can make punishment ineffective in stopping problem behavior.

Other drawbacks include the fact that punishment does not teach anything new. It only stops or decreases behavior that it follows consistently. If no alternative is available to the child, either because of a lack of skill or a lack of opportunity, the improvement will be temporary at best. Punishment also can create fear in the child, and fear can distract the child from learning or disrupt relationships in the family. Finally, punishment given in anger can become excessive and even harmful.

These drawbacks can be overcome by never punishing without having a plan to reward an alternative, desirable behavior. In addition, many techniques have been developed to avoid the need for physical punishment. One of the best known of these is called timeout from positive reinforcement. Timeout has been used very successfully by numerous parents and teachers to decrease undesirable behavior. But one must be sure that the exact nature of the timeout experience truly represents the temporary withdrawal of something that the child values.

Structure has a place in every family. A large proportion of problem situations can be avoided through firm limit setting, by enthusiastic attention and appreciation for good behavior, and by providing good examples for children to follow.

Discipline is important to all children. A structured approach sometimes is needed to deal with particularly difficult problems, and many professional psychologists and special educators can give needed advice at such times. As with many of the teaching strategies discussed here, additional readings are available to help you adapt these approaches to your needs.

ACKNOWLEDGMENTS

Contributions have been made to this chapter by James A. Mulick, Ph.D., and Ellen I. Rollins, Ed.D.

◀   Chapter 29   ▶

Going to School

Like other school-age children, youngsters with developmental disabilities need appropriate education. In the past, this was not always an accepted fact, and many handicapped children were deprived of essential educational services.

In 1975, the Education for All Handicapped Children Act (PL 94-142) became law. As a result, a free and appropriate education is now available to all disabled children regardless of the severity of their condition. The law provides for special education and special related services to meet the unique needs of handicapped children from ages 3 to 21. In 1986, Public Law 99-457 was passed, which provides an incentive for all states to develop programs for infants and preschool children with special needs. How children are identified as handicapped by the school system, the educational options available, and the role of the parent as a member of a team planning for the child are discussed in this chapter.

REFERRAL PROCESS

In order for children with handicaps to be brought to the attention of special education personnel, they must be referred. Ordinarily a child's name is submitted by the classroom teacher. Most children are referred to special education programs because they have difficulty keeping up with the other students in the regular classrom or because they are presenting behavioral problems that interfere with learning. However, referrals can also be made by parents or professionals outside of the educational system on behalf of the family. In addition, most communities have Child Find Programs in place that offer screening services in order to identify those younger children (beginning at age 2½ years) who may be in need of special education services. Also, diagnostic and evaluation centers where children can undergo comprehensive assessments often recommend special education services for children with special needs.

EVALUATION

Before children can be enrolled in a special education program, they must undergo a thorough evaluation. However, an evaluation cannot be initiated or acted upon by the school without written permission by the parents. From the start, therefore, you will be aware of the school's interest in identifying any academic or behavioral difficulties that your child may have. This system is designed to encourage parents to function as partners in the evaluation process. The school will notify you in writing about the specific tests that will be administered and the professionals who will be evaluating your child. You should also be given a copy of your rights or procedural safeguards, developed by the state Department of Education in accordance with directives of the Education for All Handicapped Children Act.

The purpose of your child's evaluation is to determine whether he or she needs special education services, and if so, in what areas he or she qualifies for assistance. In the process, the special methods, techniques, and materials needed in the educational program also are identified. The results of the evaluation are then used as a guide in judging your child's future likely performance educationally, behaviorally, and vocationally.

In some circumstances only psychological and educational evaluations are necessary. This is particularly true in children who will remain in a regular classroom while receiving resource assistance. As a general rule, evaluations are more comprehensive when it is felt the child may need a self-contained special class or residential school placement. For the child who will need a special class or a more restrictive setting, the educational and psychological assessments are usually accompanied by at least a medical and a social appraisal. It is not uncommon also to include speech and language, hearing, occupational therapy, and physical therapy assessments.

A comprehensive evaluation can be accomplished in a child assessment center where professionals including pediatricians, social workers, educators, psychologists, physical and occupational therapists, audiologists, speech therapists, and others work together to identify the child's strengths and weaknesses.

Although requirements vary by state, there are regulations as to the length of time it should take to complete an evaluation. These and other stipulations of state regulations are available from the director of special education in your community or from the Special Education Office in your state Department of Education.

TEAM MEETING

Once an evaluation is completed, a multidisciplinary team from the school department will meet and discuss the individual assessments to determine whether your child has a handicapping condition. If you are not satisfied with their judgment, you have a right to disagree and request another opinion at the school department's expense. If it is felt that your child does not have a specific handicap, he or she may not be eligible for any special education services outside of what would ordinarily be provided in the regular education program. However, if the multidisciplinary team concludes, based on the assessments, that there is a specific handicap, the team and the parents are responsible for developing an individualized education program, also referred to as an IEP.

What constitutes a handicapping condition is usually defined in the state regulations. These regulations typically cite disabilities such as hearing impairment or deafness, speech impairment, mental retardation, visual impairment or blindness, multihandicapping conditions, orthopaedic impairments, serious emotional disturbance, or learning disabilities. Each of these categories has a specific definition. If a child has one of these handicaps, he or she is eligible for special education services.

Some states consider the identification of handicapping conditions as "labeling" the child. These states, as well as some local educational agencies, have dropped these labels and have instead decided to serve the children based on their educational need. Much can be said pro and con regarding classification, labeling, and stigmatization, issues that were discussed in detail at the beginning of this book.

Development of an IEP for students identified as needing special education services is discussed next.

THE INDIVIDUALIZED EDUCATION PROGRAM

The individualized education program is the single most important school document about your child that you will ever possess. It is a written statement about your child's abilities and impairments, developed by you and the professionals who performed the evaluations. It contains a clear, individualized plan of instructions designed to deal with your child's disability.

Who Will Attend the IEP Meeting?

Your school department must give you ample notice of the time and place of the individualized education program meeting. At this meeting, personnel representing the school will ask for your input. This is a major opportunity for you to provide helpful information about your child. You will be able to discuss your child's social and academic skills as well as your own expectations for him or her in school. Although many recommendations and decisions are made by various school personnel, you should know that you have an equal role in the decision-making process and play a major function in developing goals and objectives for your child.

According to the Education for All Handicapped Children Act, the student, when appropriate, may attend the individualized education program meeting. Personnel from the school who are required to be present at this meeting include a school administrator—such as the special education director—the child's teacher, and members of the evaluation team. If your child will be leaving a regular education program to attend a special education setting, the receiving teacher also should be present.

In the case of a learning disabled student, a professional who is knowledgeable about learning disabilities may be asked to participate in this meeting. A vocational education teacher may attend the conference if your child is at an age when a vocational program needs to be discussed. Representatives from other agencies also might be asked to contribute, such as a vocational rehabilitation counselor who might be assigned to the school. In addition, the school department reserves the right to invite other professionals.

Preparing for the Meeting

To prepare for your first conference, you may wish to contact other parents regarding their experiences at IEP meetings. You may want to talk to trusted professionals and advocates of handicapped children and consider whether you would like them to accompany you. You have the right to bring anyone with you to the individualized education program meeting. A professional who has evaluated your child or someone who has a knowledge of the IEP process may be very helpful to you, as sometimes these meetings can be overwhelming and intimidating to parents.

Prior to the meeting, you should have some idea of what you want to contribute to the individualized education program and what you think would be best for your child. When considering your own recommendations, keep in mind the need to maintain the least restrictive environment, which means your child should be kept in a classroom that is as close to normal as possible, while at the same time receiving the required special services. The more special the classroom, the more restrictive or out of the mainstream the educational environment will be. All parties in an IEP meeting are supposed to work toward the goal of providing the most appropriate education for your child. All services needed by your child must be made available through your school system even if they cannot be provided locally.

If you anticipate significant disagreements with the school department, you may consider the counsel of a professional outside the school system who is either an attorney familiar with educational matters or a parent advocate. With such support and proper advice, problems that might be encountered can often be resolved without the need of an impartial hearing later. If you cannot reach an agreement, however, you will need to ask for an impartial hearing as mandated by the Education for All Handicapped Children Act.

How Will the IEP Meeting Proceed?

Usually, the director of special education will chair the individualized education program meeting. The members of the school department who are present will be introduced to you. You may want to write down their names and positions. After such introductions, usually an update of the child's present academic skills and behavioral status are presented. Also, the child's psychomotor abilities and his or her self-help and adaptive skills are discussed. Medical, psychological, and educational assessments that have taken place previously, in addition to classroom observations, are reviewed. If your child is an adolescent, his or her vocational talents and interests will be considered. Thus, many aspects of your child's overall functioning contribute to an evaluation of his or her strengths and weaknesses.

What Is Contained in an Individualized Education Program?

Federal regulations mandate the following content for an individualized education program:

A statement of the child's present level of educational performance
A statement of the annual goals
Appropriate procedures for determining whether the short-term objectives are being achieved
A statement of specific educational and related services to be provided to the child
Identification of the providers of the various services
Dates for initiation and expected duration of treatment
A statement of time to be spent in the regular educational program and the date of the next individualized education program review.

Each of these statements is discussed next.

Level of Performance

The first statement written into the individualized education program is the present level of educational performance. The term *educational* is used in a broad sense, referring not only to specific academic achievements but also to the child's behavior, special abilities, motor skills, communication capabilities, and adaptive behavior. Not all current levels of educational performance need to be listed; only those relevant to your child's disability. For example, if your child's primary problem is behavioral, the specific behavioral characteristics, such as aggressive behavior toward peers, would be listed.

Annual Goals

Likewise, the annual goals and short-term objectives are only written for those educational concerns that relate to your child's special education needs. For instance, a child who has difficulties only with mathematics might receive special education or resource teacher assistance for this subject only.

At a minimum, the annual goals must be revised on the anniversary date of the original writing of the individualized education program. The school or parents may request a change in the annual goals at any time during the year and need not wait for the anniversary date.

Goals are written according to the priorities of the student's educational needs. They are based on the child's abilities and educational performance. Of course, other concerns also may affect the goal selection. If, for example, a child has severe behavioral difficulties, significant academic growth might not be expected until the behavior is better under control. Hence, a host of variables must be considered in writing the general goals.

Short-Term Objectives

The short-term objectives are developed in conjunction with the annual goals and focus on the specific steps to be taken to reach these goals. For example, if a child does not recognize upper-case letters, the annual goal might indicate that the child will be able to name all 26 capital letters in one year. The short-term objectives, however, might state that the child will be able to name 7 capital letters in 10 weeks, 7 more during the following 10 weeks, and so on until reaching the final total of 26 at the end of the year. Specific criteria for such objectives might state, "The child will be able to name the upper-case letters A–G correctly 90 percent of the time on five occasions by a specified date." As a parent you may gauge your child's progress by using a teacher-made test that, for instance, asks your child to name each of those letters on five separate occasions, with an expectation of 90 percent accuracy.

School systems often will develop objectives that are written for each quarterly period, usually every 10 weeks. In this way, parents can review with the teacher the previously specified objectives to see if they have been met. If they have not been met, the teacher and parent can then discuss what might have caused this and what steps should be taken to correct the situation.

Other Related Services

In addition to special education, other services also may be provided to your child such as occupational therapy, physical therapy, speech therapy, transportation, and others. These should be listed on the IEP, along with the names of the involved professionals. How often such services should be provided and how long the individual sessions should last need to be spelled out. For example, the IEP may read: "David will receive individual speech therapy by the speech and language therapist, Ms. Murray, three times a week for a 30-minute period each." Also, the date when speech therapy will start and the length of time that it is expected to continue should be clearly indicated.

It is important for you to know what the term *related services* entails. According to federal regulations, *related services* is defined as

> transportation and such developmental, corrective, and other supportive services as are required to assist a handicapped child to benefit from special education, and includes special individualized assistance in mathematics and remedial reading, speech pathology and audiology, psychological services, physical and occupational therapy, recreation, early identification and assessment of disabilities in children, counseling services, and medical services for diagnostic or evaluation purposes. The term also includes school health services, social work services in schools, and parent counseling and training. (Education for All Handicapped Children Act, PL 94-142)

Related services usually complement the special education program in which the child is placed. For example, the school may have to provide occupational therapy services for a child with severe visual perceptual motor problems, or an individual with a significant orthopaedic handicap may need to be trained in certain self-care skills such as dressing and self-feeding. Another child with spina bifida may need intermittent catheterization by the school nurse. The related services used most often are special transportation, physical therapy, occupational therapy, speech and language therapy, social work intervention, and adaptive physical education.

Participation in Regular Education

The individualized education program will also contain a statement about the amount of time your child will remain in a regular education program. This is usually reported as a percentage of time for the number of hours per day that are to be spent in this setting. For example: "Jane will be in a regular class 75 percent of the time and in special education 25 percent. Out of a 6½-hour school day this will be slightly less than 2 hours spent in special education."

USING THE IEP AS A TOOL

The individualized education program is not a contract or legal document, and, therefore, the teachers or school cannot be held liable if a student does not progress as expected. However, school personnel must demonstrate that they made a serious attempt to help the child meet the goals and objectives specified in the IEP. Through the IEP, you may determine the progress your child makes on a yearly basis. If you observe that your child does not advance according to the specified objectives within a defined time period, or if other unforeseen circumstances (such as prolonged hospitalization of the child) should make the objectives unrealistic or unreasonable, you may request that the IEP be revised at any time during the school year. You may ask for another meeting and do not have to wait for the annual conference.

Although you may sign the IEP immediately at the end of the annual meeting, you also have the option to take the document home for further study and review. Read it carefully to be sure that you are comfortable with the instructional program and that it meets your child's needs. Be certain that the priorities you have identified for your child are clearly listed in the annual goals and short-term objectives. Make sure that all the services that your child needs are detailed in this report. Finally, be positive that the principle of the least restrictive environment is followed and that your child is integrated with nonhandicapped students as much as possible.

If Agreement Cannot Be Reached

As mentioned, if you do not agree with the individualized education program, you have the right to request an impartial due process hearing. You should first indicate to the school authorities why you disagree with the IEP, and give them an opportunity to revise it. However, you may also reject the IEP and request a second independent evaluation of your child at the school department's expense. At times, the disagreement between parent and school can be resolved on the basis of the results of the second evaluation, thus eliminating the need for a hearing. If the matter goes to a hearing, it will be conducted by an impartial hearing officer, an individual from outside the school department. However, the child must remain in his or her present educational program until the hearing settles the issues that are contested.

**PLACEMENT INTO THE LEAST
RESTRICTIVE EDUCATIONAL ENVIRONMENT**

Once children have been evaluated and identified as handicapped, and an individualized education program has been developed, they must be placed in their specially designed educational program. However, since we have come to realize that developmentally disabled children are more like their normal peers than they are different from them, the goal should be to place the child in an educational setting that is as close to normal as possible. This approach has come to be known popularly as *mainstreaming* or *least restrictive alternative*.

Actually, the word *mainstreaming* is not mentioned in the Education for All Handicapped Children Act, but *least restrictive educational alternative* is clearly spelled out in that document. Whether the child can remain in regular education or needs a special environment depends on his or her specific needs. The multidisciplinary team and the parents decide together on the least restrictive educational alternative for a particular child in developing the IEP.

The range of services includes regular education settings with resource help, self-contained special classes in regular schools, private special education day schools, residential schools, and, finally, hospitals or home-bound instruction. These alternatives are discussed in the next several paragraphs.

Probably the least restrictive situation possible for a student with special needs is to remain full-time in a regular class with special education monitoring. The special educator may function as a consultant advising the regular classroom teacher and the parents, but not providing any direct education services to the child. A somewhat more handicapped child, while continuing in a regular education setting, might be seen individually by a special education teacher once or twice a week for individual training in the problem area. In a slightly more restrictive educational alternative, a child would be seen perhaps five times a week by a special educator who would serve as a resource teacher to the child and as a consultant to the classroom teacher and parents. For the individual with more significant needs, a regular education classroom with special education services 2 hours or so per day in a resource room might be appropriate.

A partially integrated self-contained special class would be the next educational alternative for a more severely impaired student. In this situation, the child usually needs academic instruction in the special education program but can remain mainstreamed into the regular education setting for nonacademic subjects such as physical education, art, and music. The next step is a self-contained special class in the regular public school, a class in which the student spends 100 percent of the time in special education, although the child might participate with the regular education students in recess, lunch, and student assemblies.

Some children's impairments are so severe that they cannot be placed in a public school setting. They may need an educational placement in a full-time day program for handicapped children. A student may continue to live at home but go to a school outside of the regular education setting during the day. An even more developmentally disabled student might attend a residential special education facility where 24-hour treatment services are provided.

Probably the most restrictive setting is home-based tutorial assistance. Here the child is not exposed to other children, and social contacts, other than family members, are very limited. The special educator usually comes to the child's home and provides tutoring on a minimal basis. Such an educational program should be avoided unless the problems are so severe that this is the only setting in which the child can be educated adequately.

WHAT IS SPECIAL EDUCATION?

Parents often ask how special education differs from regular classroom instruction. Ordinarily, academic education in the special education classroom is given by trained special educators who provide a variety of services. Special education methods, techniques, and materials usually involve a step-by-step approach. Teaching assignments are often carried out on an individual and small-group basis, especially for reading, spelling, and mathematics. Besides the specially designed instructions, a great deal of help is provided in the behavioral and emotional domain. The presence of a stable and structured environment helps the student to get the most out of the program and learn most effectively. In addition, teacher aides often participate in special education programs and may provide special tutoring. In special education, many types of adaptive equipment are available. Also, computerized systems for physically handicapped persons, and other learning aids, may be utilized. Equipment to enhance communication for hearing impaired and deaf children, electric wheelchairs, and materials necessary for the education of visually impaired and blind children are available for students with such special needs.

CONCLUSION

The Education for All Handicapped Children Act is clear in its mission to include parents as active participants in the education of their children. Learning your child's rights—which include a free and appropriate education, the development of an individualized education program, participation in planning an educational program, instructions in the least restrictive educational environment, and due process procedures to settle educational disputes—is of utmost importance. The most obvious parental contribution is their involvement in the planning and development of their child's educational and instructional program, as the individualized education program cannot be written and approved without parental participation. The authors of the Education for All Handicapped Children Act realized the pivotal role parents play as participants in the team process, a role that should help ensure an optimal education for their children.

ACKNOWLEDGMENT

Contributions have been made to this chapter by James P. McEneaney, M.Ed.

◄   Chapter 30   ▶

Legal Issues in Developmental Disabilities

In American society, knowing one's legal rights and how to protect them is becoming increasingly difficult as the legal system becomes more complex. It becomes even more complicated when a parent must deal with the needs of a handicapped or retarded child. On the one hand, the child may never be able to grasp and exercise his or her own rights adequately. On the other hand, the young handicapped person may have more ability to exercise his or her rights than the courts are prepared to recognize or grant.

This chapter does not offer you specific advice about solving legal dilemmas. Its purpose is to discuss some of the common legal issues that arise in developmental disabilities. For expert advice and opinion, there is no substitute for a competent lawyer. As a parent you should plan to consult a lawyer should legal difficulties arise that you are not prepared to handle.

BASIC RIGHTS OF HANDICAPPED PEOPLE

The U.S. Constitution guarantees all citizens the right to life, liberty, and the pursuit of happiness. In the past, these most basic rights often have been denied to persons with physical or mental handicaps.

The United States has witnessed sweeping social changes in this century, and especially in the past 20 years. One by one, groups that have been deprived of their civil rights—women and racial minorities among others—have come forward to demand social and legal equality. Among them are also persons with handicapping conditions. No longer can basic human privileges be denied to a particular group on the assumption that its members will be unable to use those privileges. Myths have been challenged and proven wrong. For example, it now is taken for granted that women are as capable as men of voting intelligently and that members of various racial and ethnic minorities can achieve economic and social independence. Likewise, mentally retarded persons can vote, hold jobs, care for their own needs, and benefit from education to a far greater extent than was once believed.

The modern conception is that developmentally disabled citizens have the same rights as citizens without such disabilities. Parents are sometimes unaware that their handicapped or mentally retarded sons or daughters deserve certain rights and privileges. Because some of these rights are easier to understand than others and because their denial has been so widespread, they warrant more detailed discussion here.

Right to Life

Above all else, mentally retarded people and other individuals with developmental disabilities have the same right to live as all other citizens. To deny this right is contrary to the most basic principles of American society. This right should not be threatened on the basis of economics, appearance, perceived or expected intellectual abilities, or the expense required to preserve life.

Right to Education

The law guarantees the right to a free public education, and yet it was only within the last 15 years that this right was extended to persons with developmental disabilities. Prior to that time, children with mental retardation, chronic illnesses, cerebral palsy, or orthopaedic defects often remained at home and were deprived of educational services because a school was not wheelchair accessible or equipped to teach children with mental retardation. Their nonhandicapped peers attended public schools designed for the average student. Parents of mentally retarded children paid taxes to support public education; yet, their children were denied the benefits that those taxes purchased.

Right to Freedom of Choice

Denial of choice is a particular problem for mentally retarded persons. Because of the limited intellectual abilities of such persons, society has tended to make decisions for them or to deny them goods, services, and experiences that are available to others. It must never be assumed that individuals are incapable or undeserving because they have been categorized under the broad label of mental retardation. Like anyone else, a mentally retarded individual must be granted freedom of choice within his or her capacity to make decisions, and with the same limits imposed on his or her freedom as those of nonretarded persons.

Right to Live in the Community

The first institutions for mentally retarded children in America began in New England in the 1800s. They sprang from the desire to educate and provide medical care to a deserving and needy minority. But the concept went wrong. Institutions grew by leaps and bounds, care and training

were neglected, and only custodial care was provided. Gradually, institutions became warehouses, and lifetime commitment often became the norm for persons identified as mentally retarded. Eventually, the low level of functioning of mentally retarded persons in institutions was used as evidence that most of them were incapable of acquiring the skills necessary for living in the community.

Until recently, placement away from home was often recommended to parents as soon as a disability was diagnosed, particularly if the diagnosis was made at birth. Many parents of youngsters with spina bifida or with Down syndrome recall that after hearing the diagnosis, institutionalization was the next thing mentioned, even though the majority of children with Down syndrome are only mildly to moderately retarded and the outlook for many children with spina bifida is fairly positive.

Today, placement outside of the natural home and community is done only as a last alternative, when the need is compelling, and when it clearly serves the best interests of the disabled person. Only a small proportion of the mentally retarded population cannot be maintained within the community. To meet any individual's best interests, placement in a residential facility must include habilitation and should enhance the person's life.

Right to Work

The right of handicapped persons to work has been violated in several ways. For example, many have been forced or induced to do labor within an institutional facility without reimbursement, or without reimbursement to match the earnings of a nonhandicapped person who performs the same task. In addition, many handicapped persons have been denied any opportunity to train or work at all. The disabled person, like any able-bodied person, shares in the right to a fair day's pay for a fair day's labor.

Right to Contract for Goods and Property

Mentally retarded persons often are presumed to be incompetent and in need of help in making contractual arrangements. As a result, many mentally retarded individuals become wards of an appointed legal guardian. Once appointed, a guardian typically becomes totally responsible for the management of the person and of his or her property. Limited guardianships that allow more freedom to the ward are gradually finding their way into the law. Overprotection of a person with a developmental disability can be as unfair as underprotection. The right to make binding legal agreements, small and large, and the right to contract should be preserved whenever possible.

Right to Equal Protection under the Law

It can be difficult for mentally retarded persons to know their rights and to take advantage of them. The services of an advocate, a responsible, impartial individual who works on someone's behalf, may be required to help a person with mental retardation know, enjoy, and benefit from his or her lawful rights, privileges, and protections. If such advocate services were not available, mentally retarded and other disabled persons essentially would be deprived of their legal rights. For this reason, Title II of the 1975 Federal Developmentally Disabled Assistance and Bill of Rights Act required that as of October 1, 1975, states receiving certain federal grants for persons with developmental disabilities must have a formal advocacy system for people with handicapping conditions, and that such a system have the authority and the independence needed to provide effective protection. If you are concerned about your child's rights, your local Association for Retarded Citizens-U.S. should be able to direct you to a legal advocacy agency that can help.

Right to Sue

As Patricia M. Wald wrote in *The Mentally Retarded Citizen and the Law*, "The right of any citizen to gain access to the courts for the vindication of his legal rights is fundamental. It is not to be denied or curtailed without compelling justification" (Wald, 1976, p.24). Again, it should not be presumed that an individual does not have the ability to use the courts. Competent advocacy must be provided to aid the mentally retarded individual in making use of the legal system.

Other Civil Rights

For voting, holding public office, or serving on a jury, the requirements for persons with mental retardation should be the same as those for the nonretarded population. A truly incompetent individual will not be able to find his or her way through the procedures necessary to register to vote; will not bear the scrutiny necessary to gain public confidence and to be voted into office; and will not demonstrate sufficient understanding to be chosen for jury duty. Even among nonretarded and nondisabled people, not all voters are well informed; not all politicians are scholars; not all jurors are entirely rational, informed, unbiased, and perfectly literate. If there is to be some minimum standard of judgment or comprehension, it should be applied to all.

Right to Marry

Many states limit the right to marry for those who are labeled incompetent or intellectually limited. Enforcement of such laws varies, but is generally quite lax. There is no accurate way of predicting which marriages will be unsuccessful or end in divorce. As the record for successful marriages among the nonmentally retarded and nonhandicapped populations is far from sterling, it is hard to justify denying mentally retarded persons the right to marry.

Right to Sexual Expression

Persons with mental retardation have been the victims of myths about their sexual drive and habits, which have resulted in great hesitancy about sexual freedom for them. However, there is no evidence to suggest that mentally retarded and other developmentally disabled persons as a group differ from the norm in their sexual needs. The myths have arisen primarily because of abnormal restrictions placed on sexual expression among mentally retarded individuals, separation of the sexes, denial of privacy, exploitation of mentally retarded persons by others, lack of training in normal and acceptable sexual behavior, and unacceptable acts by some individuals that have received wide attention. In the past, sexual misconduct has been used as an excuse for institutionalization in some cases, and yet special education programs have offered little sex education. The need is not for greater restriction, but for more training and information.

Right to Bear Children

In the past, laws allowing involuntary sterilization grew from inaccurate theories about the heredity of mental retardation and the erroneous assumption that most mentally retarded persons are criminally inclined. Although there is generally a higher risk that a mentally retarded person will give birth to a handicapped child, mentally retarded couples can have children with normal intelligence, just as nonhandicapped parents can produce mentally retarded offspring. Even in cases where "normal" adults are carriers of serious genetic conditions, there is no mechanism for legally restricting those individuals' right to have a child. Genetic counseling and information concerning the risk of having a developmentally disabled child should be provided to the parents, however. The mentally retarded parent deserves to enjoy the same basic right in the absence of evidence of harm.

Right to Raise Children

The same argument that applies to the right of handicapped people to bear children applies to the right to raise them. There are competent and incompetent parents at nearly all levels of intellectual ability. Proof of mental retardation is not proof of certain neglect or of harmful ignorance about childrearing. The standards for proving neglect and for assessing adequate parenting should be uniformly applied, and training should be provided through the educational system before the parent-to-be reaches adulthood.

To summarize, it is difficult to change assumptions about mentally retarded and handicapped persons that have been held for generations. Double standards are no more acceptable when applied to persons with developmental disabilities than they are when applied to two different races or sexes. The denial of any constitutionally guaranteed right must be based upon objective and valid individual assessment. It must be demonstrated that the individual's exercise of that right will result in harm to himself or others. Discrimination against mentally handicapped citizens and different treatment of them have made many of these individuals *appear* very different. This difference has then been used to justify further discrimination. Differences between retarded and non-retarded citizens can be diminished by minimizing the differences in treatment.

ROLE OF THE ADVOCATE

Advocacy refers to any activity in which a person acts on his or her own behalf or on behalf of another, to defend a cause, maintain a cause, or meet a need. In developmental disabilities, there are two important types of advocacy. In *citizen advocacy,* a citizen volunteer represents the interests of another citizen who cannot do so because of some impairment. Such an advocate steps in when needs cannot be met without special assistance from a third party. *Legal advocacy* is a more specific term referring to efforts to address the needs of developmentally disabled persons by changing legislation or administrative rules, or by pursuing court action. Some legal advocacy tasks such as representing a client in court require a lawyer, but others do not.

Legal advocacy usually takes two forms. *Law reform advocacy* tries to achieve recognition of the basic legal rights for the disabled population as a whole or for a broad segment such as mentally retarded persons. In *case advocacy,* a single individual is represented in a particular dispute. Legal advocacy for persons with mental retardation is not just a privilege. It is now a right recognized by law. The logic behind the law is that only an advocate system can guarantee mentally retarded citizens the ability to exercise basic legal rights. Without advocates, mentally retarded persons essentially would be deprived of their constitutionally guaranteed rights. As mentioned earlier, the federal government mandated that as of October 1, 1975, each state receiving federal funds for individuals with developmental disabilities had to provide a protection and advocacy system that was independent of other service providers.

One example in which advocates can serve a critical role is in commitment cases. It now is recognized that mentally retarded individuals need legal counsel when parents or guardians institute proceedings that are intended to lead to placement in an institution. The courts view such an attempt as adversarial; they no longer assume that the parents' objective is necessarily in the best interests of the mentally retarded person. The individual now has a right to be represented by legal counsel in court proceedings, to dispute the grounds for commitment, to permit the court to hear the other side of the issue, and to ensure that his or her own best interests will be determined by the court.

Because of the lack of lawyers knowledgeable in issues regarding persons with mental retardation, many states have formed agencies with full-time trained personnel. Mentally retarded individuals and their families should explore the services their home state has to offer. A good source for information about such advocacy systems is the local Association for Retarded Citizens-U.S. (See also section on "Advocacy" in Chapter 31.)

TRUSTS AND WILLS

A trust is a legal tool by which one person, the donor, can give something to a second person, the "trustee," but specify that it will be used for the benefit of someone else. It is designed to allow the giver or donor to control the use of his or her property as he or she chooses, but is not designed to assert control over the receiver or beneficiary.

There are several advantages of a trust over a gift or a will. First, the property in question does not actually belong to the beneficiary. Therefore, the trust in many cases can be arranged so that it will not cause a developmentally disabled individual to be ineligible for help from other sources. A trust can be created before the death of the parents, so that they have the opportunity to observe the plan in action during their lifetimes. This allows for changes or additional planning. It also can be reassuring to see the trust in effect. Concern about waste or misuse of funds is lessened because the terms of a trust can be detailed and enforceable. A trust is more like a contract than a gift. There can be restrictions on the use of funds, whereas it is more difficult to place legal restrictions upon a gift. A trust can guard assets from mismanagement, but is less restrictive than a guardianship. It can leave the beneficiary some decision-making power. With the proper terms, the trust can be tailored to the need of the individual. The disabled person gets the maximum income from the trust while safeguarding the principal. When the trust is ended, the assets that remain can be distributed among other family members without death taxes or the expense of probate, the legal process of establishing that a will is genuine.

Willing property to a third party who is nonhandicapped, with provision in the will for a mentally retarded family member, is generally not recommended for a variety of reasons. It can be costly and risky, and it lacks the flexibility of a trust, which can adapt to the needs of the child as times change. Directly giving the retarded person legal title to the assets by inheritance or gift is also unsatisfactory. In some cases, a mentally retarded person may be vulnerable to exploitation. Service providers can take the assets and consume the funds in compensation for their services. Moreover, the individual may become ineligible for some types of governmental assistance.

There are many variables to take into account in determining whether a trust is appropriate for your family. These include the size of the family's estate (the sum total of their assets and liabilities), the severity of the disability, benefits and support systems already available to the disabled person, the cost of care for the beneficiary, the individual's potential to be self-supporting, specific abilities and limitations, educational level, and others. Although it may be difficult to find an attorney with training in estate planning for families with a mentally retarded member, it is important to try, because great care must be taken to find a reliable trustee and to set realistic terms or provisions for the trust.

Establishing a trust is complicated but valuable and highly recommended for families with adequate assets. It is of the utmost importance to identify a reliable individual as trustee or cotrustee. This should be someone who is familiar with the beneficiary's needs, and who can be relied upon to exercise care and good judgment in managing funds. The trust plan should allow the trustee flexibility to take advantage of new developments and opportunities for the beneficiary, as they arise. Provision must be made for an annual review of the trustee's accounts. The trust plan itself should be reviewed at intervals to take advantage of changes in services for persons with mental retardation or changes in trust law. When appropriate, if governmental agencies are providing for the basic life necessities of the beneficiary, the donor can and should make sure that trust funds are to be used for items not provided by other sources. Trust plans involve numerous considerations and can take many shapes. The help of an informed and competent attorney is a necessity.

COMPETENCY AND GUARDIANSHIP

Guardianship is a legal mechanism that grants an individual the legal power to make decisions for someone who is considered incapable of making these decisions on his or her own. Although guardianship is often used for deciding financial matters, it is typically granted in an all-or-nothing fashion. The ward legally is considered to lack the abilities to act on his or her own behalf; specific capacities are not considered.

The need for a guardian should be based upon an individual's actual ability to make decisions in his or her own best interest. Courts historically have relied upon medical testimony to determine competency, even though the issue is legal, not medical. Often in the past, no attempt was made to analyze the affected person's capabilities in regard to his or her needs. The ability of the handicapped individual to make, or to learn to make, an adequately well-informed decision on his or her own behalf was not considered or assessed. "Due process of law," the right to have any law applied fairly and reasonably and with adequate safeguards, often has been ignored. Guardianship should be used in cases where a substantial incapacity can be demonstrated, and should be limited to the particular area in which ability is lacking.

There are several types of guardianships:

1. In a *general guardianship*, the guardian has the same relationship to the ward as a parent to a minor child. The ward is stripped of his or her ability to make binding decisions, and the guardian assumes the role of determining the wishes and best interests of the ward, who has no personal or property rights left intact. This is the traditional form of guardianship. The ward may not be able to make legal contracts, buy or sell property, sue or be sued, engage in financial transactions, vote, marry, choose his or her place of residence, or decide for or against medical treatment without legal approval of the guardian.

2. Some states allow *guardianship of the person,* which often is sufficient to meet the ward's needs, even though a general, more restrictive guardianship may have been sought. Guardianship of the person usually is not granted alone without guardianship of the property, but it may be appropriate in some cases. A guardian of the person has the power to make decisions about where and how the ward will live, as well as other judgments regarding education, training, and personal welfare.

3. A *guardian of the property* (or estate) has the power to manage property and financial affairs. The guardian may also be termed a curator or conservator.

4. A *guardian ad litem* is a special court-appointed guardian whose function is to litigate (prosecute or defend) on behalf of a person who is unable to represent himself or herself adequately. Guardians ad litem often are attorneys, but are not required to be.

5. A *temporary guardian* may be appointed when a quick decision is needed to protect life or property. In such a case, the courts generally have more freedom to bypass the usual requirements of due process.

When guardianship is considered, several questions must be asked. Is it necessary? What needs to be accomplished? Can the handicapped person's interests be protected by another, less restrictive means?

Less restrictive means are becoming more available. One way is to distinguish between personal and financial affairs. Another example is the U.S. Social Security Administration's "representative payee," or "substitute payee method." This is a mechanism by which social security benefits are paid to someone named as a representative, on the condition that they will be used only for the benefit of the beneficiary. Some laws permit a court to authorize a particular transaction without appointing a guardian of the property. A guardian ad litem can be appointed for the sole purpose of conducting litigation on the ward's behalf.

A "facilitative guardianship" has been proposed in which the ward maintains his or her right to decision making and the guardian assists in achieving the individual's stated goals. The retarded person may need help in making minor or major purchases and contracts, in finding shelter, or in gaining access to training. The facilitative guardian functions as a guide.

Perhaps the most important alternative to guardianship is the provision of social services to minimize the need for guardianship at all. Guardianship, by definition, limits the individual's choices; service, however, can expand choices. In many cases, the need for a guardian arises purely out of the lack of proper education, inability to control one's actions or behavior, lack of vocational skills, inadequate monetary management, and dietary needs. With the provision of proper services, such as homemakers and counselors, the need for control may disappear.

In all arenas of life, the right of the developmentally disabled person to least restrictive alternatives is being recognized. As restrictions loosen in other areas, it becomes obvious that guardianship laws need revision and refinement as well. The evolving, modern idea is that guardianship should be limited and invoked only as a last resort, because it involves a substantial loss of rights. How well one is able to care for oneself, not one's intellectual level, should be the primary determinant of the need for a guardian. Legal capability to care for one's own interests should be presumed in most cases, unless it can be proven the capacity is substantially lacking. The ward should retain as much of a voice and as much self-sufficiency in his or her own affairs as possible. Guardianships should come under the scrutiny of monitoring systems. It bears repeating that guidance, training, and protective services can substantially lessen the need to place handicapped persons under the control of guardians. The primary consideration should be the welfare of the ward, not the estate, where the good of one is incompatible with the other. As in other areas, in providing alternatives to guardianship, society is moving in the direction of developing more meaningful procedures for meeting the basic needs of handicapped persons, while ensuring their individual rights and freedoms.

ACKNOWLEDGMENT

Contributions have been made to this chapter by Leesa H. Mann, M.A.

◀ **Chapter 31** ▶

Resource Development

Services for children with special needs are found throughout the United States. Yet, the availability of services differs from region to region, and programs to meet your child's precise needs may not be immediately available to you. Even programs that have national chapters differ in quality on the local level, depending on the personnel involved and the community support available. This is also true in the field of education. Anyone who has moved from one town to another knows that educational standards differ from locality to locality. There is even more variability in special education. One community may take its mandate to provide special education services seriously and offer a full range of services, whereas another narrowly interprets the law and does just enough to meet minimum standards. Also, the quality of medical care, funding sources, and the availability of parent groups and outreach programs may vary from community to community.

DETERMINING YOUR CHILD'S NEEDS

In order to obtain appropriate services for your child, it is paramount to determine his or her needs. If you are uncertain of what your child's specific needs are, you may want to request a comprehensive assessment. An evaluation clinic or a child development center can provide an interdisciplinary examination of your child. A complete assessment by a team of professionals including pediatricians, neurologists, nutritionists, nurses, social workers, psychologists, educators, physical therapists, occupational therapists, speech therapists, and others can identify your child's strengths and weaknesses. Based on such an evaluation, the various needs of your child, including medical, educational, psychological, recreational, and other needs, can be determined.

WHERE TO BEGIN LOOKING FOR SERVICES

Once you know your child's specific needs, your task is to find appropriate services to meet these needs. One way to begin to explore what is

332 / Assessments, Education, and Resource Development

available is to ask the people who first brought your child's problems to your attention. Whether it is the pediatrician, school personnel, or members of an interdisciplinary team, these professionals should be able to steer you toward appropriate and available resources in your area.

If the suggestions made by these professionals are unsatisfactory, you may want to investigate on your own. Try calling your local school department and various state agencies such as the Developmental Disabilities Council and state Departments of Mental Health, Mental Retardation, Health, and Human Services. You also may want to contact local chapters of national organizations such as United Cerebral Palsy, Easter Seal Society, March of Dimes, and the Association for Retarded Citizens-U.S. If your child has a specific disorder or syndrome such as spina bifida or Down syndrome, the respective parent organization often can provide you with valuable advice concerning optimal services and resources in your community. In addition, you could consult resource books that list human services in your town and state. Such guides often describe the services each agency offers, the eligibility criteria, age range, costs, and other important information.

Other parents who have handicapped children of similar age may provide advice regarding the availability and quality of services and the personnel providing those services. You may benefit from visiting various programs in your community. After observing what each has to offer, you can make an educated decision of where you would like to enroll your youngster.

ADVOCACY

For parents of the developmentally disabled child, the term *advocacy* is important. Simply stated, an advocate is a person or agency who promotes, recommends, or argues in favor of a cause. In the case of developmentally disabled children, advocacy means efforts to obtain or maintain these children's rights, privileges, and services.

Many of the services currently provided for persons with developmental disabilities originated because of the hard work of parent advocates who joined forces and requested that their children be provided the same services and education available for nonhandicapped children. Thus, during the past decades, numerous parent associations have developed advocacy to a fine art.

Learning to Be an Advocate

In general, the more facts you gather, the better prepared you are to serve as an advocate. An informed person can act more effectively than one who lacks the facts. Initially, your efforts will involve identifying needs and getting in touch with knowledgeable parents and professionals. You soon will find out what needs to be done, which methods worked for others, which ones did not, and why not. This type of information may save you time and frustration and may assist you in making an informed decision regarding the appropriate course of action.

It also is important to familiarize yourself with the rights and laws governing the specific concerns you have identified. For example, you may want to know the extent of your medical coverage, the state regulations pertaining to special education, or how to contest your child's ineligibility for Supplemental Security Income. With each of these questions you will have to deal with a different administrative system and a different set of regulations and laws. Moreover, within each of these systems, there can be great differences between what the law provides and how the bureaucracy interprets these laws. Upon reviewing your rights and the laws, you may find out that your child is entitled to a particular service, but is not getting it. If you believe that your rights are being violated, find out who is in charge of making the decision and what you can do to appeal. By learning how the system works, you can avoid wasting valuable time. Do not be afraid to appeal a decision, because decisions made at one level may be overturned on another. Nevertheless, if you appeal, you may want to enlist the aid of an agency that specializes in advocacy.

Advocacy Agencies

Many communities have advocacy agencies to assist persons with developmental disabilities. Advocacy in these agencies usually takes two forms: citizen advocacy and legal advocacy. Each organization may offer one or both types of advocacy.

Citizen Advocacy Citizen advocates are usually volunteers who assist disabled individuals and their parents in obtaining services. These citizen advocates have been trained and usually are supervised by experienced people who know the steps involved in "getting through" the networks of bureaucracies. Citizen advocates also serve disabled persons by supporting innovative programs and encouraging change.

Legal Advocacy Legal advocacy involves helping to ensure that a person's or group's legal rights are not violated, and involves more formal procedures than citizen advocacy. A legal advocacy group often employs lawyers and paralegal aides to work on individual cases or group problems, called class action. They can pursue litigation (use of the judicial process) if there is a violation of a person's civil rights. They are helpful in resolving problems such as determining which agency is responsible to provide the services your child requires. Correctly used, legal advocacy is a powerful resource and can lead to major changes for many developmentally disabled children. Because parents of handicapped children have resorted more and more to this kind of strategy, many states have been forced to improve the quality of care given to their citizens with mental retardation. This type of action also fueled the deinstitutionalization movement in the 1970s, which allowed residents of institutions to be relocated in appropriate community settings such as group homes and supervised apartments. Legal advocates are often involved in legislative activity to help improve or create new services for persons with developmental disabilities.

COMMON RESOURCES

All parents are concerned about the practical issues involved in raising children, including finances, health insurance, life insurance, and many other facets of daily living. Many families of handicapped children are particularly anxious about these concerns. Many of the common issues families face as they start planning for their developmentally disabled children are discussed in the following pages.

Specialized Health Care

Today, many options are available for health care. In addition to the traditional primary care physician, who may be a general practitioner, family physician, internist, or pediatrician, there are physician assistants, nurse practitioners, physiatrists, and osteopaths, all serving as health care providers. Children with complicated health problems, including those with chronic illnesses and developmental disabilities, usually require specialized health care at one time or another. The multiple needs of handicapped children have resulted in the development of numerous medically based, multidisciplinary evaluation and treatment facilities. In such centers, professionals from a number of disciplines work together to assess the youngster's abilities and disabilities and develop a coordinated treatment plan. If your child has complex developmental problems, you may find obtaining services at such a facility easier and more efficient than seeking out each professional individually in their private office.

If you are unsure whether such a center exists in your area, you may want to contact your state Department of Health. The state Developmental Disability Council also will be able to guide you. In addition, the American Association of University Affiliated Programs for Persons with Developmental Disabilities publishes *A Resource Guide to Organizations Concerned with Developmental Handicaps,* which lists available programs throughout the United States (see address of this organization in the Resource Organizations list at the end of this book).

Alternatives to Hospitalization

Not only do many handicapped children require specialized health care, but many youngsters frequently need to receive services in a hospital. Children with chronic illnesses or severe disabilities may require recurrent hospitalization. However, with advances in medical technology, many of the services that once were available only in the hospital now also can be provided in the home. A range of services are available today that can either shorten a hospital stay or enable an individual to remain at home.

One such service is called skilled home nursing care. This service involves a qualified nurse visiting the home and performing any necessary or prescribed duties, such as providing intravenous hyperalimentation, changing dressings, giving injections, and catheter care. Most nurses providing home care work for profit or nonprofit agencies. Other licensed nurses provide this service on a fee-for-service basis. Medical insurance carriers often cover much of the necessary expense.

If general assistance but not nursing care is needed, a *home health aide* might be able to help. Home health aides provide personal care to disabled individuals such as taking temperatures and bathing.

Homemaker services also can be very useful, as they relieve families of housekeeping chores during busy times of the day. In addition, some of these programs provide other services such as physical and occupational therapy, nutritional counseling, and social work services.

Another resource that can be beneficial to families is *hospice care.* Hospice programs provide supportive care for terminally ill patients and their families. The support given by hospice workers can be invaluable during such a difficult period.

As you look for alternative services, try not to make assumptions about what an agency can or cannot provide. Often, creative thinking and perseverance both by you and an agency can result in provision of specialized programs that meet your family's specific needs. Be sure to inquire about costs and available funding sources. In many instances, the agencies themselves suggest means of obtaining funds to cover the costs of services. To find out more about the preceding services, contact your local visiting nurses association, hospital coordinated home care program, or home care agencies.

Residential Programs and Rehabilitation Centers

When time-limited, intensive treatment is needed for developmentally disabled or behaviorally disordered individuals, a residential treatment program sometimes is an appropriate option. Residential programs can be found in private and public institutions including hospitals, schools, and rehabilitation centers. Residential placement may be appropriate if the individual's behavioral or physical difficulties are such that he or she cannot be maintained in a less restrictive environment. Generally, the option is considered only after all other community services have been tried.

Residential programs are specialized and designed to help children with certain disabilities—for example severe neuromuscular handicaps or severe emotional disorders. Types of programs and the range of services offered will depend on the facility's focus and general goals. The admission process, except for emergencies, can be long and involved and may require completing a detailed application, a multidisciplinary evaluation, interviews, and approval from the state or from a private or local funding source. Treatment philosophy, types of intervention used, staff to client ratio, and attitudinal concerns are important considerations to keep in mind. You will also want to carefully evaluate the physical surroundings. For more information on this kind of service, consult a directory of community services or social service agencies within your state.

Nursing Homes

At times, an individual's health problems may require ongoing nursing care, necessitating a nursing home placement. Nursing homes may be either privately or state operated. Like other residential programs, they differ in terms of the types of services and levels of care provided.

Before individuals are admitted to a nursing home, they must be referred by a professional, social worker, nurse, or physician, and certified to be in need of nursing care. There are different types of nursing homes:

1. Skilled Nursing Care services are less intensive than hospital care, but provide 24-hour inpatient nursing supervision as well as intensive rehabilitation services.
2. Level I Intermediate Care nursing homes provide 24-hour preventive and supportive nursing services to patients with chronic illnesses.
3. Level II Intermediate Care nursing homes provide minimal nursing care.
4. Intermediate Care Facilities for the Mentally Retarded offer supervision for persons with mental retardation and nursing needs.

When looking for a nursing home for a disabled family member, it is important to evaluate the types of services provided, how well they meet your family member's needs, the quality and attitude of the staff, and the general atmosphere of the nursing home. It is often difficult to find nursing homes or similar facilities that are geared solely to the care of children. However, such facilities are increasing in number as parents advocate for their medically involved youngster's needs.

LIFE INSURANCE

How to financially protect your loved ones is a major concern. In matters of life insurance, it is important to consult financial experts who are familiar with issues pertaining to handicapped people. A disabled child can be named the beneficiary of an insurance policy. By doing so, parents assume that the child will receive care for which they have planned. Unfortunately, this may jeopardize other benefits your developmentally disabled child may receive, such as Supplemental Security Income.

It may be difficult to obtain life insurance for a disabled family member, especially if the individual has a life-threatening illness. Because of the variability in policies, you are advised to explore the feasibility of this directly with insurance companies or other experts in this area.

HEALTH INSURANCE

Private Health Insurance

Several options are available for covering medical expenses. The most common resource is a private or company-sponsored policy for health insurance. You should inquire, however, about whether your developmentally disabled youngster is eligible for coverage once he or she turns 21, because family policies usually cover children only until they reach adulthood. Blue Cross often covers handicapped, dependent youngsters beyond the age of 18 years.

Health maintenance organizations in which you pay a monthly fee for medical services are also popular. Here the monthly fee is used to provide medical coverage for all contingencies. Your child with a developmental disability should be covered as any other family member.

Public Health Insurance

Federal and state governments have created health benefit programs for eligible individuals with certain disabilities and for those who meet other criteria such as low income levels. At present, there are two primary programs: Medicaid and Medicare.

Medicaid is a state-run, federally reimbursed program that pays for needed medical care for eligible persons. An applicant's medical diagnosis, finances, and age are used in determining eligibility. Under current regulations, disabled individuals with chronic medical problems are eligible for what is known as the Katie Beckett Amendment. This program enables certain disabled persons to obtain medical coverage with no regard to their parents' income. Previously, children would be ineligible if their parents' income was in excess of a certain specific amount. However, there are other eligibility criteria to be met. The program is basically for children with complicated medical problems. Some states or local offices are more lenient than others in interpreting this policy. Also, some states have elected to make some individuals eligible for Medicaid under so-called waivers in Medicaid programs. You can explore these options through your Medicaid Office, Division of Retardation or, in some cases, the state Department of Health.

Medicare is a federal health insurance program for individuals who are over 65 years old or for those who are permanently disabled.

Catastrophic Health Insurance

Some states offer plans that protect their citizens against the staggering costs of catastrophic illness or injury. In this instance, the state offers financial assistance based on the parents' personal resources and the disabled individual's resources. Your local or state departments of Health or Public Welfare will have more information on this provision.

Hill-Burton Act

According to federal law, if a hospital received federal money, it is required to offer free service under the Hill-Burton Act to medically needy individuals, provided they meet the eligibility criteria.

Private Charitable Organizations Covering Medical Expenses

Some hospitals also have programs for particular disabilities or are associated with organizations that help fund various medical conditions. The Palestine Shriners, for example, have such programs in some hospitals, but also run their own facilities. There are private and nonprofit organizations that service specific kinds of problems such as the Lions Club, which is particularly concerned with vision. Other organizations may cover special equipment or specific services.

FINANCES

Raising children is expensive. Raising a handicapped child can be more expensive. Regardless of your financial situation, knowledge of various kinds of public and private financial assistance that are available on the local, regional, state, and federal levels can be helpful. Obviously, new laws and programs are enacted and reenacted frequently, so it is important to keep informed on changes in them.

The best way to obtain information is to consult federal, state, city, and county agencies directly. Available services and programs change often as new laws are passed. For example, it was only recently that the Katie Beckett Amendment, already mentioned, made Medicaid available to families with private incomes.

Various nonprofit service agencies also can be contacted. Such programs may not offer cash benefits, but provide services such as special treatment programs, payment for equipment, or camp scholarships.

Cash Benefits

Supplemental Security Income The federal government's Supplemental Security Income (SSI) program provides supplemental income to certain individuals with disabilities. It was designed to assist those who may be unable to support themselves completely. The Social Security Administration is the primary agency responsible for payments. Basically, the SSI program is a jointly funded federal and state program that guarantees a minimum income to disabled children and adults. In addition, medical coverage is provided. Certain eligibility requirements must be met to receive benefits. An individual must have a disability or a combination of impairments that are expected to last for a given length of time and have a serious prognosis. Specified income levels and resources must also be met. The Social Security Administration maintains a list of potentially qualifying impairments. The specific aspects of each impairment and how each affects the individual's functioning are important considerations.

You can apply for your child by contacting the Social Security Office. Information about your child's disability and level of functioning will be needed by the Social Security Office to evaluate eligibility. The examiner will request reports from agencies and physicians who have evaluated or treated your child. Make sure the various professionals include information on the test procedures and the signs and symptoms used in arriving at a diagnosis. All information should be clear and objective. Once the documentation is received, it is assigned to an examiner and the Disability Determination Service Branch of the Social Security Office. Sometimes, further tests or evaluations may be requested. If it has been decided that an individual is not disabled and therefore is ineligible, you can appeal the decision.

Aid to Families with Dependent Children, General Public Assistance, and Other Forms of Public Aid Other state and local programs that provide financial or medical assistance to eligible individuals and families include the federally funded, state-run Aid to Families with Dependent Children (AFDC), General Public Assistance (GPA), or Medical Assistance. To learn more about what is available and the eligibility requirements, contact your local, county, or state Public Welfare Departments or other social service agencies.

Although finding sources of assistance can be difficult, you should at least try. Do not assume that a program does not exist. It never hurts to investigate the resources in your area. For example, there may be a little-known city fund for paying transportation costs for persons with disabilities or a slush fund for holiday baskets. Knowing what resources exist increases your choices when a particular need arises.

Other Services

Certain private, nonprofit organizations offer financial aid to people with disabilities. Some agencies serve the population in general, whereas others focus on specific disabilities or a particular need. Religious groups, community action programs, the American Red Cross, Salvation Army, and others provide social and health care services. Many communities have mental health clinics, family service agencies, and counseling if you need mental health services. Also, organizations such as the Muscular Dystrophy Association, Cystic Fibrosis Foundation, United Cerebral Palsy, and March of Dimes offer specialized services that may assist you.

RECREATION

Day-to-day recreational activities are another concern of families with developmentally disabled children. To begin exploring recreational opportunities, start with your local recreational department or community center. Church groups, YMCA, YWCA, Boy Scouts of America, and Girl Scouts of America also can provide assistance. The Association for Retarded Citizens-U.S. and Special Olympics often sponsor athletic activities and fitness programs for persons with mental retardation and other developmentally disabled people. Camping experiences—either day or residential camping—provide recreation for children and their families.

Whenever possible, begin with recreational programs that are available to the general public. Do not assume that because your child has a particular disability, he or she will not be accepted. If you find that your child will not fit into a regular program, you may want to look into programs specifically designed to serve persons with developmental disabilities.

SUMMARY

In summary, there are a large number of social services and resources available. Often, we do not realize that the services we need do exist until we begin looking for a particular program or we begin to notice an unmet need. Identifying the need and then searching within the community takes time and energy. Creativity and endurance is essential. Some states have information and referral services or community councils that will ease your task. Becoming informed is the only way to assess whether a service exists in your community. If it does not exist, perhaps you need to take the initiative to foster its development. Many of the most successful programs for children with special needs are the result of motivated parents and interested professionals who joined forces and advocated for specific services.

ACKNOWLEDGMENTS

Contributions have been made to this chapter by Sarah J. Gossler, M.S.W., and James C. Bernier, M.S.W.

Resource Organizations

Administration on Developmental Disabilities Office of Human Services
Department of Health and Human Services
200 Independence Ave., SW
Washington, DC 20201

Alexander Graham Bell Association for the Deaf, Inc.
3417 Volta Pl., NW
Washington, DC 20007

American Academy for Cerebral Palsy
P.O. Box 11086
Richmond, VA 23230

American Association of University Affiliated Programs for Persons with Developmental Disabilities
8605 Cameron St.
Suite 406
Silver Spring, MD 20910

American Association on Mental Deficiency
1719 Kalorama Rd., NW
Washington, DC 20009

American Bar Association
Child Advocacy Center
1800 M St., NW, Suite 200
Washington, DC 20036

American Brittle Bone Society
1256 Merrill Dr.
Marshallton
West Chester, PA 19380

American Civil Liberties Union
132 W. 43rd St.
New York, NY 10036

American Coalition of Citizens with Disabilities
1012 14th St., NW
Suite 901
Washington, DC 20036

American Council of the Blind
1010 Vermont Ave., NW
Suite 1100
Washington, DC 20005

American Deafness and Rehabilitation Association
P.O. Box 55369
Little Rock, AR 72225

American Foundation for the Blind, Inc.
15 W. 16th St.
New York, NY 10011

American Heart Association
7320 Greenville Ave.
Dallas, TX 75231

American Printing House for the Blind, Inc.
1839 Frankfort Ave.
Louisville, KY 40206

American Society for Deaf Children
814 Thayer Ave.
Silver Spring, MD 20910

American Spinal Injury Association
Northwest Memorial Hospital
Room 619
250 East Superior
Chicago, IL 60611

Arthrogryposis Association
c/o Mrs. Mary Ann Schmidt
PO Box 5192
Sonora, CA 95310

Associacion de Padres Pro-beinstar de Ninos Impedidos de Puerto Rico
PO Box 21301
Rio Peidras, Puerto Rico 00928

Association for the Care of Children's Health (ACCH)
3615 Wisconsin Ave., NW
Washington, DC 20016

Association for Children and Adults with Learning Disabilities
4156 Library Rd.
Pittsburgh, PA 15234

Association for Education and Rehabilitation of the Blind and Visually Impaired
206 North Washington St.
Suite 320
Alexandria, VA 22314

Association for Retarded Citizens of the United States (ARC-US)
2501 Avenue J
P.O. Box 6109
Arlington, TX 76005

Association for the Visually Handicapped
1839 Frankfort Ave.
Louisville, KY 40206

Autism Society of America
1234 Massachusetts Ave., NW
Suite 1101
Washington, DC 20005

B.O.L.D., Inc.
Broader Opportunities for the Learning Disabled
P.O. Box 546309
Surfside, FL 33154

Bureau on Developmental Disabilities
Office of Human Resources
U.S. Department of Health & Human Services
Switzer Building
Room 3070
330 C Street, SW
Washington, DC 20201

Canadian Association for Community Living
Kinsmen Building
York University Campus
4700 Keele St.
Downsview, Ontario, CANADA
M3J1P3

Canadian Hearing Society— Head Office
271 Spadina Rd.
Toronto, Ontario, CANADA M5R2V3

Compassionate Friends, Inc.
National Office
PO Box 3696
Oak Brook, IL 60522-3696
(for parents of children who have died)

Coordinating Council for Handicapped Children
20 E. Jackson Blvd.
Room 900
Chicago, IL 60604

Cornelia de Lange Syndrome Foundation
60 Dyer Ave.
Collinsville, CT 06022

Cri du Chat (cat-cry syndrome)
The 5p- Society
11609 Oakmont
Overland Park, KS 66210

Cystic Fibrosis Foundation
6931 Arlington Rd.
Bethesda, MD 20814

Dental Guidance Council for Cerebral Palsy
122 East 23rd St.
New York, NY 10010

Dysautonomia Foundation, Inc.
370 Lexington Ave.
Room 1504
New York, NY 10017

Epilepsy Foundation of America
4351 Garden City Dr.
Suite 406
Landover, MD 20785

Especially Grandparents
The Grandparents Program
ARC of King County
2230 Eighth Ave.
Seattle, WA 98121

**Families of Spinal Muscular
Atrophy (SMA)**
P.O. Box 1465
Highland Park, IL 60035

**Federation for Children with
Special Needs**
312 Stuart St.
Boston, MA 02116

Federation of the Handicapped
211 W. 14th St.
New York, NY 10011

**Foundation for Child
Development**
345 E. 46th St.
New York, NY 10017

**Foundation for Children with
Learning Disabilities**
P.O. Box 2929
Grand Central Station
New York, NY 10016

Fragile X Foundation
P.O. Box 300233
Denver, CO 80220

**Friedreich's Ataxia Group in
America, Inc.**
P.O. Box 11116
Oakland, CA 94611

**Guardians of Hydrocephalus
Research Foundation**
2618 Avenue Z
Brooklyn, NY 11235

Hydrocephalus Support Group
225 Dickinson St.
H-893
San Diego, CA 92103

**International Institute for
Visually Impaired, 0–7, Inc.**
230 Central St.
Auburndale, MA 02116

**International Rett Syndrome
Association**
8511 Rose Marie Dr.
Fort Washington, MD 20744

Little People of America
Box 633
San Bruno, CA 94066

Lowe's Syndrome Association
222 Lincoln St.
West Lafayette, IN 47906

**Maple Syrup Urine Disease
Family Support Group**
24806 SR 119
Goshen, IN 46526

**March of Dimes Birth Defects
Foundation**
303 S. Broadway
Tarrytown, NY 10591

**Muscular Dystrophy Association,
Inc.**
810 Seventh Ave.
New York, NY 10019

**National Association for the
Visually Handicapped**
22 West 21st St.
6th Floor
New York, NY 10010

National Association of the Deaf
814 Thayer Ave.
Silver Spring, MD 20910

**National Association of
Developmental Disabilities
Councils**
1234 Massachusetts Ave., NW
Suite 103
Washington, DC 20005

National Ataxia Foundation
600 Twelve Oaks Center
15500 Wayzata Blvd.
Wayzata, MN 55391

National Autism Hotline
Autism Services Center
Douglas Education Building
10th Ave. and Bruce
Huntington, WV 25701

National Birth Defects Center
30 Warren St.
Brighton, MA 02135

National Down Syndrome Congress
1800 Dempster St.
Park Ridge, IL 60068

National Down Syndrome Society
141 Fifth Ave. Seventh Fl.
New York, NY 10010

National Easter Seal Society
2023 W. Ogden Ave.
Chicago, IL 60612

National Federation of the Blind
1800 Johnson St.
Baltimore, MD 21230

National Foundation for Facial Reconstruction
550 First Ave.
New York, NY 10016

National Head Injury Foundation (NHIF)
333 Turnpike Rd.
Southboro, MA 01772

National Hearing Aid Society
20361 Middlebelt Rd.
Livonia, MI 48152

National Hydrocephalus Foundation
Route 1, River Rd.
Box 210A
Joliet, IL 60436

National Information Center for Children and Youth with Handicaps
1555 Wilson Blvd.
Suite 700
Rosslyn, VA 22209

National Institute for Rehabilitation Engineering
P.O. Box 841
Butler, NJ 07405

National Maternal and Child Health Clearinghouse
38th and R Sts., NW
Washington, DC 20057

National Multiple Sclerosis Society
205 East 42nd St.
New York, NY 10017

National Neurofibromatosis Foundation, Inc.
141 Fifth Ave., Suite 7-S
New York, NY 10010

National Organization for Rare Disorders
P.O. Box 8923
New Fairfield, CT 06812

National Rehabilitation Information Center
4407 Eighth St., NE
Catholic University of America
Washington, DC 20017

National Reye's Syndrome Foundation
P.O. Box 829
Bryan, OH 43506

National Scoliosis Foundation, Inc.
93 Concord Ave.
P.O. Box 547
Belmont, MA 02178

National Self-Help Clearinghouse
33 W. 42nd St.
New York, NY 10036

National Spinal Cord Injury Association
600 W. Cummings Rd.
Woburn, MA 01801

National Spinal Cord Injury Hotline
2201 Argonne Dr.
Baltimore, MD 21218

National Tay-Sachs and Allied Diseases Association
385 Elliot St.
Newton, MA 02164

National Tuberous Sclerosis Association
P.O. Box 612
Winfield, IL 60190

Orton Dyslexia Society
724 York Rd.
Baltimore, MD 21204

Osteogenesis Imperfecta Foundation
P.O. Box 245
Eastport, NY 11941

Prader-Willi Syndrome Association
5515 Malibu Dr.
Edina, MN 55436

Retinitis Pigmentosa (RP) Association International
P.O. Box 900
Woodland Hills, CA 91365

Scouting for the Handicapped
Boy Scouts of America
1325 Walnut Hill Lane
Irving, TX 75062

Sibling Information Network
Connecticut's University Affiliated
Program on Developmental
Disabilities
Department of Educational
Psychology
24a Glenbrook Road
Box U-64, The University of
Connecticut
Storrs, CT 06268

Siblings Helping Persons with Autism through Resources and Energy (SHARE)
c/o Autism Society of America
1234 Massachusetts Ave., NW
Suite 1017
Washington, DC 20005-4599

Spina Bifida Association of America
1700 Rockville Pike #540
Rockville, MD 20852-1631

Tourette Syndrome Association
42–40 Bell Blvd.
Bayside, NY 11361

United Cerebral Palsy Associations, Inc.
66 E. 34th St.
New York, NY 10016

United Leukodystrophy Foundation
2304 Highland Dr.
Sycamore, IL 60178

U.S. Department of Education
Office of Special Education and
Rehabilitative Services
Program Information and
Coordination Staff
Clearinghouse on the Handicapped
Room 3132, Switzer Bldg.
330 C St., SW
Washington, DC 20202

U.S. Department of Health & Human Services
Office of Child Development
P.O. Box 1182
Washington, DC 20013

U.S. Department of Health & Human Services
Rehabilitation Service Administration
Washington, DC 20201

Williams Syndrome Association
P.O. Box 178373
San Diego, CA 92117-0910

References and Suggested Readings

PART I CHILDREN WITH SPECIAL NEEDS, THEIR PARENTS, AND THE PROFESSIONALS WHO CARE FOR THEM

Chapter 1   Who Are the Special Children?

Darling, R.B., & Darling, J. (1982). *Children who are different: Meeting the challenges of birth defects in society.* St. Louis: C.V. Mosby.

Ross, B. (1977). *Our special child: A guide to successful parenting of handicapped children.* New York: Walker and Company.

Chapter 2   Discovering Your Child Has a Problem

Cross, L., & Goin, K. (1977). *Identifying handicapped children: A guide to case finding, screening, diagnosis, assessment, and evaluation.* New York: Walker and Company.

Thompson, R.J., & O'Quinn, A.N. (1979). *Developmental disabilities—Etiologies, manifestations, diagnoses, and treatments.* New York: Oxford University Press.

Chapter 3   Developmental Disabilities Are a Family Affair

Buscaglia, L. (1975). *The disabled and their parents: A counseling challenge.* Thorofare, NJ: Charles B. Slack.

Featherstone, H. (1980). *A difference in the family: Life with the disabled child.* New York: Basic Books.

Goldfarb, L.A., Brotherson, M.J., Summers, J.A., & Turnbull, A.P. (1986). *Meeting the challenge of disability or chronic illness—A family guide.* Baltimore: Paul H. Brookes Publishing.

Pearlman, L., & Scott, K.A. (1981). *Raising the handicapped child.* Englewood Cliffs, NJ: Prentice-Hall.

Powell, T.H., & Ogle, P.A. (1985). *Brothers & sisters—A special part of exceptional families.* Baltimore: Paul H. Brookes Publishing Co.

A reader's guide: For parents of children with physical or emotional disabilities (Publication Number [HSA], 77-5290). Washington, DC: U.S. Government Printing Office.

Chapter 4   Parents and Professionals: A Working Partnership

Esterson, M.M., & Bluth, L.F. (1986). *Related services for handicapped children.* San Diego: College-Hill Press (Division of Little, Brown).

Mulick, J.A., & Pueschel, S.M. (1983). *Parent-professional partnerships in developmental disability services.* Cambridge, MA.: Ware Press.

Mulliken, R.K., & Buckley, J.J. (1983). *Assessment of multihandicapped and developmentally disabled children.* Rockville, MD: Aspen Systems.

PART II   COMMON PROBLEMS AND DISABILITIES IN CHILDREN WITH SPECIAL NEEDS

Chapter 5   Mental Retardation

Grossman, H.G. (Ed.).(1973). *Manual on terminology and classification in mental retardation* (Special Publication No. 2). Washington, DC: American Association of Mental Deficiency.

Seltzer, G.B. (1983). Systems of classification. In J.L. Matson & J.A. Mulick (Eds.), *Handbook of mental retardation* (pp. 143–156). Elmsford, NY: Pergamon Press.

Szymanski, L.S., & Tanguay, P.E. (1980). *Emotional disorders of mentally retarded persons: Assessment, treatment, and consultation.* Baltimore: University Park Press.

Chapter 6   Minimal Brain Dysfunction

Denhoff, E., & Stern, L. (1979). *Minimal brain dysfunction: A developmental approach.* New York: Masson Publishing USA.

Chapter 7   Learning Disabilities

Ludlow, B.L. (1982). *Teaching the learning disabled.* Bloomington, IN: Phi Delta Kappa, Educational Foundation.

Stevens, S.H. (1984). *Classroom success for the learning disabled.* Winston-Salem, NC: John F. Blair Publisher.

Chapter 8   Sensory Disorders

Batshaw, M.L., & Perret, Y.M. (1986). *Children with handicaps: A medical primer* (2nd ed.). Baltimore: Paul H. Brookes Publishing Co.

Chapter 9   Communication Disorders

Hersor, L.A. (1980). *Language and language disorders in children.* Elmsford, NY: Pergamon Press.

Chapter 10   Autism

Koegel, R.L., Rincover, A., & Egel, A.L. (1982). *Educating and understanding autistic children.* San Diego: College-Hill Press (Division of Little, Brown).

Schopler, E., & Mesibov, G. (1984). *The effects of autism on the family.* New York: Plenum.

PART III   INHERITED AND ACQUIRED DEVELOPMENTAL DISABILITIES

Chapter 11   Chromosome and Genetic Disorders

Abuelo, D.N. (1983). Genetic disorders. In J.L. Matson & J.A. Mulick (Eds.), *Handbook of mental retardation* (pp.105–120). Elmsford, NY: Pergamon Press.

Pueschel, S.M., & Goldstein, A. (1983). Genetic counseling. In J.L. Matson & J.A. Mulick (Eds.), *Handbook of mental retardation* (pp. 259–270). Elmsford, NY: Pergamon Press.

Pueschel, S.M., & Thuline, H.C. (1983). Chromosome disorders. In J.L. Matson & J.A. Mulick (Eds.), *Handbook of mental retardation* (pp. 121–141). Elmsford, NY: Pergamon Press.

Pueschel, S.M., Tingey, C., Rynders, J.E., Crocker, A.C., & Crutcher, D.M. (Eds.). (1987). *New perspectives on Down syndrome.* Baltimore: Paul H. Brookes Publishing Co.

Chapter 12   Environmental Events

Hoyme, H.E. (1988). Teratogenic causes of developmental disability. In S.M. Pueschel & J.A. Mulick (Eds.), *Prevention of developmental disabilities* (pp. 82–112). Cambridge, MA: Academic Guild Publishers.

Scola, P., & Pueschel, S.M. (1988). Infections during pregnancy. In S.M. Pueschel & J.A. Mulick (Eds.), *Prevention of developmental disabilities* (pp. 142–165). Cambridge, MA: Academic Guild Publishers.

Chapter 13   Birth Defects

Adams, F.H., & Emmanouilides, G.C. (1983). *Heart disease in infants, children and adolescents* (3rd ed.). Baltimore: Williams & Wilkins.

Feingold, M., & Pashayan, H. (1983). *Genetics and birth defects in clinical practice.* Boston: Little, Brown.

President's Commission for the Study of Ethical Problems in Medicine and Biomedical and Behavioral Research. (1983). *Screening and counseling for genetic conditions* (Library of Congress, Card Number 83-600502). Washington, DC: U.S. Government Printing Office.

Smith, D.W. (1982). *Recognizable patterns of human malformation: Genetic, embryologic, and clinical aspects.* Philadelphia: W.B. Saunders.

Chapter 14   Problems in the Newborn Period

Batshaw, M.L., & Perret, Y.M. (1986). *Children with handicaps: A medical primer* (2nd ed.). Baltimore: Paul H. Brookes Publishing Co.

Lott, I.T. (1983). Perinatal factors in mental retardation. In J.L. Matson & J.A. Mulick (Eds.), *Handbook of mental retardation* (pp. 97–103). Elmsford, NY: Pergamon Press.

Chapter 15   Cerebral Palsy

Healy, A. (1983). Cerebral palsy. In J.A. Blackman (Ed.), *Medical aspects of developmental disabilities in children birth to three: A resource for special service providers in the educational setting* (pp. 31–37). Iowa City: University of Iowa.

Wolraich, M.L. (1983). Seizure disorders. In J.A. Blackman (Ed.), *Medical aspects of developmental disabilities in children birth to three: A resource for special service providers in the educational setting* (pp. 215–221). Iowa City: University of Iowa.

Wright, F.S. (1984). Epilepsy in childhood. In Symposium on chronic disease in children. *The Pediatric Clinics of North America, 31,* 177–188.

Chapter 16   Sensory Disorders

Schord, P. (1983). Visual impairment. In J.A. Blackman (Ed.), *Medical aspects of developmental disabilities in children birth to three: A resource for special service* providers in the educational setting (pp. 227–231). Iowa City: University of Iowa.

Chapter 17 Neurological Disorders with Associated Skin Findings

Mincus, J.H. (1984). Textbook of child neurology (2nd ed.). Philadelphia: Lea & Febiger.
Riccardi, M.D., & Eichner, J.E. (1986). Neurofibromatosis: Phenotype, natural history, and pathogenesis. Baltimore: Johns Hopkins University Press.
Wiedenmann, H.R., Grosse, K.R., & Dibbern, H. (1985). An atlas of characteristic syndromes: A visual aid to diagnosis. Chicago: Yearbook Medical Publishers.

Chapter 18 Diseases of Muscles and Bones

Brooke, M.H. (1977). A clinician's view of neuromuscular diseases. Baltimore: Williams & Wilkins.
Dubowitz, V. (1978). Muscle disorders in childhood. Philadelphia: W.B. Saunders.
Siegel, I.M. (1986). Muscle and its diseases: An outline primer of basic science and clinical method. Chicago: Yearbook Medical Publishers.

Chapter 19 Metabolic Disorders

Schultz, F.R. (1983). Phenylketonuria and other metabolic diseases. In J.A. Blackman (Ed.), Medical aspects of developmental disabilities in children birth to three: A resource for special service providers in the educational setting (pp. 197–201). Iowa City: University of Iowa.
Scriver, C.R., & Rosenberg, L.E. (1973). Amino acid metabolism and its disorders. Philadelphia: W.B. Saunders.

Chapter 20 Endocrine Disorders

Hung, W., August, G.P., & Glasgow, A.M. (1983). Pediatric endocrinology. New Hyde Park, NY: Medical Examination Publishing Co.

PART IV SPECIAL CARE FOR YOUR CHILD: PROCEDURES, APPLIANCES, AND MEDICAL AND SURGICAL TREATMENTS

Chapter 21 Strategies for Helping Your Child

Fraser, B.A., & Hensinger, R.N. (1983). Managing physical handicaps: A practical guide for parents, care providers, and educators. Baltimore: Paul H. Brookes Publishing Co.
Horner, R.H., Meyer, L.H., & Fredericks, H.D. (Eds.). (1986). Education of learners with severe handicaps: Exemplary service strategies. Baltimore: Paul H. Brookes Publishing Co.
Musselwhite, C.R. (1986). Adaptive play for special needs children: Strategies to enhance communication and learning. San Diego: College-Hill Press (Division of Little, Brown).

Chapter 22 Tests and Procedures

Miller, W.A. (1988). Prenatal genetic diagnosis. In S.M. Pueschel & J.A. Mulick (Eds.), Prevention of developmental disabilities (pp. 114–129). Cambridge, MA: Academic Guild Publishers.

Schultz, F.R. (1983). Computerized axial tomography (CAT) and other imaging techniques. In J.A. Blackman (Ed.), *Medical aspects of developmental disabilities in children birth to three: A resource for special service providers in the educational setting* (pp. 61–64). Iowa City: University of Iowa.

Chapter 23 Adaptive Equipment

Bergen, A.F., & Colangelo, C. (1985). *Positioning the client with CNS deficits: The wheelchair and other adaptive equipment* (2nd ed.). Valhalla, NY: Valhalla Rehabilitation Publications.

Finnie, N. (1975). *Handling the young cerebral palsy child at home* (2nd ed.). New York: E.P. Dutton.

Fraser, B.A., Hensinger, R.N., & Phelps, J.A. (1987). *Physical management of multiple handicaps: A professional's guide.* Baltimore: Paul H. Brookes Publishing Co.

Jones, S., & Clark, S. (1982). *Adaptive positioning equipment: Directory of available services.* (Available from Georgia Retardation Center, 4770 North Peachtree Road, Atlanta, Georgia).

Williamson, G.G. (1987). *Children with spina bifida: Early intervention and preschool programming.* Baltimore: Paul H. Brookes Publishing Co.

Chapter 24 Medications May Be Necessary for Your Child

Gadow, K.D. (1986). *Children on medication: Vol. 1. Hyperactivity, learning disabilities, and mental retardation.* Reston, VA: Council for Exceptional Children.

Gadow, K.D. (1986). *Children on medication: Vol. 2. Epilepsy, emotional disturbance, and adolescent disorders.* Reston, VA: Council for Exception Children.

Hanson, C.R., & Cohen, D. (1984). Multimodality approaches in the treatment of attention deficit disorders. In Symposium on learning disorders. *The Pediatric Clinics of North America, 31,* 499–513.

Chapter 25 Some Children May Have to Undergo Surgery

Jones, P.G., & Woodward, A.A. (1986). *Clinical pediatric surgery* (3rd ed.). Melbourne, Australia: Blackwell Scientific Publications.

Maher, B.W. (1981). *Pediatric anesthesia.* Philadelphia: J.B. Lippincott.

Turek, S.L. (1984). *Orthopedics* (4th ed.). Philadelphia: J.B. Lippincott.

Chapter 26 Hospitalizations and Aftercare

Coleman, W. (1981). *My hospital book.* Minneapolis: Bethany Publishers.

Howe, J. (1981). *The hospital book.* New York: Crown Publishers.

McCollum, A. (1981). *The chronically ill child: A guide for parents and professionals.* New Haven, CT: Yale University Press.

Petrillo, M., & Sanger, S. (1980). *Emotional care of hospitalized children: An environmental approach.* Philadelphia: J.B. Lippincott.

PART V ASSESSMENTS, EDUCATION, AND RESOURCE DEVELOPMENT

Chapter 27 Assessing Developmental Disabilities: Psychological Tests and Procedures

Fewell, R.R. (1983). Assessing handicapped infants. In S.G. Garwood & R.R. Fewell (Eds.), *Educating handicapped infants* (pp. 143–169). Rockville, MD: Aspen Systems.

McLoughlin, J.A., & Lewis, R.B. (1986). *Assessing special students* (2nd ed.). Columbus, OH: Charles E. Merrill.

Morganston, M. (1983). Standard intelligence tests and related assessment techniques. In J.L. Matson & J.A. Mulick (Eds.), *Handbook of mental retardation* (pp. 201–214). Elmsford, NY: Pergamon Press.

Mullen Scales of Early Learning (MSEL) [ages 15 months to 6 years]; *Infant MSEL* [ages 0 to 15 months]. (Available from [T.O.T.A.L. Child, Inc., Cranston, RI 02920])

Mullikin, R.K., & Buckley, J.J. (1983). *Assessment of multihandicapped and developmentally disabled children*. Rockville, MD: Aspen Systems.

Simeonsson, R.J. (1986). *Psychological and developmental assessment of special children*. Newton, MA: Allyn & Bacon.

Ulrey, G., & Rogers, S.J. (1982). *Psychological assessment of handicapped infants and young children*. New York: Thieme-Stratton.

Wodrich, D.L. (1984). *Children's psychological testing: A guide for nonpsychologists*. Baltimore: Paul H. Brookes Publishing Co.

Wodrich, D.L., & Joy, J.J. (Eds.). (1986). *Multidisciplinary assessment of children with learning disabilities and mental retardation*. Baltimore: Paul H. Brookes Publishing Co.

Chapter 28 Helping Children Learn

The argument for early intervention. (1981). (Available from ERIC Clearinghouse on Handicapped & Gifted Children, 1920 Association Dr.,Reston, VA 22091)

Baker, B.L., Brightman, A.J., Heiftez, L.J., & Murphy, D.M. (1976). *Behavior problems*. Champaign, IL: Research Press.

Becker, W.C. (1971). *Parents are teachers: A child management program*. Champaign, IL: Research Press.

Foxx, R.M., & Azrin, N.H. (1973). *Toilet training the retarded*. Champaign, IL: Research Press.

Handleman, J.S., & Harris, S.L. (1986). *Educating the developmentally disabled: Meeting the needs of children and families*. San Diego: College-Hill Press (Division of Little, Brown).

Osofsky, J.D. (Ed.). (1979). *Handbook of infant development*. New York: John Wiley & Sons.

Public Law 94-142. (1977, August). The Education for All Handicapped Children Act. *Federal Register 163*, 42474–42518.

Chapter 29 Going to School

Algozzine, B., & Maheady, L. (1986). In search of excellence: Instruction that works in special education classrooms. Special edition of *Exceptional Children, 52*[6].

Falvey, M.A. (1986). *Community-based curriculum: Instructional strategies for students with severe handicaps*. Baltimore: Paul H. Brookes Publishing Co.

Orelove, F.P., & Sosbey, D. (1987). *Educating children with multiple disabilities: A transdisciplinary approach*. Baltimore: Paul H. Brookes Publishing Co.

Wilcox. B., & Bellamy, G.T. (1982). *Design of high school programs for severely handicapped students*. Baltimore: Paul H. Brookes Publishing Co.

Winton, P.J., Turnbull, A.P., & Blacher, J. (1984). *Selecting a preschool: A guide to parents of handicapped children*. Baltimore: University Park Press.

Chapter 30   Legal Issues in Developmental Disabilities

American Association on Mental Deficiency. (1975). *Rights of mentally retarded persons: Position papers of the AAMD.* Washington, DC: Author.

Apolloni, T., & Cooke, T.P. (eds.). (1984). *A new look at guardianship: Protective services that support personalized living.* Baltimore: Paul H. Brookes Publishing Co.

Effland, R.W. (1976). Trusts and estate planning. In M. Kindred, J. Cohen, D. Penrod, & T. Shaffer (Eds.), *The mentally retarded citizen and the law* (pp. 115–132). New York: Macmillan.

Kindred, M. (1976). Guardianship and limitations upon capacity. In M. Kindred, J. Cohen, D. Penrod, & T. Shaffer (Eds.), *The mentally retarded citizen and the law* (pp. 62–87). New York: Macmillan.

Vitello, S.J., & Soskin, R.M. (1985). *Mental retardation: Its social and legal context.* Englewood Cliffs, NJ: Prentice-Hall.

Wald, P.M. (1976). Basic personal and civil rights. In M. Kindred, J. Cohen, D. Penrod, & T. Shaffer, (Eds.), *The mentally retarded citizen and the law* (pp. 2–26). New York: Macmillan.

Chapter 31   A Guide to Resource Development

Ballard, J., Ramirez, V., & Zantal-Wiener, K. (1987). *PL 94-142, Section 504 and PL 99-457: Understanding what they are and are not.* Reston, VA: Council for Exceptional Children.

Budoff, M., & Orenstein, A. (1982). *Due process in special education: Going to a hearing.* Brookline, MA: Brookline Books.

Plasse, D.P. (1986). *Litigation in special education* [Special Edition]. *Exceptional Children, 52*(4).

Index

Skilled home nursing care, 335
Skin findings, neurological disorders with, 139–142
Skin graft, 258
Sleeping problems, chloralhydrate for, 235
Sleeping sickness, 105
Slow learner, 49
Small for gestational age (SGA) infants, 128
Smoking, pregnancy and, 108–109
Social/emotional problems, signs of, 8
Social service intervention, 167–168
Social skills, assessment of, 288–289
Social worker, 41–42
Sonography, prenatal diagnosis with, 10, 169
Sorrow, chronic, 21
Spastic cerebral palsy, 131
Spasticity, medications for, 230–232
Special children, definition of, 3–4
Special education, 307–318
    definition of, 317–318
    see also School
Specialists, *see* Professionals; *specific type*
Speech pathologist, 42
    see also Communication disorders
Speech therapy, 165
Sphingolipidoses, 149–150
Spina bifida, 113–116
    prenatal diagnosis of, 171
    surgical repair of, 245
Spinal anesthesia, 243
Spinal cerebellar degeneration, 143
Spinal deformities, surgery for, 254–255
Spinal fusion, 255
Spinal muscular atrophy, 143–144
Spinal tap, 106
Splints, 199
    static versus dynamic, 200–201
Spoons, adapted, 217
Squint, 65
SSI (Supplemental Security Income), 339
Staff, *see* Professionals
Standing, aids and devices for, 196–198
Standing boxes, 197–198
Standing frames, 203–204
Standing tables, 197–198
Stanford-Binet Intelligence Scale, 274
State programs, adaptive equipment and, 191
Static splints, 200
Stelazine (trifluoperazine hydrochloride), 232
Stenosis
    aortic, 121
    duodenal, 247
    pulmonic, 121
    pyloric, 247
Stimulant medications, 228–230
Stomach problems, 34
Stool softeners, 236
Strabismus, 65
    surgery for, 258
Sturge-Weber syndrome, 140–141
Stuttering, 77
"Substitute payee" method, 329
Suctioning, 266
Supplemental Security Income (SSI), 339

Support groups
    adaptive equipment and, 192
    see also Associations
Surgeon, 42
Surgery, 159–160, 241–258
    anesthesia for, 242–243
    eye, 257–258
    for feeding problems, 249
    gastrointestinal, 246–249
    general considerations for, 241–242
    for hearing disorders, 256–257
    heart, 249–251
    for hydrocephalus, 243–245, 246
    musculoskeletal, 251–255
    reconstructive, 258
    for spina bifida, 245
    urinary tract, 256
Sweat test, 172–173
Switches, adapting, 216
Synthroid (levothyroxine), 236

Tay Sachs disease, 149
Teachers, 33–34
Teaching strategies, 299–301
Teeth, care of, 33
Tegretol (Carbamazepine), 225–226
Temporal lobe seizures, 136
Temporary guardian, 328
Tendon lengthening, 251–252
Tenotomy, 251–252
Teratogens, 105, 106–109
Terminology, 3–4
Test age, 284
Tests, *see* Assessment; *specific test*
Tetralogy of Fallot, 120
    surgery for, 251
Therapeutic interventions
    occupational therapy, 164–165
    physical therapy, 163–164
    psychological, 166–167
    respiratory therapy, 165–166
    social service, 167–168
    speech and language therapy, 165
Thioridazine hydrochloride (Mellaril), 232
Thiothixene hydrochloride (Navane), 232
Thoraco-lumbar-sacral orthoses (TLSO), 205–206
Thorazine (chlorpromazine hydrochloride), 232
Thyroid hormone deficiency, 153–154
Thyroid medications, 236
Tobacco, pregnancy and, 108–109
Tofranil (Imipramine Hydrochloride), 235
Toilet training aids, 218–219
Tonic-clonic seizures, 135
Tonic seizures, 135
TORCH titer, 105
Toxoplasmosis, 103–104
Trabeculectomy, 258
Tracheoesophageal fistula, 247
Tracheostomy care, 264–265
Traction, 198–199
Transfer devices, 218
Translocation, 91–92